Cambridge Studies in Social Anthropology

General Editor: Jack Goody

62

THE HULI RESPONSE TO ILLNESS

The Huli response to illness

STEPHEN FRANKEL

Senior Lecturer
Department of Epidemiology and Community Medicine
University of Wales College of Medicine

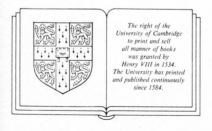

The right of the
University of Cambridge
to print and sell
all manner of books
was granted by
Henry VIII in 1534.
The University has printed
and published continuously
since 1584.

CAMBRIDGE UNIVERSITY PRESS

Cambridge

London   New York   New Rochelle

Melbourne   Sydney

Published by the Press Syndicate of the University of Cambridge
The Pitt Building, Trumpington Street, Cambridge CB2 1RP
32 East 57th Street, New York, NY 10022, USA
10 Stamford Road, Oakleigh, Melbourne 3166, Australia

First published 1986

Printed in Great Britain by
the University Press, Cambridge

British Library cataloguing in publication data
Frankel, Stephen
The Huli response to illness. –
(Cambridge studies in social anthropology; v. 62)
1. Folk medicine – Papua New Guinea
2. Huli (Papuan people)
I. Title
615.8′82′09953   R683.P25

Library of Congress cataloguing in publication data
Frankel, Stephen.
The Huli response to illness.
(Cambridge studies in social anthropology; 62)
Bibliography.
Includes index.
1. Huli (Papua New Guinea people) – Medicine.
2. Huli (Papua New Guinea people) – Medical care.
3. Medical anthropology – Papua New Guinea.
I. Title.   II. Series: Cambridge studies in social
anthropology; no. 62.
DU740.42.F73   1986   615.8′82′09953   86-6170

ISBN 0 521 32524 2

UP

For my mother and father

Contents

Figures

Tables

Glossary of some key Huli terms

agali	man, also the illness in men caused by female pollution
amali	a chronic chest disease
bamu	for no reason
Bayebaye	literally 'perfect', the boy who was killed in error in an earlier performance of *dindi gamu*
bu	breath, or life force
dama	spirit(s)
dindi gamu	literally 'earth spell', the major earth fertility ritual sequence
dinini	a shade
Duguba	the collective term for all the peoples of the Papuan Plateau, including Etoro, Onabasulu, Kaluli, Tsinali and Petamini
gamu	spell or rite
hameigini	a parish or parish section
hambu	a type of sorcery
ibagiya	the bachelor cult
Ibatiri	a water spirit, or a scruffy pauper
kanaka	rural bumpkin, also a pagan
kebanda	a sacred site dedicated to the ancestor spirit Kebali, or the temple built on such a site
kuyanda	the leech-like parasitic mass that grows within the chest of a child that has swallowed some of the birth flow
lingi	an illness caused by others' covetousness
mana	lore
mbingi	literally 'time of darkness', a fall of volcanic ash from the sky
mogo laya	startled
nambis poisin	a novel form of sorcery
tawa timu	Ibatiri's arrow
tene	agnate
yamuwini	non-agnatic cognate

A note on orthography

Murray Rule's 'Statement of the phonology and grammar of the Huli language', and his Huli dictionary were invaluable aids in this research. I have followed his orthography here, with two exceptions. First, he underlined nasalised vowels. Here I have marked nasalised vowels with a tilde, thus: *tõle*. Secondly, I have neglected to mark tone patterns. I will make no detailed comment on Huli pronunciation. The only major departure from English sounds in Rule's orthography is the '*y*' between vowels in words such as *kuyanda*. This is frictionalised, and resembles the English 'j'.

Preface

This is a study of the response to illness of the Huli people of the Southern Highlands of Papua New Guinea. There are many accounts of traditional responses to illness in societies such as the Huli. Some information is available on levels of disease. There are also some quantitative data on the utilisation of Western health services. But there have been few attempts to bring together these aspects of the modern experience of illness in such societies and to examine their interrelationships. This broad aim guided the design of this research.

A long-standing wish to become an anthropologist became a firm plan when I worked as a medical officer in Papua New Guinea from 1972 to 1974. The view from a clinic offers little opportunity to understand what leads people to seek treatments of different sorts. The anthropological approach allows a unique opportunity for examining the context and meaning of such decisions. However, despite this potential, the particular theoretical concerns of the subject have produced only a partial picture of societies such as the Huli in the literature of medical anthropology.

It is often difficult to relate anthropological studies of illness to the common problems that concern all people in their everyday lives. When I first worked in Papua New Guinea as a medical officer I was struck by the gulf between the accounts of illness in the anthropological literature and the people's responses to illness as I observed these in my clinical practice. I assumed that this gulf was explained largely by my own ignorance of what people were really thinking and doing, a deficiency I hoped to correct in one area at least through the research project described in this book. However, this research and other recent work in Papua New Guinea and elsewhere suggest that the apparent rarity of sorcery victims, for example, in the queues outside my clinic reflected the true picture as much as it reflected my lack of anthropological sophistication at that time.

One aim of this book is to demonstrate the merits of introducing a more epidemiological approach than is usual in anthropological studies of illness. The approach I have favoured here is to combine findings derived from intensive observation with those derived from extensive surveys. This synthesis of qualitative and quantitative methods is in my view essential, both to give a representative analysis of responses to illness, as well as to understand the processes of change which underlie the current pattern of response in any society exposed to a complex array of alternative strategies in illness. In addition, this approach allows the findings to be applied to questions of health policy. However, the question of the relevance of anthropological methods to the planning and evaluation of health services is beyond the scope of this book. It is treated at length in a number of works listed in the references.

Field work was conducted during three periods. The bulk of the study was completed during the two years that I lived with my family in Hambuali parish during 1977 to 1979. I returned alone for three months in 1982, when I was generously included in the household of Howard Hegele Puma. I returned twice to Tari during 1983 while I was attached to the Papua New Guinea Institute of Medical Research. The first period of field work was supported by the Social Science Research Council. Subsequently the research was supported by the Leverhulme Trust. I am most grateful for the generous support of both these bodies.

Field work in New Guinea combines rich companionship in a beautiful physical environment with intermittent physical and social discomfort. My first personal note of gratitude therefore goes to my wife Hermione for the flexibility and wit with which she tackled the experience of caring for a small child in unfamiliar circumstances.

A number of members of the Papua New Guinea Institute of Medical Research have contributed to this research both in terms of their expertise, as well as with that invaluable commodity to a field worker, hospitality. In particular I would like to mention Dr Deborah Lehmann, Dr Peter Heywood, and Dr David Smith. Dr Jack Simpson of the Forest Research Station, Bulolo, helped me with the identification of mushrooms, and Mr M. Galore of the Lae Herbarium identified the plant specimens. Brian Cheetham, an applied linguist formerly of the Language Department, University of Papua New Guinea, was also engaged in field research with the Huli, and our discussions whilst in the field were very rewarding. He kindly read and commented on a draft of this work. In Cambridge, my main intellectual debt is to Dr Gilbert Lewis. Colin Duly guided me through my first experiences of computing and has helped in numerous ways since.

I am grateful to D. Reidel, Dordrecht, for permission to use material that first appeared in *Culture, Medicine and Psychiatry*, vol. 1, 1980; *The Culture-Bound Syndromes*, ed. C. Hughes and R. Simons, 1985.

However skilful an anthropologist's analysis, the validity of the work must also be a reflection of the quality of particular relationships with individual people. A large number of individual Hulis have helped me with this research. Here I can only single out a few people for special mention. Bareagua was always generous with his considerable knowledge of healing and lore.

Preface

Hulia-Hewabe and Hubi-Hondomogo (who sadly has since died) taught me about the present and past practice of major ritual. Tabali and Kaume told me of women's knowledge and concerns. In Hambuali, Howard Hegele Puma, Stephen Baya Haroli and Handipa Kara have been constant companions who have shared the fascination of exploring the differences and similarities between our various traditions.

S.J.F.

1

Introduction

Death and disease are the lot of all peoples. The knowledge and techniques which every culture evolves to combat them must in some sense be adaptive for the society to survive. This knowledge also provides the means whereby individuals come to interpret the threat that disease represents to them, and guides the measures they use to attempt relief. Besides such knowledge, a number of influences combine to affect the patterns of behaviour in illness which characterise each society. These include the nature of the particular diseases to which people are exposed; environmental influences of benefit or disadvantage to health; and aspects of the social order which may affect the incidence of illness, and which set the manner in which the sick are cared for. The interaction of these diverse influences is such that each society displays a distinctive pattern of response to illness. This study is an investigation of the responses to illness of the Huli people of the Southern Highlands of Papua New Guinea. My intention is to trace the various strands that combine to produce the pattern of behaviour in illness that is particular to them. In this introduction, I first make explicit the considerations which led me to select for study certain areas of Huli life.

The scope of the study and the premises underlying it

The universal characteristics of bodily functioning, growth and development represent limits to the extent of cultural variation. Certain bodily changes have implications which are broadly similar whatever significance the particular culture attaches to them. For example, the pain and incapacity that follow the breaking of a leg have similarities wherever they occur. This does not imply that the practical consequences of such an injury may not differ between, say, a mountain farmer and an urban telephone operator. Also, interpretations of such an injury may vary widely according to the particular views of those affected, and the types of explanation favoured by their culture. The social implications of the injury will be influenced by the interpretation of its cause. Where it is seen as largely accidental, the effects may be confined to the immediate consequences of the sufferer's incapacity upon close kin. The ascription of blame to others may lead to litigation and disputes. The injury

1

could be seen as evidence of divine displeasure, and ceremonies may be performed to secure healing. Even the most straightforward lesions can lead, therefore, to a wide range of social responses. But various constants follow from the medical aspects of the lesion. In this simple example it is likely to have developed suddenly, probably by the application of considerable force. The limb probably will not support the person affected without some sort of mechanical assistance. The period of recovery will be counted in weeks and months rather than days. Complete recovery is possible, and an adequate return of function likely. These aspects, which derive from the biological nature of the lesion, clearly pattern the experience of the sufferer and the outcome.

In this study I am therefore assuming that disorders of the body and mind have sufficiently common features in the sorts of undesirable discontinuities they imply for those experiencing them that one society's responses to them can properly be compared with another's, and that both responses are in some measure referable to the knowledge of scientific medicine. This approach is applicable both to the paradigmatic diseases clearly describable in biological terms, and to the 'penumbra where the dubious cases lie' (A. J. Lewis 1953). The dubious cases include deformities, blemishes, mental illness and other marginal categories where moral judgements are clearly involved in the significance ascribed to the affliction. Where there are differences in the inclusion or exclusion of such attributes within a particular society's general category of illness, the isolation of the area of study on biological grounds makes such variations more, not less, discriminable.

Such an approach, first advocated by Gilbert Lewis (1975:146–51), seems preferable to the exclusion of aspects of illness behaviour on grounds that may not be clearly defined. Such exclusion usually occurs tacitly, guided by the theoretical concerns of the anthropologist and the conspicuousness of different sorts of illness behaviour. Defining the field of study according to local priorities is likely to reflect the dominant concerns of the culture in question, but it does not allow us to determine the criteria by which the people of that culture come to stress some aspects of illness and not others. Glick (1967) suggests that this tacit exclusion of illnesses which do not lead to elaborate explanations and cures should become explicit. He proposes that 'ailments', which he defines as conditions which have no socially significant cause and are treated by simple means, should be omitted from an anthropological analysis of illness. Such an approach would make comparisons between the medical responses of different societies impossible as the boundaries of each would differ greatly, and within the same society such boundaries would alter with time.

In delimilating my area of study I am therefore assuming that illness, with its general, though varying, relation to man's biological basis, is on a priori grounds a distinct aspect of all peoples' experience. Of course there are wide differences in illness behaviour between different societies. As Freidson (1970:206) points out, medical practice 'constitutes a social reality that is distinct from (and on occasion virtually independent of) physical reality'. However, the social construction of illness, and the cultural variations that this allows, are more apparent in the expression of illness and the social organisation of care than in definitions of what does and does not constitute illness in each society. Of course, this does not imply that there is any necessary relation between the biological and social aspects of illness in all cases. There are many examples of folk diagnoses in cases where a Western doctor would be unable to discover disease. For example, the Huli diagnosis *kuyanda* (p. 101) may be applied in the absence of disease as this is defined medically. Conversely, changes that might be defined medically as pathological might be regarded by lay people in the West or all people in other cultures as unexceptional, or even desirable. The shaman who might also be seen as suffering from a psychosis is perhaps one instance of a culturally valued disorder, though Devereux's (1956) view of the shamanic role as an adaptive cloak for the schizophrenic is not borne out by empirical studies of the personalities of practising shamans (Fabrega 1972:33–39).

A number of medical conditions that people of other cultures do not classify as illness are cited in introductory texts to the field of medical anthropology to illustrate the point that illness is culturally defined. However, in view of the importance of such conditions in suggesting the possible limits to cultural variation, it is interesting how poorly supported these stock examples actually are. The Mano of Liberia are said not to regard yaws as an illness. Ackerknecht (1946) is the usual source of this observation. Ackerknecht derives it from Harley (1941). Harley, a medical missionary, does indeed quote the Mano as saying of primary and secondary yaws 'Oh, that is not a sickness,...Everybody has that' (ibid:21). But the significance of this observation in the discussion of the cultural definition of illness turns on the referents of 'sickness'. Harley's point in the passage from which the quotation is taken is that primary and secondary yaws are so common that they are treated by what he refers to as 'rational treatment' and not attributed to witchcraft. He does not say that the Mano regard their yaws lesions as unexceptionable and so ignore them. Indeed elsewhere (ibid:67) he details the various illness terms that relate to yaws, and describes the range of measures that they apply to obtain relief from the 'considerable discomfort' caused by these lesions.

One of the most widely cited examples of this sort is the condition *pinta* (dyschromic spirochaetosis), which leads to discolouration of the skin. The affliction is said to be so common amongst some Amazonian peoples that those whose skins are disfigured with *pinta* are thought of as normal. Ackerknecht (ibid) cites Biocca (1945) as the source of this observation. However Biocca, who was Professor of Medicine at the University of Rome, was concerned in his paper with likely means of transmission of *pinta*, and not with native concepts of normality. The condition was common amongst the peoples of the Icana River, but the paper does not suggest that those affected regarded the condition as normal. The ethnography is sketchy, but his discussion of 'criminal transmission', where *Pintados* would secrete infected blood from the edge of a lesion into the food of unwelcome guests, suggests that *pinta*, though very common at that time, was nevertheless regarded as an abnormal and unwelcome affliction.

The Thonga are similarly well known in this literature, not only for not regarding infestations with intestinal worms as illness, but for even considering them necessary for digestion. The source here is again Ackerknecht (ibid), who cites Junod. However Junod (1912:(I)46) also tells us that the Thonga believe convulsions and diarrhoea in childhood to be caused by the intestinal worm 'which is in every child and must always be combated because, if unchecked, it will pass from the bowels to the stomach: it will come and beat the fontanella and will finally penetrate the chest. Then the little one will turn his eyes, be seized by convulsions and die. Happily there are some drugs which have a wonderful effect on this dangerous guest!' These conditions are cited to suggest that there are wide cultural variations in the definition of what constitutes illness. However, I suspect that unequivocal examples of this sort that would withstand careful scrutiny are very rare. As Kleinman (1980:83) points out, 'the problem with most ethnomedical studies is not that they impose an alien category on indigenous materials, but rather that they fail to apprehend a profound cross-cultural similarity in clinical interest and praxis'.

One of the concerns in anthropological writing about illness is to examine the pattern of response to illness in each society, and to show the relationship between the society's social organisation and the particular form of expression and resolution of illness favoured by its members. Turner's account (1967:385) of an Ndembu doctor's practice is an elegant example of this approach. But the patient's symptoms 'consisted of rapid palpitations of the heart; severe pains in the back, limbs, and chest; and fatigue after short spells of work. He felt that "people were always speaking things against" him.' Such symptoms are commonly found to be somatic expressions of psychiatric disorders, and Turner felt that they were 'mainly neurotic' in this case. Somatisation of psychic distress accounts for the symptoms in many cases that are analysed in such terms. Other studies concerned with the cultural patterning of illness deal with behavioural disorders. A number of exotic syndromes have been described (Simons and Hughes 1985; for Papua New Guinea see Frankel 1976). This literature seeks to demonstrate that the stresses to which individuals are responding are explicable in terms of the conflicts inherent in their society, and that the particular expression of such conflict is appropriate or even adaptive for the members of each society. The cultural origin and the cultural moulding of illness has been clearly demonstrated in such behavioural disorders. But this task is made easier by the fact that, to a degree, the illness *is* the behaviour. Illnesses explicable largely in terms of the somatisation of psychic distress and behavioural disorders are the most plastic disorders, and so the most amenable to analysis in terms of cultural influences.

In this study I am following the convention of using the term 'disease' to refer to disorders of the body or mind which are describable in terms of medical science, and 'illness' for the individual's experience and expression of such disorders. Disease is thus defined in terms of biology and psychology, while illness is a necessarily social phenomenon. Coughs, colds, belly aches, sprained ankles, bronchitis and the like are of course illnesses as well as diseases. But the place of cultural influences in determining the experience, expression and outcome in such illnesses has received considerably less attention from anthropologists than it has in behavioural disorders. This study is intended to redress the imbalance.

One of the concerns that guided the design of this research, therefore, was that the findings should be representative of the range of Huli responses to illnesses of all sorts. An adequate description of a society's responses to illness should include the more common complaints. First, illnesses of this sort are quantitatively the most pressing concerns of the people themselves. Secondly, unless we can place the relatively rare cases where more exotic explanations are applied within the total body of illness, we cannot understand the importance of such explanations in the range of responses to illness. Nor can we distinguish what may set such cases apart for more detailed consideration by the people themselves. In addition to following the normal practice in anthropological research of studying the community in which I lived by means of participant observation, the considerations I have outlined led me to gather in addition data of a more epidemiological nature. A further factor here was the level of social change. I therefore collected quantitative information on how they explained instances of illness and what they did for them as a way to study their choices between alternatives and their relative commitment to different kinds of treatment. Finally, unless we take note of conditions that most concern the people we are studying and not only those that relate to the established anthropological debates, the findings of research of this sort will not be relevant to problems of evaluating and planning improvements in rural health services.

I am therefore handling two distinct analytical frames: on the one hand the Huli's particular culturally determined set of ideas through which they interpret instances of illness, and which guides their responses to it; and on the other the disease pattern which can be described in medical terms. These two areas interact at the analytical level. Disease patterns are in some aspects the product of culturally specific adaptations to the environment. And

5

conversely, characteristics of the culture may represent particular responses to noxious environmental influences. Most importantly for this study, these frames come together at the level of the individual. A key characteristic of illness is an indesirable discontinuity in an individual's experience, entailing discomfort, incapacity or even the threat of dying. The recognition of this state on the part of individuals or of those caring for them will be guided by a number of issues particular to the society, such as their conceptions of normality. Similarly, the ensuing experience and events will be guided by circumstances peculiar to that culture. But most such illness events may equally be described in biomedical terms. The varying importance of these influences will emerge only from the study of ill Hulis, rather than Huli illnesses.

In his stock-taking paper Prins (1981) applied the metaphor of the three-legged Lozi cooking-pot to the study of therapy and affliction, with the supporting legs representing the contributing specialisms of medicine, anthropology and history. Epidemiological aspects of Huli health and illness are introduced here where appropriate, though the more medical aspects of this research and the detailed exploration of its relevance to questions of health care are considered in accounts which are intended to complement this one (Frankel 1984 and 1985; Frankel and Lehmann 1984 and 1985; Frankel and Lewis forthcoming). I have already indicated the cut of the anthropological leg. It therefore remains to introduce the third support of this account of Huli medical pluralism: the historical background to current practice.

The early controversies concerning the place of historical material within an anthropological enquiry have no relevance here. The rejection of 'conjectural history' was in part a response to the excesses of the speculations of some diffusionists, and in part a means of establishing the academic respectability of the novel subject of social anthropology. Nevertheless, while ahistorical ethnographies are no longer the norm, accounts of the sort of timeless 'Anthropologyland' so scathingly debunked by Cohn (1980) still appear. Such an approach would be especially inappropriate here. The past is of great relevance to the Huli. The way that they use history is in some respects similar to the use of myth as charter, a familiar concept in anthropological writing from Malinowski onwards. But the Huli are perhaps unusual in that they do not, as many other such societies are said to do (Leach 1961:126), remain in a constant relationship with the distant past. Huli creation myths are not 'like concertinas' (I. M. Lewis 1976:122). Instead, the Huli consider that the progression of the generations is accompanied by predestined moral and social changes, so that for them time does have 'depth' (Leach:ibid). They interpret the present and anticipate the future in terms of this progression. Their own historicism cannot be understood without considering their particular view of the past, and the nature of the past events that they deem significant.

An historical perspective is also essential for understanding the current medical mix. Ethnographies of illness have until recently stressed the symbolic or ideological coherence of the medical practice of other cultures. Modern responses have been seen as marginal to this project. The Huli did not come under direct outside influence until the 1950s. Many former treatments were used only rarely if ever by most people by the time I made my study, but knowledge of their rationale, procedures, materials and spells was still retrievable by observing the relatively rare occasions when a traditional rite was employed, or by talking with retired specialists about techniques now generally discarded. Methods such as these can be used to reconstruct an ideal 'traditional medical system'. However, this approach would be based on the false assumption that for these societies it was usual for a timeless tradition to be disturbed by the physical arrival of colonial intruders. In the case of the Huli, and most such societies, the limited evidence available concerning their experiences in the early part of this century and beyond suggests the meaninglessness of dubbing a particular historical period as representing 'tradition'. In Papua New Guinea the rate of change has certainly increased markedly over the last twenty years, but our preoccupation with the adoption by members of other cultures of the trappings of Western living can distract us from the significance of other and earlier changes, changes which may or may not have been prompted by the secondary effects of colonial expansion.

The shifting scene of medical choices is a difficult one to capture. The methodology employed in this study was designed to derive as representative a picture as possible. The result is primarily an analysis of the range of Huli responses to illness that I observed during the particular years I have spent with them. This account is thus a single slice across an evanescent subject. The analogy with a microtome is apt. The two-dimensional image examined by the microscopist is essential for the appreciation of form, but it cannot offer more than grounds for speculation about process. My intention here is to understand the process of decision-making and the process of change. The Huli are responding to a profusion of novel influences, both in terms of new ideas and of new techniques. Their acceptance or rejection of these novelties is not a passive process. Innovations are assessed according to the empirical evidence of their value. Their incorporation or rejection is also influenced by resonances between particular novelties and traditional knowledge. This process is both creative and dialectical. The pattern of medical pluralism that emerges in the following pages is commonly informed by the syncretistic resolution of discrepancies between traditional thought and the elements of Western thought that are presented to them.

The organisation of the data

Scientific medicine categorises its knowledge of diseases according to their aetiology, clinical features and pathological changes discernible through special investigations. On the basis of such categorisation, statements concerning likely prognosis can be made, and treatment strategies are selected. Diagnoses in most cases refer to the particular pathological lesion deemed responsible for the illness, and may also define the causative agent. Diagnosis is an important aspect of all medical systems. Through diagnosis the amorphous threat represented by illness may become definite, and particular strategies of treatment are indicated. Amongst studies of diagnosis in other cultures, Frake's (1961) account of diagnosis among the Subanun is unusual in the coherence of the classification of disease that is presented. One reason for the rarity of such elegant accounts of disease taxonomy in the ethnographic literature may be that data of this sort have not in general been relevant to the concerns of anthropologists investigating illness, and so, like Evans-Pritchard, they may therefore have 'tired of the fruitless labour of collecting the names of innumerable diseases and medicinal plants' (1937:481). While the preoccupations of their ethnographer may have had some influence here, the Subanun are distinguished from many other societies in the extent of their knowledge of medicinal plants, and the consistency of their criteria for prescribing one rather than another. Schemes of classification do not exist in the abstract. In this case, the Subanun's intricate discrimination between diseases is an essential preliminary to the selection of one of 724 different herbal remedies.

The ordering of Huli illness terms reflects their cultural preoccupations, just as the Subanun system reflects theirs. But the Huli possess no complex taxonomic hierarchy of disease names comparable to that described by Frake. Their language of illness is rich and varied, but to attempt to arrange all their illness descriptions into sets of contrasting categories distinguished according to the nature of the symptoms would not reflect their view. As we shall see, the nature of the symptoms can be important in a number of Huli diagnoses, though in others the symptoms may be of little interest. In some circumstances the symptoms may follow from the diagnosis. The symptomatology therefore comprises one aspect only of the complex set of interactions between the disease process, culturally grounded interpretations of the significance of the illness, and social influences that guide responses in particular cases of illness. Good (1977:27) stresses these wider ramifications of diagnosis when he refers to a disease category as 'a syndrome of typical experiences, a set of words, experiences, and feelings which typically "run together" for the members of a society. Such a syndrome is not merely a reflection of symptoms linked with each other in natural reality, but a set of experiences associated through networks of meaning and social interaction in a society.' A presentation of Huli responses to illness according to sorts of symptoms would be similarly inappropriate. Instead, a breakdown of their concepts according to the level and type of explanation that they imply does reflect their concerns. And this approach is convenient for analysing the relationships between their beliefs about illness and their responses to it. However, the detailed distinctions that Hulis make can only emerge from the analysis of instances of illness. Here I will outline the scheme which has guided my presentation of that material.

In a large proportion of cases, Hulis become aware of the presence of illness, but offer no complex interpretations of it. In such instances their illness terms are largely descriptive, addressed to the question, What is wrong? In addition, Hulis have theories about a number of physiological and pathological processes. In a number of cases they may describe illnesses in terms of the nature of the lesion, referring to the bodily process that is disordered. Illness descriptions of this sort are broadly addressed to the question, How did this illness occur? Where such diagnoses are applied, specific therapies are often indicated which are understood to reverse the pathological changes. I consider their understanding of and responses to illnesses of these two sorts in chapter 6. One aspect of bodily processes that is particularly important to the Huli, and which is central to their concepts of health and illness, is that concerned with sexuality, growth and development. I consider this separately in chapter 7.

The number of occasions when they present an unequivocal view of the specific circumstances that led to the development of the illness is relatively small. Illness descriptions of this sort are addressed to such questions as, Why did this illness occur? Why did it afflict me? Why did it develop now? What did I do to deserve it? Who is responsible? or Which spirit have I offended? The relationships between the answers to questions such as these and the social organisation of the society is the stuff of most anthropological writing concerned with illness. I discuss illnesses with explanations grounded in social relations in chapter 8, and those relating to religious ideas in chapter 9. Illnesses of these sorts will in addition usually be describable in terms of their concepts of bodily processes, and according to the nature of the lesion or symptoms. These features of the illness may also guide aspects of therapy. But in illnesses where answers to the question, Why? are known, responses are likely to be directed to whatever harmful influences the illness is ascribed.

Distinctions of this sort are guided by a number of issues, including the nature of the illness, and the attributes of the sufferer. In their turn, they guide the level of concern, the significance attributed to the illness, and the particular treatment. Before proceeding to the detailed discussion of these interactions I will set the scene from a number of perspectives. Chapter 2 places their present concerns in terms of their historical experience. Chapter 3 describes key features of current social organisation. In chapter 4 the broad themes of their views of health and illness are introduced. Chapter 5 presents various quantitative data concerning the burden of illness, explanations of illness and the selection of treatment strategies.

2

Historical Perspectives

The Tari Basin is now traversed by a network of roads that connect to the Highlands Highway, and thus most of the major highland and coastal towns. Many Hulis now spend much of their time away from the Southern Highlands working or visiting, often travelling in trucks driven and owned by Hulis. The air in Tari is filled by the thrumming of twin-rotored helicopters which maintain a constant shuttle to remote oil exploration camps. The bachelor cult through which young men were expected to receive their preparation for manhood is now all but defunct. Traditional healing is now rarely practised. The vast majority of Hulis are at least nominal Christians, and the majority attend church services regularly. These and other aspects of change represent radical departures from traditional experience. Glasse (1968) tells us that in 1959 the impact of the administration and the Christian missions was limited, and that rituals were still practised regularly. The seeming abandonment of traditional practice and adoption of the novelties, such as Western medicine, described here, were thus condensed into two decades or less. In this chapter I describe this remarkable change, first in terms of the development of administrative control, and secondly in terms of the traditional perceptions which have guided their adoption of new ideas and practices. Many of these traditional concerns relate to the Huli's earlier historical experience. Prins (1979) points out the importance of distinguishing 'superficial change and underlying continuity from underlying change and superficial continuity.' The material presented here allows us to make this distinction in relation to the pattern of medical pluralism expressed in the Huli's response to illness.

Administration and development
First contact

On 21 April 1935 the Huli had their first experience of an administration patrol. Jack Hides, Jim O'Malley, ten policemen and twenty-eight carriers emerged from the lowlands and entered Huli territory at a place called Yubaya, some 10 kilometres south-east of the present administrative centre of Komo (see figs. 2 and 3). This meeting was marked by inevitable

10

Fig. 1 The Tari Basin

misconceptions. Hides (1936:77) describes his sense of wonder at his first sight of the 'rolling timbered slopes of a huge valley system. On every slope were cultivated squares, while little columns of smoke rising in the still air revealed to us the homes of the people of this land. I had never seen anything more beautiful.' Besides his delight at discovering 'a population such as I had sometimes dreamed of finding' (ibid:78) his arrival in Huli territory meant relief from the hardships of the four months journey from the Papuan Plateau, and the possibility of fresh vegetables and pork for his hungry band. At first the people would not approach the patrol. They allowed Hides to help himself from the gardens, but made it clear that they wanted these intruders to go back whence they came. On the second day a leader came forward. Hides dubbed him 'Besoso', Motu for 'big beard', and was impressed by his bearing, describing him variously as 'a splendid figure of a man,' 'this imperial figure,' and 'like a military officer.' 'He jerked his head to me questioningly. I thought he was asking where we had come from, so I pointed south-westwards over the limestone barrier' (ibid:82). Hides was pointing towards *humbirini andaga*, the place of the dead. Informants who as young men had been present at this encounter told me that the leader (Dabure-Puya) who approached Hides recognised in Hides' face the features of his brother Barina who had recently died. Dabure-Puya told the people gathered there that Barina had returned, and he went off to kill a pig for his brother. 'As evening approached...Besoso beckoned to me once more. When I came up

11

Key

‑ ‑ ‑ ‑ ‑   Huli area

Capital letters
   e.g. DUNA   language group

●   Tari Administrative Centre

Fig. 2 The Huli area and nearby peoples

to him, he took my arm and pointed northwards across the canyon..."Na bobi, Na bobi", he said, and shook his head vigorously' (ibid:85). Dabure-Puya was telling his brother to be on his way and not to kill him (*nababe, nababe*, 'Don't kill me, don't kill me').

The next day the patrol set off to the north-east. Hides suspected 'Besoso' of planning an attack, and 'fired over the men in ambush. The latter removed themselves with surprising speed...And as we went on...there, waiting brazenly a few yards off the road with about fifty men, was the bombastic Besoso. I fancied I could see his chest still heaving with the exertion of his

12

Fig. 3 Witnesses to Hides' 1935 patrol identifying 'Besoso's' photograph from Hides' (1936) account of the patrol.

run from the place of ambush to this retreat' (ibid:87). In fact fear is a more likely explanation of Dabure-Puya's heaving chest. The Huli still regarded these interlopers as spirits. This is clear from Hides' own account. For example, he describes how a particular 'chief...would point to our white skins, our clothes and steel, and then pointing to the sky, would look at us questioningly, as though to confirm his statements' (ibid:96). The claims of surviving witnesses to these events that the Huli did not initiate combat is therefore plausible.

On 28 April a further suspected ambush resulted in the deaths of two Huli men amongst a group who were shadowing the patrol. That afternoon Hides was led by a man he refers to as 'Mambu' (*mambo* is a Huli term for 'friend') to a suitable camp site. He offered pork, and 'brought us genuinely friendly people whom he indicated belonged to him. Among them was a fine old man. He appeared to be suffering from asthma, and asked me to cure him...to please him I gave him a little sugar with a few drops of kerosene. After he had taken it the look on his face told me that he was cured already' (ibid:100). The Huli were particularly troubled by *dama* at the time of Hides' appearance. *Dama* had always existed, but in the past were said to have impinged little on the affairs of men. A range of afflictions experienced during this period

13

were interpreted in terms of intense and novel predation by *dama* (see pp. 24, 27–8). The old man presented to Hides was taking advantage of this opportunity for making an appeal to a spirit (*dama*) in such uniquely concrete form. As an informant recalled the event: 'We thought that we squander so many pigs to give to *dama*, but we had never seen the face of one. Now a real *dama* has come amongst us. We thought it would be good to take this sick man to ask the *dama* to remove his illness... the sick man was delighted with the cure. We wanted to give more pork, but the *kiap* didn't understand, so we left it at that.' Such readiness to accept novel circumstances and often to attempt to gain advantage from them has been characteristic of their responses to the changes of recent decades.

There was one more Huli death, a girl who was killed by a policeman. There is no record of this incident in Hides' patrol report, and it is most likely that he was ignorant of it. The patrol left the Tari Basin on 30 April 1935 leaving the Hulis with their first experience of outsiders. Hides had left understandably threatened by the press of armed Huli men, yodelling as they followed his progress. But his exaggerated sense of danger resulted in many unnecessary deaths during this patrol, most of which occurred before and after he entered the Huli area. At the inquiry into these deaths, Hides reported the firing of 133 rounds of ammunition during the course of the patrol. The following year Ivan Champion, a less romantic and otherwise steadier figure, completed a similar patrol without a single shot being fired.

The consolidation of administrative and mission influence

A base camp was established beside Lake Kutubu in 1937. A limited number of patrols passed through Huli territory, but further exploration and the extension of administration control were interrupted by the Pacific War. The post at Lake Kutubu was abandoned, and during the early 1940s the Hulis' lives were influenced not by European patrol officers, but by Enga men travelling through Huli territory (pp. 28–9). The administration did not return to Lake Kutubu until 1949. From there they made regular patrols, and in 1952 established a patrol post at a site known to the Hulis as Lumulumu. This administrative centre is known as Tari, a name which derives from a mishearing of the name of the major river which drains the basin, the Tagali. Pacification was more or less completed throughout the Huli area by 1960.

By the 1950s opportunities for proselytising large uncontacted populations had become rare. Tari was therefore an attractive prospect for the Christian missions. Four groups promptly established themselves there. Methodists (now United Church), the Asia Pacific Christian Mission (now the Evangelical Church of Papua), an undenominational fundamentalist group, Capuchin Catholics, and Seventh-day Adventists.

The process of change has in some respects been slower for the Huli than for other highland groups of similar size and population density. Reasons for this include the isolation of their region from commercial centres, and the absence of settlers or plantations. The Huli were not encouraged to plant cash crops until recently, so the favoured means for most people to earn money has been migrant labour. At the time of Papua New Guinea's attainment of Independence in 1975 it was recognised that the Southern Highlands Province was one of the least developed in the country. Government policy was directed towards equalisation of incomes among different areas of the country, and hence towards favouring the poorer areas. In the Southern Highlands this policy was expressed in the Southern Highlands Integrated Rural Development Project which was established in 1978. The main component of the Project was to construct an all-weather road from Tari which would connect with the Highlands Highway. This was completed in 1981. Other components included the promotion of cash cropping, primarily coffee and tea, educational projects, particularly establishing two new high schools in the province, research and extension projects in subsistence agriculture and nutrition and a health component. The health component consists of two new health sub-centres in the eastern half of the province, a nurse training school at the provincial capital, Mendi, and an in-service training programme for health workers.

The main treatment facility now available to the Huli is Tari Major Health Centre. This is the referral centre for the Koroba, Kopiago and Komo Districts, and so serves a population of over 100,000. Staffing varies, but two doctors and some ten nurses are usual, assisted by some thirty nurse aides and fifteen hospital orderlies. There are about 100 beds, and facilities include an out-patient department, operating theatre, labour room, laboratory, dental clinic, radiology section and malnutrition ward. Only in exceptional cases are patients referred to the provincial hospital at Mendi, so for most cases of illness, to be admitted to the health centre is to reach the top of the pyramid of available Western health services.

Simple treatments and referral to the health centre for more serious conditions are obtained through the network of aid posts. These are the basic tier of Papua New Guinea's rural health services. Each serves a population of about 1,000, and is manned by orderlies who, on completion of six years or less of primary schooling, are trained in the diagnosis and treatment of most common complaints. Maternal and child health clinics for the Tari area are based on the health centre and four health subcentres which are run by the United Church and Asia Pacific Christian Missions.

These are the bare facts of the rapid changes of recent years. The Huli's reception of the first patrol demonstrates the importance of Huli presuppositions in guiding their reactions to novel events. The principles underlying their attempts to reconcile such innovations with their own cosmology are the subject of the next section.

Huli sacred geography and the appreciation of change

Huli mythology, and in particular the lore of their major ritual (*dindi gamu*, literally 'earth spell'), offers a set of assumptions about the world. These assumptions supply a grid which orders some of the Huli responses to the changes of recent times. For example, their response to Christianity, highly relevant to current choices of treatment, can only be understood in terms of certain continuities between Christianity, as this has been represented, and the lore of *dindi gamu*. This lore is clearly derived from certain geological, geographical and social givens and comprises a set of premises concerning past and future relationships with their land, with the neighbouring peoples and with each other. Recent novelties are readily accommodated within this overarching scheme. Indeed, the events of the last decades are seen as confirmation of the fundamental truth of this lore. In this section I will therefore outline elements of the *dindi gamu* lore and consider other features of their historical experience that are relevant to understanding Huli enthusiasm for aspects of Western culture.

The range of their geographical horizons and the extent of change have increased greatly with the intensive outside influence that has occurred since the 1950s. But their culture cannot be said to have been isolated or static prior to contact with Europeans. The Huli saw themselves as being in the centre of a group of peoples all of whom were descended from a common ancestor, Hela. (This is a particularly Huli view which is not reciprocated in the mythology of the other groups concerned.) In addition to Huli, Hela fathered Obena (the Enga, Ipili and Paiela to the north), Duna (the Duna people to the west), Duguba (all peoples of the Papuan Plateau, but especially the Etoro, Onabasulu, Kaluli, Tsinali and Petamini), and Hewa (the groups around Lake Kutubu, primarily Foi and Fasu; see fig. 2). The Huli maintained trading relations with these peoples, most importantly on a north–south axis. From the Duguba in the south they obtained bows, sago, hornbill beaks, rope and the tree oil used in decoration and ritual. Hulis travelled as far south as the Kikori River to obtain these articles. From the Obena they obtained traditional salt and stone axe blades. Besides these practical links, their relations with the neighbouring cultures find expression in religious thought. It was held to be essential that Hulis should act as intermediaries between Obena and Duguba. Should men of these groups meet, the balance of the world would be disrupted, and the 'earth would deteriorate' (*dindi ko holebira*). Duguba and Duna dancers were required for some major rituals at the sacred sites (*kebanda*) closest to the boundaries with these other groups. In other *kebanda* Hulis dressed up as Duguba to perform their dances (known as *dawa gereya*). Most of their ritual is uniquely Huli, but the willingness to experiment with and incorporate new religious ideas, apparent in their response to Christian proselytisation, is also shown in the way they previously adopted practices from their neighbours. The healing rite *nogo golo* (p. 158) is said to have been learned from the Enga. The Duguba are feared as sorcerers and *hambu* sorcery (p. 145) techniques are said to derive from the Papuan Plateau. The Duguba were said to decide when to initiate the *dindi gamu* cycle. Other types of sorcery are said to come from Duna, and it may be that the common traditional practice of treating illness by divination and sacrifice to the spirit (*dama*) deemed responsible may have come to the fore as a healing strategy through recent Duna influence.

No archaeological work has been done in the Tari area, so any account of Huli pre-history must be based largely on oral history. Their oral history gives no indication of the geographical origins of the present population. On the contrary, the creation myths describe the emergence of the ancestors of each clan at the sacred sites (*kebanda*) in each parish or group of parishes where the main fertility rituals were held. They also talk of other populations having lived before the time of the founders of the present generation. Three or four epochs are commonly cited. These previous populations are said to have been destroyed by water, and the present epoch begins with the founding ancestors emerging in a land of mud and water, until they succeeded in causing the rivers to flow and the land to be drained. Besides their mythology, Hulis cite the frequent discovery of fragments of wooden spades, digging sticks and other artefacts when they are digging drainage ditches as evidence for these previous epochs. It therefore seems reasonable to assume that the Huli have occupied the Tari Basin for a considerable period.

Accounts of a number of geological events are presented in the oral history with great immediacy. This body of knowledge is imbued by the Huli sense of the interconnectedness of geological and human affairs. The earth, mountains and rivers are seen as animate, and responsive to men's deeds or misdeeds. The Tari Basin was formed by the disruption of drainage by volcanic activity. While the major changes would have been complete long before people arrived in the area, ash layers indicate significant falls of tephra during the period of settlement. The most recent of these has had a major influence upon Huli thought. The dramatic event of a heavy fall of volcanic ash is remembered in the mythology of many New Guinea societies (collated in Blong 1982). The Huli remember this not as a disaster, but as something desirable. The last major ash fall probably arose from an eruption of Long Island *c.* 1700 AD (Blong ibid), and the Huli refer to its effects as *mbingi* (literally 'time of darkness'). The myth of *mbingi* is more than an account of its last occurrence. It also comprises the lore to guide people in their preparations for and survival from the next *mbingi*. These concerns are still current, and inform contemporary interpretations of events and ideas. This version of the myth is from Bareagua of Hambuali.

First they heard thunder, and the rumbling of mountains. When they heard this they said '*mbingi* will come, we must build houses. We must build these *mbingi* houses on high ground.' Each parish built one huge house. They roofed them not with thatch, but with slabs of the hardest timber. When the houses were completed they said, 'We must prepare food', and they stored food and water in the houses. They stacked firewood in the houses, and put male and female pigs inside. Sisters returned to their brothers. The lore of *mbingi* told that men must be apart from their wives. They had waited three months, and in the fourth month it became dark. The people stayed inside their *mbingi* houses. When darkness fell, snakes, lizards, frogs, rats, possums, cassowaries and other birds followed the people into the houses. The lore had said that something to frighten you will come inside, but you must not kill it, and that game will come inside, but you must let it live. It became dark, and they said 'We must wait now to see what falls from the sky.' And black earth fell. As this rained down, all their old houses were buried and destroyed. Trees were destroyed, sugar cane and bananas were buried. On the first day after this, an only son was permitted to go out. Those with one sibling could go out on the second day, and so on. When they looked out they could not recognise where their gardens or houses had been. The land was covered with black earth. It had fallen with rain, and was like mud. But no one was killed. They all stayed in their *mbingi* houses, and none of these collapsed. When it became light again, the animals went out. When the people went outside, they found that the stuff that had fallen (*dapindu*) had covered trees, filled creeks and made their land unrecognisable. But soon the crops grew again, and grew more quickly and more plentifully than before. Where sugar cane had been before, sugar grew again. Where sweet potatoes had been, sweet potato grew again. Where bananas had been, they grew again, more prolifically than before. The ground is poor now, so you don't see the stuff that fell (*dapindu*) in garden soil any more. Though sometimes when you are digging in swamps you see some of the black earth from that time. One woman went into the *mbingi* house pregnant, and carried her son there. He was called Mbi (darkness). We are the eleventh generation since his time.

The Huli world view entails a strong sense of entropy. The fertility of the earth must inevitably deteriorate, and only through the return of *mbingi* can a new era of plenty begin. This is also a moral view. The physical decline of the earth is paralleled by a moral decline into anarchy and promiscuity. The properly controlled return of *mbingi* will summon a new age of plenty and harmony. The major ritual sequence, *dindi gamu*, was intended to effect this.

Whatever the material feasibility of such a project, it is important to point out that in its most ambitious form, the full *dindi gamu* ritual sequence was not politically feasible. Extended cooperation between members of a single parish was unusual. *Dindi gamu* would have required the cooperation not only of all Hulis, but of all the neighbouring peoples as well, and would therefore have embraced peoples of several language groups over an area of some 2,500 square miles. In practice, individual parishes and groups of parishes performed their rituals in their own sacred sites (*kebanda*). These local rituals were staged to address local problems such as drought or disease. However, in addition to these local concerns, the *kebanda* rituals performed at key sacred sites were also conceived as contributing to the grand scheme of the *dindi gamu* sequence, and were thought to be ultimately directed to the more ambitious aims of *dindi gamu*, particularly the arrest of moral and physical decline through the recall of *mbingi*. This assumption was protected both by political reality and by the social organisation of knowledge in Huli society. The dangers of travel in former times prevented any individual from experiencing all the putative components of a completed sequence. In addition, detailed knowledge of such fundamental importance was secret, so that inconsistencies between different experts' conceptions of *dindi gamu* were not revealed. This lore and the ritual authority that flowed from it was associated with a small number of specialists, *dindi gamuyi*, 'those who hold *dindi gamu*'. This knowledge was passed from father to son within the clans whose land contains one of the principal sacred sites. The names of these key ritualists, some eight men in all, were known to all Hulis. The account I present here is a composite of the views of the surviving ritual specialists from the key sacred sites. In particular I have drawn on the knowledge of Yaliduma-Dai of Gelote, Hubi-Hondomogo of Bebenete, Dabu-Togoiya of Daberanda and Wara-Timbabu of Hari Hibira.

The geographical dimension of the *dindi gamu* cycle concerns the flow of ritual power broadly from south-west to north-east, from the Papuan Plateau to the central highlands. Key sacred sites are said to be joined by the 'root of the earth', which has the physical form of a thick liane entwined by a python, and provides a channel through which flow water and, during performances of *dindi gamu*, smoke. The muffled roar of an underground stream is said to mark the passage of the root of the earth. It is conceived as both a pathway of power for *dindi gamu*, and as the physical support of the earth. Active points along this pathway are marked by the major sacred sites. Such places are referred to as, literally, 'the knots of the earth' (*dindi pongone*), where the key strands of the earth's fabric interweave, and so gain strength. The root of the earth is said to be accessible to ritual manipulation at these points. The major sacred sites were hidden in groves of hoop pines (*Araucaria cunninghamii*). The sanctum consisted of a cave, a pool or other striking natural formation associated with the founding ancestor. The significant features of each site, the buildings constructed there, and the details of the ritual performance enacted there, followed the creation myths of each area.

The principal sacred sites are to be found on either side of ranges, as if to mark the re-emergence of the root of the earth from its passage through mountains. The source of ritual power is said to lie in the lowlands of the Papuan Plateau. The major *dindi gamu* cycle capable of summoning *mbingi* is said to be initiated by ritual activity on the Plateau. All Plateau groups are referred to as 'Duguba' by the Huli, but the orientation of each Huli ritual centre affects the particular Plateau group to which this term refers.

At Hari Hibira (site B, fig. 4), the southernmost major Huli site, the central feature was a cave in which a pool of water was said to cover the liane of

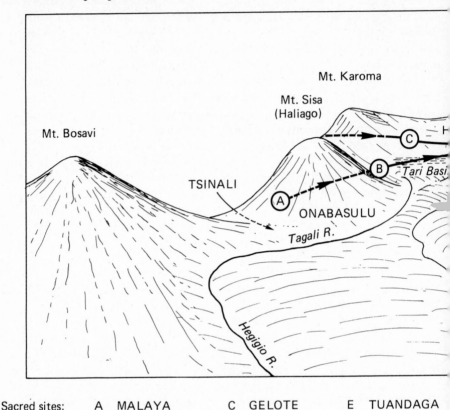

Sacred sites:
A	MALAYA	C	GELOTE	E	TUANDAGA
B	HARI HIBIRA	D	BEBENETE	F	BIBIPAITE

Fig. 4 Huli sacred geography

the root of the earth. As the fertility of the earth declines, so the water level
in this pool falls. It can only be replenished by the performance of *dindi gamu*.
The ritual leader at this site, Wara-Timbabu, initiated some performances in
response to local need alone. But on occasions of generalised adversity, such
as widespread drought, he believed that he was taking his cue from the Papuan
Plateau people to the south. The peoples of the Plateau were thought to hold
their own *dindi gamu* at such times, though instead of pigs they were believed
to sacrifice fish, frogs, possums, birds and human corpses. Huli traders and
travellers were not invited to Plateau rituals, but it is possible that the Huli
accounts of 'Duguba *dindi gamu*' are misinterpretations of the Plateau
hunting-lodge rituals described by Schieffelin (1982). The Plateau sacred site
was said to be on the other side of Mount Haliago, at a place called Malaya
(site A, fig. 4) which was joined to the cave at Hari Hibira by the root of the
earth. Smoke was said to travel through the root of the earth to emerge at

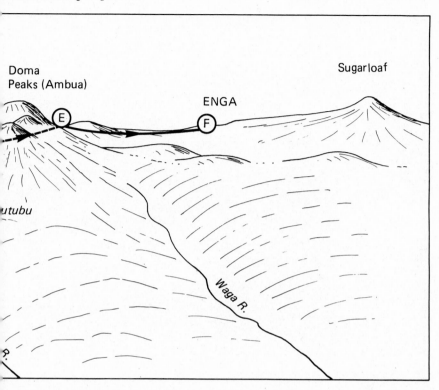

this cave. When Wara-Timbabu saw smoke on the mountain he interpreted this as evidence of a call from the Plateau people to instigate his *dindi gamu*. The Plateau peoples of the Malaya area were not aware of their putative role in *dindi gamu*. Nevertheless, the name the Huli use to refer to the sacred site on the Papuan Plateau, Malaya, is said by the Kaluli, Onabasulu (on whose land the site is) and Etoro peoples of the Papuan Plateau to be the origin place of all Plateau peoples, and for all these groups has considerable cosmological significance (Schieffelin, pers. comm.).

Hulis at Gelote (site C, fig. 4) orientate themselves to a different set of 'Dugubas', the Tsinali, who inhabit the Papuan Plateau to the west of Gelote. The sanctum there is also a cave which was approached along a great avenue through the pine grove. Inside are stalactites, the breasts of the creatress, which were annointed with red pigment and tigasso oil as the culmination of the Gelote ritual (fig. 5).

At Bebenete (site D, fig. 4), the sanctum was again reached by means of a broad avenue through the hoop pines. The performance there culminated in the ritualist hurling a bundle of pork, which had been bound with the cane used for hafting axes, from a cliff-top into the river Hulia. This 'axe' (*ayumbu*) is for the two water spirits that continually clear debris from the

21

Fig. 5 Yaluduma-Dai within the sanctum at Gelote

lower reaches of main rivers. If they tire of their work the rivers will flood, and this epoch, like the last, will end with the world being destroyed by water. *Dindi gamu* is intended to achieve renewal and fertility. In times of drought one purpose is to summon rain. But the need for balance and control, central to the Huli world view, is here expressed in the encouragement offered to the spirits who must maintain the drainage of Huli land.

Ceremonies were performed at these sites as well as at the lesser sites every few years, with no coordination between them other than the tendency for different groups to respond contemporaneously to parallel adversities. However, coordination between the key sites was an essential prerequisite in the ultimate goal of *dindi gamu*, the summoning of *mbingi*. For *mbingi* to be sent successfully, a *dindi gamu* ritual at the southern major sites was to be followed by a ritual at Bebenete (site D, fig. 4). The smoke from the Bebenete ceremony would pass through Mount Ambua to emerge at the sacred site of Tuandaga (site E, fig. 4). From there it would pass to Bibipaite (site F, fig. 4). Bibipaite is 40 miles to the north-east of Mount Ambua, well outside Huli territory. The Enga-speakers of that area, the Kaman, do have a sacred site in the place referred to by the Huli as Bibipaite, though they refer to it as Pipikam (Raich 1967). The ritual leaders there know of the Huli interest in the site, though they performed their ceremonies there quite independently of Huli ritual. The root of the earth is said by the Huli to emerge at Bibipaite, and from there ascends into the sky. The flow of ritual power generated by this chain of performances would climax in the fall of *mbingi*, and the physical and moral renewal that this would bring.

Their explanation for past failure to achieve the return of *mbingi* has striking parallels with Christian teaching. The fortuitous correspondence between key dogmas in the two religious traditions is a central strand in the explanation of the Huli's enthusiasm for Christianity. In an early performance of *dindi gamu* at Bebenete, variously timed at between three and ten generations ago, a boy named Bayebaye was killed in error. A little of his blood from a cut finger was to have been added to the oblation of pork, but in an excess of enthusiasm he was killed. His mother left Bebenete to return to her home amongst the Duna, the Huli's western neighbours. She keened as she left them, and this mourning lament was a curse upon future generations:

I, Bayebaye's mother, am leaving you here. I will take the propitious path. But you will find famine. You will have to slaughter your herds. You will fornicate. You will grovel for food. You will forage for rubbish. She will tell you that she is your mother, but you will take her anyway. She will tell you that she is your sister, but you will take her anyway. He will tell you he is your father, but you will kill him anyway. He will tell you he is your brother, but you will kill him anyway. You will find famine. You will be able to think of nothing but where to find food. There will be plagues, and you will find death.

Bayebaye means 'perfect,' here referring to great fertility of crops, people and pigs, and also to social harmony. But the boy was killed, and Hulis see in their current predicament evidence of the fulfilment of his mother's curse. This will not be revoked unless Bayebaye's death is compensated. This putative compensation payment would involve all Hulis, as well as the surrounding groups. Similarities between Bayebaye and Christ are apparent to Hulis to the extent that the two names are frequently used interchangeably. Many feel that the Huli are responsible for the crucifixion, and a number of attempts to give compensation payments to missionaries have been made. I will return to this point when I discuss modern resonances of *dindi gamu* below.

The mistaken killing of Bayebaye, and his mother's curse, are one expression of the Huli conviction that decline and deterioration are inevitable unless specific measures are taken to prevent this. This conviction is also basic to the wider lore of *dindi gamu*. The Huli have deep genealogies by New Guinea Highlands standards. Ten or more generations are commonly cited, particularly during the formal presentations of genealogies which constitute land titles. Theirs is a fifteen-base counting system incorporating body parts as numerals. This counting system sets the idiom for stylised statements within the *dindi gamu* lore concerning the accelerating vitiation that must accompany the unfolding of the generations. The common view is that the current generation is the thirteenth since the beginning of this epoch. The epoch will end with the fifteenth generation, either disastrously, consumed by fire, or climactically, with the return of *mbingi*. At the beginning of the epoch the earth was new and moist, but it must dessicate and age as the human body does. Just as a dry skin is a sign of debility, the Huli reference to 'dry earth' is concerned with more than its moisture content. It implies some underlying affliction which if left unchecked can only progress to a state of complete barrenness. This and other statements concerning current decline are expressed in the *dindi gamu* lore in terms of past predictions of the future. Yaluduma-Dai of Gelote put it like this:

Now it is the thirteenth generation. It was said that in the thirteenth generation, no one will listen (*halenengi hale naholebira – hale*, the ear, is the stem for the numeral thirteen. 'Listening' refers to obedience to Huli lore.) The young will not obey their parents. In the thirteenth generation the swamps will become dry. Grasses will grow where only swamp plants grew before. In the fourteenth generation they will have seen all this with their eyes (*denengi deme handai holebira*, where *de*, eye, is the stem for the numeral fourteen). Babies will speak as soon as they are born, young boys will develop beards and pubic hair, young girls will develop breasts, it will be a time of frantic theft and fornication. That was the lore. And it is proving true. Now young men mature too soon. They refuse to work the land, dig ditches or look after pigs. They just roam around fighting, stealing, fornicating, and will not listen to their fathers. People take what is not theirs, they help themselves to others' belongings and wives. This is the time for us to die. It is now the afternoon. There is not much time left to us now. The world is dry. Where we are now was once a swamp. Before boys could not walk across it as the water would have been over their heads. Before it was new ground, but now the earth is old and worn out. (Yaluduma-Dai of Gelote)

Another aspect of degeneration that must accompany the unfolding of the generations is epidemic disease. This development too is said to have been predicted in the lore of *dindi gamu*, and began to become a reality during the last generation. It is expressed in terms of an assault on the Huli by a horde of spirits (*dama*). Until the last generation they were confined within the sacred site at Gelote. Since their escape they have wreaked havoc amongst the Huli, causing disease and death while satisfying their inordinate appetites for human flesh. They have also caused distrust and conflict through their malign interventions in human affairs.

These demons (*dama*) emerged in my time. When you whites were ready to come to our land, these demons preceded you. They consumed people voraciously. They show us many roads that lead to death. Men are few, demons are many. When I was a boy they emerged. All this sacrificing pigs to *damas*, that began then. In my father's time they did not sacrifice for this profusion of *damas*. They sacrificed for the spirits of their ancestors. In those days life was good. Since the *damas* emerged, life has become hard for us. In former times wars were only small, and we did not kill women or destroy houses. But just before the whites came there were terrible wars, with many people killed. (Hubi-Hondomogo of Bebenete)

24

The Huli view is that a fixed pool of human knowledge and ability was created by the founding ancestors to equip the first and subsequent generations. This knowledge is contained in creation myths and ritual lore. They therefore scrutinise and reinterpret such lore, and particularly the *dindi gamu* material, in their endeavour to render intelligible the radical changes of recent decades. Even the arrival of Europeans is said to have been predicted. Their purpose and the outcome of their presence are also explained in the *dindi gamu* lore. Various objects held at the sacred sites are now interpreted as evidence that Europeans were present in the distant past, and have chosen this time to return. It is said that some red cloth, a rosary, three shoes and some hair from the head of a European woman were preserved at Daberanda, a sacred site near Tari, as mementoes of the earlier presence of Europeans. The roads that Europeans were so concerned to build were reminiscent of the broad avenues maintained within sacred sites. 'We used to build roads inside the *kebanda* too, like the whites do. We are brothers.' When the whites first came they announced that they were 'kiaps', the pidgin title for patrol officers. The title 'kiap' was confused with 'Kebe', the founding ancestor or ancestors of each group. This interpretation was confirmed by the 'kiap's' interest in the sacred groves of hoop pines, which they felled as the most desirable timber for the construction of administration and mission settlements. 'We had not planted these trees, they are Kebali's trees. When the whites wanted to fell them, we knew that the trees were theirs, that they had planted them before. They were theirs', so we let them take them away.'

However, the most striking concordance to the Huli between their lore and the arrival of Europeans concerns the past and future role of the boy Bayebaye who is said to have been killed at the last serious attempt to summon *mbingi* through *dindi gamu*, and whose death must be compensated before the attempt can be made again. Surviving key ritualists claim that in the years before Europeans arrived attempts were made to set in motion the full *dindi gamu* sequence. Compensation for Bayebaye is seen as a necessary preliminary for the recall of *mbingi*, and it is therefore likely that strategies for achieving this were under discussion. Bayebaye is described as 'red-skinned' in the mythological account of his death:

The whites (literally 'reds') did not come for no reason. They came for Bayebaye's compensation. That was my father's lore. My father said that the whites would come. He said that before they have crossed the River Tagali we must determine quickly who killed Bayebaye, and so we must pay the compensation immediately. He said that they will be like a river in flood, they will keep coming. They are behaving as we would do. When we have suffered a death, we seek retribution from the people responsible. If they do not pay us, we kill them, wreck their gardens and destroy their houses. That is what the whites did. Now they appoint councillors and committees to arrange for the compensation to be paid. (Hulia-Hewabe of Talete)

Since the whites have come, Bayebaye's mother's curse has come true. There is incest, and the ground is bad. (Hubi-Hondomogo of Bebenete).

Historical perspectives

The current predicament can only be resolved and an auspicious future secured through collaboration with the whites. The arrival of the whites is a further indication of imminent demise, but it has also offered a variety of avenues for resolution. The various avenues intended to achieve such resolution differ in the extent to which they draw on foreign or indigenous traditions. A small minority still attempt to stage traditional *dindi gamu* ceremonies, but the resulting rituals attract the support of no more than a couple of dozen mostly old men. These events are thus pitiable in comparison with past ceremonies they remember, which attracted thousands of participants. The vast majority of Hulis, while still concerned by the issues raised in their traditional lore, draw more heavily on the foreign traditions and facilities that have become available to them. Though even here the continuities between the concerns expressed in the *dindi gamu* lore and the aspects of modern teaching that have been most accepted are quite explicit. It is to these current expressions of long-standing preoccupations that I now turn.

Responses to the European intrusion
Ecological concomitants

The Huli preoccupations with entropy, with decreasing yields, with a recent upsurge of human and porcine disease and with increasing strife are expressed in the *dindi gamu* lore in terms of a predestined progression towards devastation that can only be averted by prescribed ritual acts. These afflictions that the Huli interpret as indicative of a fundamental deterioration in the ritual forces that maintain the natural and moral order can also be seen as the products of recent ecological changes that have affected horticulture and disease patterns.

The fertility of the soil is said to have been deteriorating for generations, but the process is thought to have accelerated rapidly since the 1930s. Older people make adverse comparisons between the stringy tubers of today and the fine harvests that they remember when they were young. The coincidence of this loss of fertility with the emergence of disruptive foreigners is said to be a part of traditional *dindi gamu* lore. This coincidence is also explicable in terms of soil science and changing land use patterns. Elsewhere in the highlands there is evidence for the appearance of agriculture about 9,000 years ago (Golson 1982). Investigations at the Kuk site in the Western Highlands have revealed intermittent phases of swamp drainage for agricultural exploitation against a background of continuous cultivation on dry land. An intensification of activity occurred some 250 years ago, which Golson attributes to the introduction of the sweet potato. The richness of Huli oral history suggests that investigations in the Tari Basin might be similarly revealing of the fluctuating relationships between earlier inhabitants and their environment. But until this is undertaken circumstantial evidence will have to suffice.

Elsewhere in the Southern Highlands, at Lake Egari, cores from sediments indicate recent phases of increased soil erosion interpreted by Oldfield *et al.* (1980) as corresponding to phases of intensification of agriculture. The first occurred between 300 and 150 years ago. This presumably represents an increase in forest clearing that followed the adoption of the sweet potato. The sweet potato is capable of producing greater yields and tolerating lower temperatures and poorer soils than former tubers, such as taro and yams, and so permitted the exploitation of land that previously could not be cultivated productively. The second phase of accelerated soil erosion is much greater, and occurred some twenty years before sampling. As Wood (1980) suggests, this recent soil degradation therefore reflects changes in agricultural practice occurring at and after contact. Forest clearing has increased since the introduction of the steel axe. Fallowing has deceased with the reduction of multiresidence (p. 50), the rarity of the forced flights that used to be a feature of warfare and the preference of young men for migrant labour rather than the labour of clearing new gardens. The population has increased since the introduction of health services, and there has been an internal migration into the Tari Basin where services are concentrated. 'The orderly succession of forest regeneration after cultivation can be upset...[by]...the repeated clearing of the same area at short intervals...In these circumstances the vegetation succession may break down, with the establishment of degraded secondary growth, ferns or grass' (Golson 1982:44). The lore of *dindi gamu* is said to predict a degradation of the environment. 'In the thirteenth generation the swamps will dry out, and they will be covered with kunai grass and *yagua* [a fern, *Pteridium aquilinum*]' (Yaluduma-Dai of Gelote).

The perceived upsurge of illness this century, attributed by the Huli to an unprecedented onslaught by *damas*, is also likely to be an accurate representation of their experience this century. Europeans were preceded by their pathogens. Trading routes with surrounding peoples were well developed, allowing the spread of novel viral epidemics, particularly influenza, chicken pox and measles. An influenza epidemic in 1969 resulted in a mortality rate of 2% despite the presence of health services. Earlier outbreaks are likely to have been at least as damaging. Hulis complain that they have become increasingly prey to chronic bronchitis (see *amali*, pp. 86–7). This complaint can be a later expression of childhood respiratory infections, and so could well be a delayed consequence of viral epidemics that occurred decades before. Devastating dysentery epidemics occurred in the early 1940s coinciding with porcine anthrax epidemics. Venereal diseases were introduced by the early patrols. More recently, malaria has become a significant problem. 'The illness of the lowlands' (*wabi warago*), as it is known, was previously seen only as a hazard of trading trips to the Papuan Plateau. Migrant labour and improving road communications have established malaria as a serious disease problem for the Huli.

Such novel predation by *dama* caused the Huli to suspect the hand of an enemy in their misfortune. Certain *dama* are said to enter contracts to kill or otherwise harm their patron's enemies in return for pork. Such indirect means of redress are not characteristic of the Huli. Sorcery accusations are uncommon, and it is significant that the only type of sorcery that currently concerns them is 'coastal sorcery' (*nambis poisin*, pp. 147–9). In the past, too, they attributed novel afflictions to exotic techniques. The most feared of the tractable *dama* was *dama* Toro. He is a Duna spirit, and Hulis were said to travel far into Duna territory to enlist his support. They paid large numbers of pigs, and were said to undergo trials to assess their fitness to control the power that Toro would bring them. Knowledge of Toro may have a long history, but the attribution of large numbers of deaths to him probably coincides with the epidemics of the early 1940s.

Eleven of my children died. I had killed some men in a war, and so they acquired *dama* Toro and killed eleven of my children. So I acquired *dama* Toro myself, and I killed fifteen of them in one day, and fourteen the next. But they sent Toro again and killed more of my relations so that I was alone. (Hubi-Hondomogo of Bebenete)

These epidemics and the Huli interpretations of them led to cycles of enmity. Older men talk of an intensification of warfare at this time. It seems that Huli society was in a somewhat disordered state at the time of contact.

Early religious experimentation and unrest

Occasional patrols passed through Huli territory from 1935 onwards, but these were intermittent disturbances only. The first coherent exotic response to these increasingly disconcerting circumstances was brought not by Europeans, but by the Huli's northern neighbours, who had developed their own ritual response to similar events. Exploration and administration in the highlands of the Mandated Territory was much further advanced in the 1930s than in the Papuan highlands, with administrative centres being established at Goroka, Mount Hagen and Wabag. Amongst the Enga one of the secondary effects of this intrusion, and the political and economic changes that followed it, was Ain's cult, which is described in detail by Meggitt (1973). The aims of this new religious movement altered as it was disseminated from its original focus, but it was broadly concerned with health, wealth and immortality. During the early 1940s the peoples of this area also experienced a number of hardships, including a severe frost which destroyed gardens, and epidemics of porcine and human disease. The new ritual was an attempt to recover from these reverses, as well as a response to the uncertainty that followed the growing influence of the administration. The cult reached the Huli by two main routes. From the north-east it was brought by Waka Enga, and from the north-west by Ipili. Men and women from these groups travelled widely in the Huli area, and trained Huli helpers who also disseminated the cult. It was known by the Huli as *mara gamu*. (*Gamu* is the Huli word for a spell or rite. *Mara* is unknown in Huli, but Megitt refers to the Ipili term '*marakali*' for 'shaking men'. Shaking was also prominent in Huli performances of the cult.) I cannot describe here the complexities of the transformations of the cult as it passed through Huli territory. Briefly, the various aspects Meggitt describes continued into Huli practice. Platforms were built and pigs killed on them. The officiants spun spears, and told people to look along them at the sun. They dammed streams, and all people bathed there, men and women together. Participants in the rites shook. Holes were dug where shells were expected to appear. The Hulis were told to break and burn their bows, to inter their dead and not raise corpses on platforms and to end the strict separation of the sexes, instructions which they later recognised as 'the path of Europeans' (*honabinaga hariga*). Besides hopes of wealth and health, some Hulis thought that *mara gamu* would prevent the arrival of any more Europeans. A particularly Huli transformation of *mara gamu* was that it represented a new means of causing the return of *mbingi*, and *mbingianda* (specially strengthened large houses to protect the population should *mbingi* return) were built in several places.

When *mara gamu* failed to secure any of the benefits that had been promised, it was abandoned. Most people said they had been tricked, and in some places demanded compensation from those who had invited the Enga proselytisers to bring the new cult to their parish. The more convinced ascribed its lack of success to the Huli's incomplete commitment to all the observances and restrictions that they had been taught. The Huli reverted to their former practices. They resumed warfare, bachelors returned to their *ibagiyanda*, married men maintained the usual distance from their wives and the rituals that had been temporarily neglected were revived.

Some ten years later the administration, closely followed by the missions, initiated the current period of intensive exposure to new ideas and opportunities. One indication of the disordered state of Huli society at this time and of the anxieties experienced during the early years of administrative control is offered by the outbreaks of stylised frenzied behaviour that greeted patrols in 1960 and 1961. *Lulu* is the Huli word for madness. Acute dissociative states of a sort common in New Guinea (Frankel 1976), which would have been called *lulu*, were not unknown in former times. But *lulu* now reached epidemic proportions (Rodrigue 1963). A man who was affected described his experience to me like this: 'It started with dizziness, then heat built up in my chest and rushed to my head. I can't remember much after that, except a sense of being surrounded by crowds of red-eyed staring people. I wanted to escape from them, but could not.' Women were also affected, but their attacks were confined to shaking and crying. Men would first shake, and then start rushing about, dressing themselves, perhaps bizarrely, in whatever finery was available, leaping over obstacles, despoiling graves and becoming randomly

29

violent, shooting arrows at anyone who came near. These usually missed, but some found their mark. It was the experience of gathering for census or similar purposes that prompted this reaction. This form of *lulu* can be seen as an expression of the anxiety generated by mingling with large numbers of allies and enemies alike at a time when customary patterns of social relations were no longer appropriate, and new ones had yet to be consolidated. Rodrigue reports that some 10% of Huli were affected by this form of *lulu* between August 1960 and December 1961. Interestingly he notes that although 'the Huli believed that mental and physical illness was the result of supernatural forces...with *lulu* it was generally agreed that a different mechanism operated and something in Western medicine would probably be effective in eradicating the condition' (ibid:278). The Huli looked for a solution to this exotic problem from those who had brought it.

This sort of *lulu* has not occurred since then. However, the shaking which was seen before or instead of the stylised frenzy has been a common feature of all the novel movements that have formed a part of the Huli response to recent changes. Shaking was a feature of the *mara gamu* cult that was brought by the Enga. And it is a prominent feature of the more recent movements of Christian enthusiasm. Before I discuss these I will consider another movement which represents the most ambitious attempt to form a synthesis of European and Huli lore.

The Damene Cultural Centre

In former times any inconsistencies between different versions of Huli lore were not readily exposed. Pacification and increased mobility have made people more aware of wide divergencies between the traditions of different areas and the knowledge of different individuals. The Huli refer to important knowledge as the *tene*, the base or foundation. It is fixed and incontravertably correct. Where there are disputes about an aspect of lore they assume that one of the protagonists must be wrong, either through dishonesty or ignorance. They cannot agree to differ. The current concern of those attempting to achieve the aims of *dindi gamu* is to determine what knowledge is indeed 'the foundation', that is, the truth. They want to scrutinise European lore in the same way in order to select elements from both traditions. This project is the main objective of the founding of the *Damene* Cultural Centre. Ostensibly this is planned as a museum for Huli artefacts and ritual objects, but the concept of a museum is not a meaningful one to the Huli. Their interest in the Centre is the familiar concern from *dindi gamu* lore:

The ground is bad. People are in a poor state. Pigs are unsound. There is no fertility in the soil, it has leaked away. Men are crippled, lantern-jawed. They have no wisdom. They are foolish and they age quickly. Children are in a poor state. Boys' skins are poor. They become bearded too young. Girls don't grow well, then their breasts develop while they are still small. Women do not menstruate. Sows and bitches do not go on heat. This is a bad time, a time of stealing and fighting, and the earth is bad. The Centre is to stop this. When they have all seen the true lore they will pay compensation for Bayebaye, and we will send *mbingi*. We must get on with this task, as those who hold this lore are old and are dying. The government is helping with nails and money, and we will organise it all.

The word *damene* means relations, those that one can call on for assistance. The choice of this term is an expression of the redefinition of political and hence ritual relationships that is fundamental to the project. The 'relations' are to include members of all the surrounding language groups, and the Europeans.

We want to build a house with six doors, with a door each for the Obena, Duna, Duguba, Huli, Hewa and Europeans. Fifteen or twenty knowledgeable old men from each group will sit in each room. In each room, these experts will each tell their origin story, and the lore. We will write these down. When they have all finished we will read out the story from each expert. Where the accounts concur they will become the true lore. Those that do not correspond are not the truth, and so we will discard them. Then we will know what has brought things to such a state of confusion and disorder, with men sharing their wives' food, and having sex with anyone at any time. They will find out where such customs came from, find out what happened before, and what is happening now. Now is a bad time, with poor soil, fighting and stealing. The Centre will allow us to curb this. When they have seen the true lore, all these bad things will cease. Then we will pay compensation for Bayebaye, and we will send *mbingi*.

This activity is conducted at two levels. On the one hand there are committee meetings, minutes, discussions of building plans with government officials, and fund-raising to build the sort of centre that is encouraged by an administration concerned to preserve elements of the country's varied cultural heritage. The true purpose of the organisers is not stated explicitly at such meetings, though this is common knowledge to Hulis. For them 'culture' is not a commodity that can or should be preserved. It is an active process directed to particular ends. The Cultural Centre represents to some a last opportunity to complete the *dindi gamu* project. There are those who regard this activity as eccentric and hopeless, but where there is scepticism it is more usually directed at the qualifications of the organisers of the Centre or at practical difficulties that they face, rather than at the feasibility of the project *per se*. Committed Christians disapprove, however, as in their view the millennium must be approached by means of Christian worship alone. Nevertheless, the missionaries' assistance is regarded as essential for the success of the Centre. Not only must all indigenous lore be examined and consolidated, but it must also be reconciled with the authentic aspects of European lore, that is, mission teaching.

We will send for the missions, each of them. We will tell them to bring their Bibles, to sit with us, to look at their Bibles, and so find out which version of their lore is the true one. Before we did *dindi gamu*, and all was well. The missions told us to stop, and so we abandoned it. So we must ask the missions, if we all contribute money to the mission as they ask, and if everyone is baptised, and everyone is united in their conviction, will that bring *mbingi*, will new earth fall from the sky then? Or will the mission people see that some are not baptised, and so instead of sending *mbingi* to renew the earth, they will send fire to destroy it.

Nevertheless, while the aims of those attempting to organise the *Damene* Cultural Centre are widely shared, the most common avenue for their achievement is now through Christianity.

Huli Christianity

The churches' current hold over Huli thought and religious observance is the product of a number of aspects of the Huli's colonial experience, of their own cosmological preoccupations and of the evangelical techniques of the Christian missions active in the Tari area. When Europeans first established control in the early 1950s Huli society was in a disordered state. The Huli were looking to both traditional and new rituals to resolve novel ecological and political threats. The missionaries were the only ones to offer what the Huli took to be the religious underpinning to the material and political supremacy of Europeans. As we have seen, the Hulis' interest in Christian dogma was enhanced by a number of fortuitous resonances between their own lore and the teaching and activities of the missionaries. Europeans' interest in the sacred groves of hoop pines, in their view planted by the founding ancestor, Kebe, indicated that blacks and whites shared a common origin, and prompted the Huli to ponder the significance of this return. 'We thought that the whites were the owners of these trees. We hadn't planted them. They had the right tools to cut them, chain saws and sawmills, but we couldn't cut them. They weren't ours.' Besides the conceptual implications for the Huli of this interest in their sacred sites, the establishment of sawmills in the pine groves was incompatible with their use in ritual. The mission stations and churches in the Tari area are largely constructed with hoop pines from these sacred sites.

A second concordance of continuing significance to the Huli is the similarity between their lore of Bayebaye, the boy killed in an earlier performance of *dindi gamu*, and Christian teaching of the crucifixion. The names Jesus and Bayebaye are used interchangeably by many Hulis, and the resolution of their responsibility for his death is a topical concern. This relates to the millennial concerns of traditional Huli ritual and the fundamentalism that dominates Christian preaching.

In the decades prior to the Europeans presence amongst them, the Huli had become increasingly concerned by what they interpreted as a concerted and unprecedented onslaught by a profusion of exotic spirits. They adopted new means of divination in their attempts to identify them, and sacrificed pigs generously in their efforts to divert and satisfy them. But many saw this as an unequal struggle. The missionaries too were preoccupied by *dama*, and their offer of combating their influence was welcomed by many. It was assumed that the Europeans' competence in other spheres would be matched here. Further, the missionaries' exorcisms and the continued protection from *dama* that they offered appeared to be without cost, whereas their own sacrifices constituted a serious economic drain. The material and political supremacy of Europeans was an important factor in the missionaries' success in gaining adherents. But the efficacy of Christianity was also assessed empirically by the Huli in the same way that they had assessed other new ritual techniques of recent decades. However, the new religion raised a major dilemma for the Huli. They wished to take advantage of the protection against *dama* that was offered by Christianity, but in doing so they found that they were expected to forgo most of the protective and strengthening ritual that in their view had nothing to do with *dama*. Missionaries saw the influence of Satan and his demons in a wide range of Huli activities, and adopted the term *dama* to refer to what they saw as satanic forces. The missionaries identified *dama* in activities which to the Huli were quite profane. Such tensions are described in Huli recollections of these years. They also emerge clearly from the missionaries' writings, as in this passage (Twyman 1961:111):

We were thankful to see some young men in the first class too, for it was hard for a young man to forgo the fun of being an *Igiri haroali*, initiate. Who would choose to take hold of God's Way rather than become an initiate? What a sensation to be dressed in the special red wig and have the adornment that went with it! What fun to hear the 'oohs' and 'aahs' of the women and girls as he walked by! What intriguing mystery to live with the initiate's teacher for months learning all the magic and filth of the tribe!...For Dindini at about seventeen years of age the choice was not easy and it brought immediate trouble. One of his best pigs took sick. This brought the usual taunt, 'The spirits are annoyed with you; kill a pig to placate them'. But instead Dindini prayed to his God. One of his clan relatives declared, 'If your god hears you and makes the pig better, I too will believe'. The pig recovered, and Dindini's relative joined the Enquirer's Class the following Sunday.

The missionaries' position of authority as Europeans and the appeal of aspects of their message facilitated the acceptance of Christianity, but these advantages are in themselves insufficient to explain the current extent of their authority. Also important is the effectiveness of their strategy for proselytisation. By the 1950s each of the missions which established itself in the Tari area had considerable experience in New Guinea evangelism, and was therefore able to consolidate its hold over the congregation through methods found to be successful elsewhere. The selection, training and deployment of local evangelists had long been standard practice and was employed here too. In addition, the mission with perhaps the greatest influence in the Tari area, the Asia Pacific Christian Mission, determined to preach in the vernacular as soon as possible, and devoted much of its early effort to achieving this aim.

The missions gradually increased their hold through individual conversions or through more public events such as 'fetish burnings' (Pethybridge n.d.:116). They offered health services, and maternal and child health clinics in particular extended their influence. Mothers were impressed by the health and growth rates of the missionaries' children, and were quickly willing to discard their own strengthening rituals in preference for mission teaching. By the early 1970s Huli ritual and initiation had been largely abandoned. Nevertheless, missionaries were becoming dissatisfied with what they saw as only a partially successful outcome for their work. The changes occurring in the newly self-governing state of Papua New Guinea reached Tari in a variety of guises, including an increasing unwillingness to comply with the authority of Europeans, particularly amongst the young. The perceived immorality of the young concerned church leaders and parents alike. In addition, the earlier momentum of proselytisation appeared to be played out, so that Christian worship was felt to have become for many a routine without true conviction. The events of the next years, while unexpected and in some respects alarming, were generally welcomed by Christians as a resurgence of faith.

In 1973 a group of Solomon Island pastors from the South Seas Evangelical Mission was invited to preach at Lake Kutubu, to the south of the Huli area. They were particularly effective evangelists who had become active since a Maori evangelist had preached on Malaita in 1970 with results similar to those that developed in the Southern Highlands. Local pastors in the Kutubu area were inspired by the Solomon Islanders' vigorous style of preaching and adopted it themselves. By the early part of 1974 the people of the Kutubu area had been engulfed in a movement of Christian enthusiasm which took precedence over all other activity. They spent most of their time in church, many collapsed, shook and were said to speak in tongues. There were reports of miraculous cures, visions and prophesies of the imminent Judgement Day. The Hulis were first affected by this activity by chance. Two young men from one of the southernmost Huli settlements had come to Lake Kutubu to buy building materials. They attended a church service there, and one of them started to shake and felt that he had 'the Holy Spirit' (*dinini holi*). When they returned home this man's preaching caused his own congregation to succumb, shaking and confessing their sins. They held exorcisms which culminated in an old man, a traditionalist who resented their disruptive fervour, being trampled to death.

Groups of pastors travelled from Kutubu to preach and tell of the Christian enthusiasm they had witnessed there. These pastors, as well as missionaries and others, caused these events to become widely known throughout the Southern Highlands. The central Huli population was most vehemently involved during the early part of 1976, when many congregations spent most of their time in church, praying, shaking and confessing their sins in preparation for the end of the world and the Last Judgement. Reports of glossolalia and miraculous healing were commonplace. By the following year

Fig. 6 A baptism

the movement had become less intense. The more dramatic manifestations were confined to a few congregations only. But these events had had a lasting effect upon most people's view of Christianity, effectively consolidating the church's earlier gains and reversing an incipient decline in their authority (fig. 6).

Since that time there have been many flurries of concern that the Second Coming is imminent. Some of these rumours have been prompted by pamphlets distributed by church groups. One of these, entitled 'Time is running out', was felt to be so authoritative that the people of one parish sent for a government official to advise them whether there was any point in replanting their gardens. When the official told them that he regarded the pamphlet as nonsense their relief was considerable, and the official was applauded enthusiastically. This preoccupation with Judgement Day is informed by avid Bible reading. One of the most pertinent texts to the Huli and their teachers is Matthew, chapter 24. News of 'wars and rumours of wars', whether concerning fights in the Tari area, or external events such as the Falklands' conflict, is held to be an indication for greater preparedness. 'Famines, and pestilences, and earthquakes' are similarly regarded. Such tribulations are predicted in *dindi gamu* lore too. There are further similarities. 'Immediately after the tribulation of those days shall the sun be darkened, and the moon shall not give her light, and the stars shall fall from heaven, and the powers of the heavens shall be shaken.' However, instead of the renewal of *mbingi*, they are now taught to expect the Second Coming.

Thus traditional concerns have become increasingly accommodated within Christian practice. It is instructive to compare Huli responses to the two eclipses of the sun that have occurred in modern times. At the first, in 1962, informants recall a certain amount of anxiety that the time of darkness that they were told to expect would prove to be the *mbingi* of their own lore. As they were not prepared for it they could expect to be destroyed by it. Some people are said to have strengthened their houses as the lore instructed them to do. In the event the darkness was only brief, and the warnings of the traditionalists were proved unfounded. A second eclipse of the sun occurred on 11 June 1983. On this occasion, the few traditionalists who still harboured hopes of recalling *mbingi* through traditional ritual, as well as those involved in transformations of this lore, such as the organisation of the *Damene* Cultural Centre, were satisfied by government assurances that the expected time of darkness would be brief and have no significance. There was none of the premonitary warnings described in the lore. The experience of 1962 confirmed them in the view that this brief veiling of the sun was in some undefined way the responsibility of the whites who could predict it, and was irrelevant to their own programme. But these traditional concerns with times of darkness and the millennium were given much more weight by the Christians, the vast majority. Some maintained that this was indeed to be Judgement Day, but the dominant view was that this eclipse would constitute one of the penultimate signs. They spent the afternoon of the eclipse in church. At the service I attended the preaching dwelt on the common themes. 'When the sign comes, then we will know that it is the last day for us. We are waiting for a sign now. Another sign I have seen is that a casuarina sapling I planted is not growing. And think of how our sons and daughters behave. You see disobedience, adultery and people ignoring God's word. He will come soon. Some of you will be ready, and some of you will not.' The time of the eclipse was met by a frenzy of clapping and incomprehensible sounds as participants performed '*Holi gamu*', the possession state that is said to indicate the presence of the Holy Spirit (fig. 7).

The complex interactions described in this chapter between traditional and exotic knowledge have guided the Huli's responses to novel circumstances. The continuities between their own concerns and the aspects of European culture that have been presented to them have influenced the particular way in which they have chosen to accommodate the colonial experience. However, it would be wrong to exaggerate the bounds of choice. Compulsion was important, particularly in the cessation of warfare. Economic pressures have also had a major impact, in the acceptance of migrant labour, for example.

Fig. 7 *Holi gamu* during the 1983 eclipse of the sun

Nevertheless, the particular quality of modern Huli society and culture is also a product of the fortuitous correspondences between their own concerns and those of the incomers. The apparent transformation of Huli cultural, and especially religious, life seems less radical when we examine the doctrinal continuity between traditional religion and their particular interpretation of Christianity. These same trends are also apparent in the Huli response to illness. The energetic syncretism characteristic of their attempts to accommodate new religious ideas is also apparent in their appreciation of the relative merits of their own and new explanations and treatments for illness. The processes described in this chapter are most explicitly revealed when we come to consider the moral and spiritual dimensions of illness. But the same active process of reconciling the differing traditions is to be found in their more pragmatic measures in illness. The picture of a seemingly wholesale abandonment of traditional healing therefore becomes more blurred when such continuities are exposed.

3

Huli society

The Huli language is classified by Wurm (1961) as a sub-family of the Enga–Huli–Pole–Wiru family of the east New Guinea Highland stock. There are some 100,000 Huli speakers inhabiting the intramontane basins and surrounding slopes of the western portion of the Southern Highlands Province of Papua New Guinea (see fig. 2). Traditionally they were not one people in any political sense. Parishes and groups of parishes were engaged in a constant round of warfare, and there were no circumstances where groupings of more than a few thousand people would unite for a common purpose. But they did have a general sense of shared identity in distinction to the surrounding cultures. The extent of Huli territory was well known, and individuals travelled widely throughout the Huli area and beyond. Most ritual was organised within a single parish but, as I have indicated, the major sacred sites were significant to many parishes, and in its ideal conception their religion aspired to the harmonious participation of all Hulis.

All Huli speakers may describe themselves as 'Huli' to distinguish themselves from members of the surrounding language groups. But the term Huli refers primarily to those groups living in the southern part of the Tari Basin. Huli speakers to the west of the Tagali river are referred to, and may refer to themselves, as 'Duna', though they speak Huli, and do not share the language or culture of the Duna people proper to the west beyond Koroba. Huli speakers to the north may similarly be dubbed 'Obena', and those to the south 'Duguba' (the general term for all the peoples of the Papuan Plateau), though they share few of the features of these neighbouring groups. This study is based primarily upon the investigation of the people of the Tari Basin. In general, these findings are applicable to all Huli areas, though there are regional variations which become more marked in the areas transitional with the surrounding cultural groups.

Most Huli speakers live at an altitude of approximately 1,500 to 2,000 metres, though some of the northernmost settlements are higher than this, and those to the south towards Lake Kutubu are significantly lower. The environment is thus broadly similar to that inhabited by many other major highland populations, and it would be superfluous to detail those well-described features here. The population density is high in the central Tari Basin, rising to 200 per square kilometre. This falls off in the surrounding areas to 40 per square kilometre and below. The subsistence pattern is common to the general area with the mound cultivation of sweet potatoes, supported by a number of crops including taro, legumes, greens, pumpkins and corn. The diet is supplemented by pandanus nuts and mushrooms when these are in season, intermittently by pork and store foods and, for the central Huli at least, rarely by game. Traditionally there was a strict separation of the sexes, to the extent that men grew and cooked their own food. Housing is still separate for almost all Huli, but most men are now willing to take food from women. The division of labour is now broadly that men do the axe work, clearing garden sites, building fences and houses, while women do the spade work, digging the mounds, planting and weeding.

Social organisation and individual allegiance

There is an extensive literature on the social organisation of New Guinea highlands societies and on the problems of characterising their group structure. Key papers include Barnes (1962), Langness (1964), de Lepervanche (1967–8) and A. Strathern (1973). Huli social organisation has been described by Glasse (1968). This topic is not my main focus and I have therefore had to approach it selectively. The following discussion has three purposes: first, to include sufficient description of their society to make later analysis of illness behaviour intelligible; secondly, to deal in more depth with issues which particularly influence their responses to illness; and thirdly, to comment on aspects of the literature on the Huli and their neighbours which may make these groups appear anomalous in comparison with other descriptions of Highland societies.

The parish

The Huli area is divided into pieces of territory with clearly defined boundaries whose inhabitants refer to themselves and to the land they occupy by a name which is usually that of the agnatic founder of the group. Each of these groups is known as a *hameigini*. *Hame* is 'father', and *igini* is 'son', so this term translates as 'sons of the father'. Where possible I shall follow the terminology used by Glasse (1968) as it will then be simpler to compare the situation in the late 1950s with my own data of some twenty years later. I shall therefore translate *hameigini* as 'parish'. Constituent units within the *hameigini* are also known as *hameigini*. The level of grouping being described is apparent to Hulis from the context, but here I shall again follow Glasse and translate the smaller grouping as a 'parish section'. I shall also introduce a third level, the 'parish sub-section'. Groups at this third level may also be

39

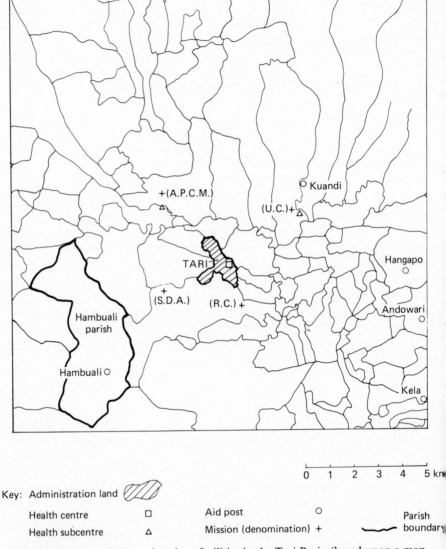

Fig. 8 Parish boundaries and various facilities in the Tari Basin (based upon a map prepared for the Southern Highlands Project by Dr A. W. Wood).

termed *hameigini*, though they are usually referred to by the name of their founder. He is likely to be a son of the founder of the parish section.

Rather than continue in generalities, I will describe the composition of the parish in which I conducted most of my research, Hambuali. The parish of Hambuali occupies 945 hectares of the western part of the Tari Basin and the ridges that rise from it (fig. 8). The total population in 1979 was 554 men, women and children. The Hambuali people say that they have always inhabited the territory they now occupy. One version of their creation myth begins: 'All things grew out of the earth, as does a mushroom. In the beginning Hambuali-Malubi was there. He was at Hambu Hiliawi.' Hambu Hiliawi is the name of the sacred site (*kebanda*) where Hambuali people performed their major fertility ritual for Kebali, the generic term for founding and other significant agnatic ancestors, here including Hambuali-Malubi. The myth tells how Hambuali-Malubi's grandson, Hambuali-Hira, originated the *kebanda* ritual. He sacrificed a pig within the grove of hoop pines at Hambu Hiliawi, performed a ritual over the rock that is buried there, and built the tall conical house, *bibi-ogo* that is characteristic of the *kebanda* ritual. This part of the myth is the lore guiding the performance of this ritual. The myth goes on to tell of the travels of Hambuali-Hira's son, Hambuali-Taiabe. His mother was killed by a cannabalistic giant Baiyage Horo, and the boy was rescued by two Duguba (southern Huli) men who killed the giant. They took him to Malenda (now known as Komo) and fed him fish and frogs. When he was grown they travelled back to Hambu Hiliawi via Duna, where he found a wife, the daughter of Adidi. Hambuali-Taiabe fathered Hambuali-Puli who fathered Hambuali-Kamianga and his son was Hambuali-Yuli. By his first wife Hambuali-Yuli fathered two boys, (Hambuali-)Wari and Hiwari. By his second wife, Gendo and Bainage. These are the founders of the four parish sections of Hambuali: Wari, Hiwari, Gendo and Bainage.

In relation to other parishes, Hambuali is seen as a political unit. When they describe major wars, people may say that another group attacked 'Hambuali'. The people of Hambuali combined to stage the *kebanda* ritual at Hambu Hiliawi. But in most contexts, the whole parish is not the effective political unit. Cooperation in warfare, compensation payments and ritual did not normally extend beyond the level of the parish section, and was most likely within the sub-section. Ideally, members of the parish should settle their differences without recourse to killing, but the parish sections did occasionally attack each other. Within the parish section formal armed attack did not occur, and any eruption of violence is strongly disapproved. The population and the territory is further divided into parish sub-sections, and members of these are likely to live near each other and cooperate in everyday tasks. Where the parish section is expected to make a large compensation payment, each of these sub-sections will be allocated their portion of the burden.

The genealogy of Hambuali parish illustrates the relationships of each of

41

Huli society

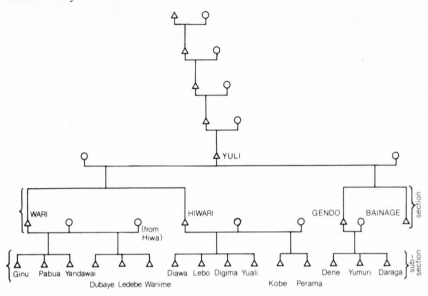

Fig. 9 Genealogy of Hambuali parish

the founders of the parish sub-sections (fig. 9). The male ancestors in this genealogy are named. The names of their wives are not retained, though the *hameigini* of origin of most of these women is known. Three of the sub-sections of Wari *hameigini* (Dubaya, Ledebe and Wanime) are grouped together as Hiwa *hameigini* after the *hameigini* of origin of the mother of these sons of Wari. Bainage is nominally a parish section of equal status with Gendo. But it is a small *hameigini* and functions effectively as a sub-section within Gendo. It is said that Bainage, as the last son of Hambuali-Yuli, found that little land was left for him by his three brothers, and so he stayed with Gendo. The founders of the sub-sections are separated by some five or six generations from the present.

The Huli distinguish between three categories of parish member according to the basis of their recruitment. *Tene* means the bole of a tree. It is also used to refer to the source of knowledge or objects and to the nub of an argument. In relation to parish members, *tene* are those who are agnatically related to the founder, in this case, to Hambuali-Yuli. It is difficult to determine the extent to which genealogies are modified by dropping female links to conform to an agnatic ideal, but the strictness of the Huli definition of agnation is supported by the convention of attaching agnatic patronymics to each person's name. The Hambuali patronymic is Hambuali-, and only true agnates are entitled to use this. Links through women are remembered over many generations. I know of men whose ancestors have lived in a particular parish for eight or more generations since their non-agnatic link who are not

Table 1 *Mode of recruitment of all Hambuali men over twenty years*

Category of membership	Number	%
Tene (agnates)	41	25
Yamuwini (non-agnatic cognates)		
ainya ('mother', first generation)	20	12
agua ('grandmother', second generation)	35	22
others (third generation or more)	35	22
all non-agnatic cognates	90	56
Tara		
wali agalini (uxorilocal men)	16	10
igiri yango (friends)	15	9
all non-cognates	31	19

regarded as *tene*, though they may be referred to as '*tene hamene*' (the brothers of the *tene*).

Non-agnatic cognates are referred to as *yamuwini* (born of women). *Yamuwini* may be distinguished according to their relationship with the female agnate through whom they are related to the *tene* of the *hameigini*. Thus those whose membership comes through a mother who was a true agnate are *ainya* (mother). Their children are *agua* (grandchildren). Their children are *aguanene*. Beyond three generations from the agnatic core, *yamuwini* may be known as *aguanali*.

The third broad category of parish members is known as *tara*. In general use *tara* means 'different'. In this context it means 'others' in distinction to 'relations' (*damene*). *Tara* includes men who have married in, referred to as *wali agalini* (literally 'husbands of women'), or *wali dalu* (literally 'those on women's land'), or *wali haga* (literally 'they stay with women') and unrelated friends, known as *igiri yango*.

The conception of the *hameigini* as the 'sons of the father' is greatly at variance with its actual composition. The 162 Hambuali men over twenty years of age belonged to these various categories of membership in the proportions shown in table 1.

Only 25% of the adult men who belong to Hambuali are true agnates, and 19% are not even related through cognatic links. The majority (56%) are non-agnatic cognates. Land is commonly given by a mother's brother to a sister's son, and the son and his descendants stay within the parish.

Social anthropologists have written extensively on this aspect of social relations in the New Guinea highlands. Mythology and rhetoric may suggest that these societies are organised according to the principles of segmentary descent groups, but closer examination of the empirical data may suggest that such descent constructs are relatively unimportant as organising principles. In the case of the Huli, besides the finding that true agnates comprise only a minority of each group, a number of other features might make the interpretation of group formation in terms of descent difficult to maintain.

First, the scattered settlement pattern and ethos of individualism combine to make Huli homes private but important centres. Each homestead is effectively a private estate. The entrance is set in an arch of sharpened stakes. Even with the increasingly popular hinged doors and padlocks this offers no insuperable barrier, but the effect is far from welcoming. The estate may be ringed by ramparts, stockades and deep ditches. These are intended as defences against pigs, and are decorative, but they are also intended to discourage trespass. Casual visiting by any but close friends and relations is often unwelcome, so that those who are not expected will call out their business from outside the gate. Uninvited visitors may be suspected of theft or other ill intentions.

Secondly, individual Hulis develop their own private networks of interest through their particular choice of kinsman, affines or just friends. These networks differ from one man to the next, and are likely to be quite independent of the *hameigini* of residence. Roads in the Huli area abound with men and women, alone or in groups, travelling from parish to parish, maintaining links, attending feasts, collecting debts or simply visiting kin or friends.

Thirdly, the Huli do not in general ascribe responsibility corporately. Grievances may be expressed against a whole parish, for failure to pay compensation for a death for example, but the individual held ultimately responsible for the events that led to the death will be sought, and he will be expected to accumulate the necessary pigs. Others, particularly members of his parish, will help him, but in doing so they are assisting him rather than accepting joint responsibility. In the case of a war death, compensation is demanded from the man who initiated hostilities, the 'source of the war' (*wai tene*).

Fourthly, there are no competitive ceremonial exchanges which involve a whole parish or parish section comparable with the Mount Hagen *moka*. In former times major ceremonial exchange was linked to the *tege* ritual cycle. *Tege* has been abandoned, and without its religious inspiration these exchanges too have lapsed. Pigs are now killed on a large scale mainly at new gatherings known as *bisnis*. The instigator builds a high fence around the chosen site. Visitors pay a gate fee and must pay cash for any pork they consume. Entertainments include courting sessions (*dawanda*) and occasionally string bands. All the proceeds go to the organiser and his helpers.

Fifthly, there is the relationship between mode of recruitment and leadership. It is possible to differentiate two sorts of leadership at the level of the parish or parish section: first, the man who is a leader by virtue of his knowledge; and secondly, the man who becomes a leader on the strength of his personal attributes. These forms of leadership may commonly be combined in the one individual leader. The significance of the first sort of prominence is partly political and partly religious. As I have described, each group's title to its land is contained in the stylised genealogy linking the present parish members to the founding ancestors. This genealogy is known as *dindi malu*. Major ritual included sacrifices to these same ancestors, and the men most knowledgeable in *dindi malu* were often also ritual experts. Such men are prominent through their possession of such knowledge, though they must also be skilful in their utilisation of it. The knowledge is possessed by particular parish sub-sections, and ideally given to the eldest son in each generation.

The second sort of leadership is founded more upon the personal attributes of the leader. Through forcefulness, being articulate, in the past through skill in warfare, through his intelligence or other qualities, such leaders may build up personal reputations. They may begin with advantages, such as being the son of another leader or rich man, or they may develop a reputation on the strength of their own efforts alone. Such men are prominent in exchanges, in dispute settlement and all public affairs. Leaders of this second sort are 'big men' of the kind well known in Melanesia. Leaders of the first sort could only be called 'big men' in the usual sense when they involve themselves successfully in secular affairs.

In Hambuali the leadership of the *kebanda* ritual passed from *tene* to *yamuwini* in the last generation. The last *tene* expert in this rite was a bachelor. He chose to give the knowledge to his sister's son. The son of this man is the present possessor of this knowledge, though the ritual is no longer practised. This man is also the expert in the origin myth and genealogy for his parish section, and when it is necessary for someone to speak for the whole of Hambuali, this man usually does so. He has been elected as local government councillor on three occasions. His brother, of course also *yamuwini*, was elected to be village court magistrate. Of the four other most vigorous leaders who consistently attempt to exert influence outside their own parish sub-section, three are *yamuwini*, and one is 'other' (*tara*, a 'woman's husband', *wali agalini*). It is clear, therefore, that non-agnates are under no disadvantage in attaining prominence in the parish.

Considerations such as these have led Sillitoe (1979) to argue that descent groups are irrelevant for understanding the social relations of a neighbouring group of highlanders, the Wola. He suggests that apparent indications that this society is influenced by the principle of descent are in fact secondary manifestations of the true principle, which he identifies as exchange. Whatever the validity of this approach for characterising the Wola, a similarly extreme response to the complexities of Huli social relations would cause us to discard some key values which are central to their characterisation of themselves, and which articulate their relations with each other.

Table 2 *Residence, land-holding and mode of recruitment*

Residence and garden site	*tene*	*yamuwini*	*tara*	total
Unilocal				
all unilocal residents	18	41	11	70
all gardens within parish section of residence	14	22	4	40
some gardens outside parish section of residence, but within Hambuali	2	1	3	6
some gardens outside Hambuali	2	18	4	24
Multilocal				
houses in two Hambuali sections	–	1	3	4
second house in a parish other than Hambuali	1	12	8	21
Non-resident members	9	24	–	33
Totals	28	78	22	128

Residence and affiliation

I consider here the relationship between the mode of recruitment to the parish on the one hand, and the patterns of residence and land-holding on the other. As we saw in table 1, true agnates are in fact in a minority, comprising only 25% of the adult males. The majority of parish members gained their land through non-agnatic links. Hulis say that land is plentiful, that if they chose they could acquire land in any number of parishes, and that land can be held simultaneously in different parishes. The patterns of residence and land-holding of 128 Hambuali men is shown in table 2.

Thirty-three of these men (26%) were non-resident. Of these, thirty had left the Tari area temporarily to work, mainly at Mount Hagen and coastal plantations. None of the non-residents was 'other' (*tara*). This suggests that non-cognates are not thought of as parish members if they are absent for extended periods. Though presumably they could reinstate themselves on their return.

Of the ninety-five men who were resident in Hambuali, seventy (74%) maintained one household, and twenty-five (26%) maintained two. Of these twenty-five, four maintained households in a parish other than Hambuali. The mode of recruitment relates to the style of residence and siting of gardens. Of all resident cognates 81% (fifty-nine men, *tene* and *yamuwini* combined) lived unilocally, while 50% of non-cognates did so. This difference is significant at the 0.01 level (chi-square = 8.28, d.f. = 1). If we compare agnates with non-agnatic cognates, 95% of resident agnates lived unilocally (eighteen men), while 76% of non-agnatic cognates did so (forty-one men). This difference is not significant (p > 0.05, chi-square = 3.20, d.f. = 1).

Cognates are therefore significantly more likely to live unilocally than non-cognates. Agnates are more likely than non-agnatic cognates to live unilocally, but this relationship is less striking. If we also consider the site of these unilocal residents' gardens, we find that 49% of resident cognates (*tene* and *yamuwini* combined, thirty-six men) possessed gardens only within the parish section where their house is sited, while 18% of resident non-cognates gardened only within this parish section. This difference is significant at the 0.01 level (chi-square = 6.72, d.f. = 1). If we compare agnates with non-agnatic cognates, we find that 74% of resident agnates (fourteen men) gardened only within their parish section of residence, while 41% of non-agnatic cognates did so (twenty-two men). This difference is significant at the 0.02 level (chi-square = 6.10, d.f. = 1). The pattern of bilocal residence of course shows inverse trends.

In summary, these findings indicate that a man's residence pattern and the geographical distribution of his garden plots relate to his mode of recruitment to the parish. Agnates are most likely to live unilocally and garden only within their parish section of residence, non-cognates least likely to do so and non-agnatic cognates show a pattern intermediate between agnates and 'others'. Although Hulis can acquire land and take up residence on the basis of a variety of links, including friendship, these findings suggest that descent, particularly agnation, may influence their choices.

Idioms of descent

A number of authors have shifted the discussion of descent in Highland societies away from its possible importance as a criterion of recruitment towards its significance as an idiom (see particularly A. Strathern 1972 and Langness 1968). The Huli view indicates that an account of their society must take account of descent.

The land occupied by parishes in the Tari area is theirs by virtue of their descent from the founding ancestors who first occupied that land. In the event of a land dispute the key interchange is where leaders of either side recite their *dindi malu*, the formal presentation of the genealogy linking present members with the ancestors. If they are able to link present members to the ancestors by agnatic links alone, they will do so. In this respect, agnation is more highly valued, though this does not mean that agnates have higher status. In Huli perception agnates are the core of the *hameigini*, as their use of the word *tene*, 'source', implies, and other categories of member are accretions onto this agnatic core. The continuity imparted by male descent is also indicated by Huli notions of the respective contributions made by either parent in the formation of a child. The bones (*kuni*) are derived from the sperm, and the flesh (*mbirini*) and blood (*darama*) from the mother's blood. Flesh is transient, while bones are permanent. The protective shades of the agnatic ancestors

47

are said to remain in the sacred sites where their bones were placed. The significance of agnation is also implied by its immutability. Whether or not genealogies are modified after five or more generations by dropping non-agnatic links, as far as the Huli are concerned this does not occur. The use of agnatic patronymics also serves to preserve knowledge of each person's agnatic origins.

Tene exist in contrast to *yamuwini*, those 'born of women'. There is an element of lower valuation here. *Yamuwini*, whose forebears have lived in a parish for four, five or more generations since their single female link with the *tene*, may say that while they are *yamuwini*, through their being long established in the parish, they are now '*tene hamene*', the brothers of the *tene*. The sense of permanence and continuity contained in the idea of *tene* is to a degree achieved by those with an extended association with the parish. For example, a man said, 'my father's father and my father lived and died on Hiwari land. I will die here too, so I am *tene*.' (*I aba ibu ababi i ababi Hiwari dindini halu homayagola o ibi homole dagola o i tene kogoni.*) He was related to the agnatic core of the parish through his FaFaFaMo (*aguanali*). In saying that he is *tene* he was not claiming that he was an agnate. He was unequivocally *yamuwini*, and his patronymic was other than Hambuali-. He was referring instead to his commitment to the parish, and his inalienable right to stay there. This is what is implied by becoming 'a brother of the *tene*' (*tene hamene*), which is what he would normally describe himself as. Such people are also said to have 'lived there for a long time' (*haabo haga*). That non-agnatic cognates should express an association with a parish that extends over generations as a claim that they are now the brothers of the agnatic core is an indication of the centrality of agnation in the Huli conception of the *hameigini*. *Yamuwini* say that they could not be evicted by *tene*, and I know of no case where this occurred. One tentative attempt was made, however, with a group of *yamuwini* whose non-agnatic link with the parish where they lived was eight generations before the present. They were asked to go back to their 'own land' (the place where they were *tene*, though they had not lived there for eight generations). The attempt was not pressed very firmly, but was anyway dismissed on the grounds that when the formal presentation of genealogies (*dindi malu*) was heard, the leader of the *tene* was unable to name as many generations since his group's establishment on the land as the leader of the *yamuwini* could name since his. While such incidents are rare, this again suggests a lower valuation of female links as a basis for parish membership. The Huli in general feel that land is plentiful, and say that if they are short of land in one parish, they can obtain some in another. It may be significant that the incident I have just described involved land that was held to be ideal for cattle and coffee projects.

In other contexts *tene* and *yamuwini* are seen as complementary components of the *hameigini*. This complementarity may find formal expression. For example in the *tege* ritual, where the sponsor of the ritual (*tege anduane*) is *yamuwini*, he will ask a man who is *tene* of his parish section to take the central role in the ritual. When the sponsor is *tene*, he will ask his *yamuwini* to take on this role. Another occasion when such complementarity is formally expressed is after a wedding, when one pig from the bride-price may be killed and eaten. If the bride was *tene*, only *yamuwini* will eat the pork. Conversely, only *tene* will eat pork from the bride-price of a *yamuwini* bride (these two examples of complementarity between *tene* and *yamuwini* are also described in more detail in Glasse 1968:57, 84–5). Particular roles are also prescribed for *tene* and *yamuwini* in the *kebanda* ritual, and there is also a more general view that *tene* or *yamuwini* should help the other in disputes, compensation payments or whenever assistance is required.

Several Hambuali parish sub-sections no longer contain *tene*. Major ritual is no longer practised, so this role for *tene* is no longer required in modern circumstances. Leadership is not the formal province of the *tene*, so the need for section leaders to be *yamuwini* presents no problems. The Hambuali leaders in this position were in any case long established, and known as *tene hamene*. But the sense of interdependence of *tene* and *yamuwini*, and the importance of *tene* as the symbolic support of the group, is expressed by leaders of groups without *tene* as sorrow for their loss. One leader of a sub-section with no surviving *tene* said:

My *tene* are gone, and I have taken their place. I find it hard to look after everyone, to pay compensation, and talk to other parishes. I say to others, 'your *tene* are here, but I have no *tene*'. It causes me great sorrow (*dara timbuni*).

'Others' (*tara*, non-cognates) include men who live in the parish as husbands or friends. Whatever the actual regard in which such men are held the position of *tara* may be regarded with derision. In general men should not be subservient to their wives, and uxorilocal marriage may be seen as evidence of subservience. Men in this position may come to be accepted as permanent residents through becoming 'rooted to the earth (of their adopted parish) by their children' (*dindi waneiginime pi beda*). As for *igiri yango*, non-cognates, it may be significant that the term *igiri* refers to minors, boys and young men, before they can be regarded as men, *agali*. *Yango* also means 'namesake'. The term may imply that such men, though able to use the name of the parish, are not seen as possessing full jural status within it. I must again stress that I am here considering the term *igiri yango*, and not the status of actual individuals who gained their parish membership in this way.

A cognatic society?

Individualism is a dominant characteristic of the Huli temperament. Their homes are clearly separated one from the other, and it is not unusual for older men to live entirely alone. They pursue their own interests, maintain private links with kin, affines and friends in parishes over a wide area, and many may take little interest in the affairs of the parish where they live. The atmosphere at gatherings is often fractious and volatile. Disputes may flare up suddenly which cause individuals who had apparently been living in amicable proximity to scatter with their possessions and take refuge in other parish sections or other parishes. But this flow of social drama is played against a conceptual grid of descent. Agnatic descent is the dominant value, but links through women may in some contexts be seen as complementary rather than secondary. Any model of Huli social organisation must take account of both these levels. Descent constructs are not thought by the Huli to be in conflict with the multiplicity of choices open to them, and it would be false for us to suggest that these elements are in opposition.

Writing before this less typological approach became current in the analysis of New Guinea highland societies, Glasse (1968) described the Huli as a cognatic society. His data differ in several important respects from my own findings. A striking difference between the Tunda area in 1959 and Hambuali parish in 1979 is the residence pattern. Glasse found that 70% of parish residents resided multilocally, while twenty years later in Hambuali, only 22% of residents did so. While Hambuali and Tunda are only 10 kilometres apart, it is difficult to make comparisons between different parishes at different times. But the 1980 census (Parish List 1980) allows us to compare the present situation in Tunda (referred to as Toanda in the Parish List) with that in 1959. Multiresidence has fallen from 70% in 1959 to 17% in 1980. An important factor in explaining this difference is likely to be pacification. As Glasse says (1968:83–4): 'The need for security is one of the strongest motives for multilocal residence, particularly in the central Tari Basin where attack may come from any quarter with little notice. A prudent man maintains two homesteads, preferably some distance apart, on different parish-territories.' This danger is no longer a major consideration.

Secondly, the population density in the central Tari Basin is greater than at Hambuali, which is on the edge of the basin. The parishes in the central basin in general occupy correspondingly smaller territories (see fig. 8). In former times, when multiresidence was a favoured strategy, in the central Tari Basin a man would therefore have had to travel smaller distances to maintain gardens and homesteads in different parish territories.

Another difference between Glasse's findings and my own is that in 1959 in the Tunda area 40% of men regarded as parish members were non-resident. In Hambuali in 1979 the corresponding figure was 26%. It is difficult to compare these figures as most of the non-resident men from Hambuali were migrant labourers, while twenty years before non-residents of one parish were residents of another. Again this difference is likely to relate to the need to maintain links with other parishes in order to be able to seek asylum in time of war. Also, formal occasions to express parish membership were more common in former times before warfare and major ritual were abandoned.

Besides this substantive difference in the data, my conclusions also differ. In as much as their model can be said to be ordered by descent, their dogma has an agnatic, not a cognatic, bias. One of the features of Huli society which led Glasse to characterise their social groups as ambilineages was the preponderance of non-agnatic cognates amongst parish members. In his description Glasse follows the Huli definition of agnate, as I have done. In comparison with other highland societies this is unusually strict. The Mae Enga are known through Meggitt's (1965) account as displaying a highly agnatic organisation, with 91% of men in each clan parish being agnates. But here Meggitt is following the Enga definition of agnate, which is considerably more lax. 'The children of the co-resident sons of female agnates are regarded simply as clan agnates' (ibid p. 32). The Huli equivalent would be for *agua*, *aguanane* and *aguanali* to be regarded as *tene*, and not *yamuwini*. By this definition of agnate, the percentage of agnates in a Huli parish would rise from 25% to 69%. Paradoxically, it is the idealogical significance which the Huli attach to agnation which causes them to appear cognatic in comparison with other highland societies.

Marriage and divorce

Marriage choices are ordered around two principles. The first is that agnatic descendants of a parish founder should not marry each other. The use of agnatic patronymics assures that this prohibition is always observed. The second is that close cognates should not marry. This rule is more flexible. Non-agnatic cognates who can trace their descent from the same section founder would not normally marry, though they may do if they live in, and so belong to, different parish sections. There are no specific marriage alliances between Huli parishes. Polygyny has become much less common. Glasse (1968:48) reports 24% of men had two or more wives in 1959. In 1979, 11% of men in Gendo section of Hambuali parish had more than one wife. This change largely reflects mission influence. Voluntary bachelordom has also become uncommon. In former times the men who ran the bachelor cult (*ibagiya*) remained unmarried through choice. Now the only two men who remain unmarried in Gendo parish section are poor and ineffectual individuals referred to as *ibatiri* (p. 58).

Approximately one-third of all marriages end in divorce. In Gendo parish section the percentages of all marriages terminating in divorce was 37% for men and 28% for women. The difference between these rates can be accounted for largely by the age difference between wives and husbands. Men may marry women much younger than themselves, and such marriages are likely to be terminated by the death of the husband. Of Gendo women's marriages, 29%

were terminated by the death of their spouses, while only 7% of men's marriages ended in this way. Gendo men said that of the thirty-six divorces they had experienced, twenty-two (61%) were initiated by the wife. Gendo women said that of their thirty-two divorces twenty-six (84%) were initiated by the wife. Members of either sex tend to stress their own roles in initiating divorce. Despite this tendency these figures show that women initiate divorce more frequently than men. Most divorce occurs early in marriage, before the birth of children. Of Gendo men's divorces, 78% were of this sort, and 81% of Gendo women's. If we exclude divorces occurring early in the union before the birth of children from the calculation of divorce rates, we find that divorces as a percentage of all marriages falls for men from 37% to 11%, and for women from 28% to 7%.

These figures are an indication of the tension between the sexes that will emerge in the detailed discussions below of the illnesses of men that relate to the complex of Huli ideas concerning female pollution, and in illnesses of women which can be seen as attempts at gaining redress in an unequal relationship. However they also indicate that, despite male dominance, women are able to exert significant influence over their own lives, both in establishing and terminating marriage.

Many Huli illnesses are clear expressions of the social order. Characteristic cuts and bruises reflect the division of labour. Diagnoses may be based upon breaches of norms, for example of hospitality, of sexual conduct or of religious observance. Such illnesses can then become strategies of social control which in these instances could lead to generosity, sexual restraint or deference to a pastor respectively. The common attribution of illness to assault offers the most explicit equation of the body and its ills with the body politic. The style of care reflects their domestic arrangements and the multiplicity of choices available to them in seeking support. The preceding analysis of Huli social organisation was necessarily somewhat two-dimensional. The subtle interplay between the nature of their society and their experience and expression of illness will emerge from the examination of actual instances of illness. But first it is necessary to establish the boundaries of their own terms for health and illness.

4

Ideas of health and illness

The bulk of this study is an examination of how Huli individuals interpret the range of illnesses to which they are exposed, and how they select between the various means available to alleviate these ills. But it is first necessary to examine the general categories that we must use in a discussion of these issues in order to isolate the range of meanings that they have for us, and so their relevance to Huli usage. The basic terms in a study of this sort are 'health', 'illness' and 'disease'. I therefore deal with these first.

Health

The word 'health' has in English a range of meanings. We may say that someone is 'in good health', 'healthy for his age' or that his 'health is broken'. One component of our idea of health is the absence of disease, but health is not simply this. An otherwise vigorous person might still regard himself as healthy despite a sprain, or what he senses to be a passing respiratory infection. He might say that he is 'basically healthy' despite such afflictions. In becoming unhealthy, in addition to being sick we become sickly. Health is thus a state of resilience, a state of comparative invulnerability to disease.

We also talk of 'health food', and have a World Health Organisation which incorporates in its charter a definition of health as a 'state of complete physical, mental and social well-being'. This conception of health as extending beyond merely adequate functioning and encompassing ideals is implied in the derivation of the word. 'Wholeness' is a moral more than a medical concept.

How does the Huli view relate to these various concepts? Such a comparison is complicated by the absence in Huli of any single term that corresponds with our word 'health'. There is instead a constellation of ideas and actions that indicate their view. I will explore these aspects of Huli thought and behaviour in order to characterise their conception of health.

53

Ideas of health and illness

Health as the absence of disease

Health in the sense of the absence of illness means broadly the same to them as it does to us. The presence of pain, discomfort and incapacity are generally undesirable. The broad distinction between health in this sense and illness is one that Hulis readily make, though in individual cases the criteria may be uncertain. But the quality of illness and its implications may differ from our own, and their ideas of health in this limited negative sense will differ correspondingly. Such differences will emerge from the discussion of their experience of illness.

Health as resilience

One way of achieving health is through the successful treatment of illness. Another is to resist the intrusion of illness by prophylactic means. For the Huli, protection from illness and thus the maintenance of health follow from the performance of protective rituals. For each person these begin a few days after birth with the *ma hiraga* (scorching taro) ceremony. Here the newly born baby lies in a net bag across its mother's lap suckling, while a ritual specialist recites a spell and scrapes scorched taro over the mother and child. An example of the spell runs as follows: 'sago palm, bark of pine grow vigorously, sago fibre grow vigorously, claw grow vigorously, cassowary bone dagger grow vigorously' (*nuli hiwa, aiane bobo, aialuni bobo, gibane bobo, kebane bobo*). The *gamuyi* (holder of the spell, thus ritualist) evokes the strength, size and fecundity of the sago palm, the ability of the pine to renew its bark, an image of indestructability, and the toughness of claws and bones. He allies these images with the exhortation 'grow vigorously' to secure the resilience and so the survival of the child. Minor rituals were performed frequently throughout childhood, but the key ceremonies included a rite (*ma ibira gamu*) to strengthen a child in preparation for the birth of a sibling, another (*angawai hangaga*) to bind the soul within the body (see pp. 136–7), and commonly *kuyanda duguaga* to remove the weakening taint of maternal pollution (see p. 101).

The employment of such protective rituals as these is one indication of a more general theme of the Huli view of health. Individuals are seen to be more or less resilient to illness, and thus more or less healthy. This quality may vary with factors outside the individual's control, such as a greater vulnerability amongst the very young and very old. But to a considerable extent one's own or one's childrens' health is regarded as evidence of one's skill and resolve in maintaining it. Their view is not that man's naturally healthy state is intermittently disrupted by disease. Theirs is a pessimistic view which sees life as a fragile state. Health is a quality to strive for through the application of ritual knowledge and prudent living. Its absence is likely to be attributed to one's own fecklessness or the wrong-doing of others.

54

Ideas of health and illness

Health and social effectiveness

A third aspect of the Huli view is that for them health is as much a social as a physical state. They are deeply concerned about their bodies and the care of them, but this care is inextricably mixed with ideas of social effectiveness, and particularly the attraction of wealth and influence. They are quite able to distinguish a bad cough from poverty, but their means of avoiding these two predicaments can be the same. Traditionally, men's achievement of this ideal state of physical resilience and social distinction required lengthy training in the bachelor cult (*ibagiya*).

The houses where young men were trained to become *ibagiya* were hidden in secluded areas of forest. Women and married men were forbidden to go near. Each training house (*ibagiyanda*) was supervised by a bachelor (*daloali*) expert in this lore. The establishment was run rather in the manner of a private college. The neophytes or their parents chose a particular bachelor house on the basis of the reputation of the *daloali*, though personal ties were also important. Young men were under no obligation to submit themselves for this training. If they chose to offer themselves, and could afford the specialist's fees, they entered a contractual relationship with him whereby he would impart his knowledge, and they would abide by his rules. While young men were not required to enter training, the knowledge of *ibagiya* was held in such high regard that most men acquired it. They entered seclusion for some eight months, learning the spells and lore that would afford protection from malign influences, especially those of women, and which would make them beautiful. They grew their hair and shaped it into the red wig (*manda hare*) that is the mark of *ibagiya*. Finally they were admitted to the house within a fenced enclosure which is the *ibagiyanda* proper, and for two nights and a day were taught the core spells and shown the magical plants which are the central mystery of the cult.

The spells, techniques, knowledge and herbs of *ibagiya* ensure that the initiate will mature physically, and be resistant to damaging influences, particularly the polluting effects of women. But his training is also intended to lead to social benefits. Some of these are explicit. For example an *ibagiya* learns spells and acquires magical plants that lead to the increase of his pig herd, an essential prerequisite for social distinction. But the implicit benefits are more significant. A fine appearance is said to have a direct effect upon others. One such effect is to increase the generosity of others in their dealings towards you. This is of obvious consequence in a society where social distinction depends to a considerable extent upon success in exchange transactions. It is therefore appropriate that the desired outcome of this training is expressed in descriptions of the skin. The skin, as the visible aspect of the body, mediates between an individual's inner state and others' appreciation of him. The quality of his inner state is itself said to influence events, and that quality becomes apparent through the appearance of the skin

Fig. 10 The male ideal of health seen in the shining skins of *mali* dancers

(fig. 10). This is a common theme in Melanesian societies. For example
Malinowski (1922:335–6) describes the Kula magic of beauty, intended 'to
make the man beautiful, attractive, and irresistible to his Kula partner'.
Andrew Strathern (1977:109) comments upon the 'physiological and sociological appropriateness' of shame being 'on the skin'. The Huli vocabulary
in this area is very rich. The shine of the skin (*tingini* or *dongone*) is described
in various ways. For example, 'the skin shines like the sun' (*tingini limilimi
deda*), or 'it gleams like a rainbow' (*domodomone*), or 'it glows like an ember'
(*loai leda*). It may be likened to natural objects, such as to *ngoedali*, a *Russula*
mushroom with a waxy indigo cap. Or they may refer to its texture with
adjectives such as *mbali mbali* (smooth). The way the light catches particular
parts of the body is indicative of a desirable state. The shine on the sides of
the nose, *ngui pindidigibi* (literally 'nose sweat') and of the eyes, *de gilibi*
(literally 'finely marked eyes') are remarked upon. These observations have
a deeper significance than our 'doesn't he look well'. The connotation of
social effectiveness is also found in some of our terms describing a pleasing
appearance, such as captivating, winning or engaging, but for the Huli the
interrelationship between physical appearance, social effectiveness and good
health is more explicit.

The fusion of health, wealth and social effectiveness in Huli thought is also
made clear in the ritual and training that surrounds marriage. I will deal with
the ritual surrounding marriage and sexuality in more detail when I discuss

the relations between sexuality and illness in chapter 7. Here I will focus upon elements of marriage training (*ndi tingi*) that offer insights into the general Huli view of health. The ritual and admonitions given to the couple in the early months of marriage by the expert in marriage lore (*ndi tingi gamuyi*) seems to be entirely directed towards teaching both bridegroom and bride how to protect his health from her polluting power. But ritual training for marriage has a second, more positive, aim. This is indicated in the content of the spells used in the final ritual before consummation, some eight months after marriage. A representative section from this lengthy and repetitive spell runs:

Portions of pork, portions of pork, he wanted it for himself, these shells, these shells, I hold them, white shells and shells that are not white, I hold them, cowrie shells, goldlip shells, I hold them, shell ear-rings, shell ear-rings, I hold them, the great pine, I hold its new shoot, I hold its branch, I hold its trunk, I gather these things and put them in my bag, I gather these things and put them in my bag, I gather these things and put them in my bag, I prepare them, I prepare them and place them there, at the meeting ground of *aiari mandi*.

(*Pilini puguni, puguni podone, o ibu inini lene, gare ogola, nagare ogola, minalu minaro, pelegola napelegola, minalu minaro, hewaliyene yene, mamaguni la, minalu minaro paguali lole o, madaliba la, minalu minaro, o gubiriye, mane mane yido, magane magan(yido, irane irane yido, obena obena yido, o mo mubi mubi o, o mo gondo gondo o, m(pogoria pogoria o, manda o, manda manda bu ngelaro, aiari mandini.*)

The spell talks primarily of wealth, pork and shells. The pine tree is the image of the indestructible strong man, and its branches his influence and extending wealth. At the gathering place his skill and presence lead to his attracting gifts, further evidence of his importance. The spell continues with images of the power of the eagle, of wealth flowing as freely as the flowing rivers and of 'holding' his relations, that is leading his group.

One idiom which clearly expresses this interrelation between health and wealth concerns the 'openness' of the nose. During marriage training the expert tells the couple that if they do not do what he has taught them one of the results will be that, literally, 'their noses will be shut' (*ngui payulebira*). Through an 'open nose' (*ngui duguhe*) flows influence and wealth. By observing the lore, they assure the bodily health of the husband but also their wealth and influence.

Ill health

The converse of 'good skin' includes more than physical illness. The terms used to refer to 'bad skin' are again varied and graphic. *Ko* (bad) may be used, which refers to anything disapproved of or undesirable. More specifically, the skin may be called dry (*tingini gabu ka*), said to be as if covered in ash (*be taguabi*, flaky like the *alualu* mushroom (*Pulveroboletus ravenelii*), soft (*gedeore*), yellowing and limp like an aging banana leaf (*baborada*), or one of many other epithets may be used. The Huli word *dodo* can mean simply 'dirt', but in relation to 'bad skin' it has the connotation of taint: *dodo ngagi lowa* (dirt stuck to the skin) implies extreme decrepitude. 'The wig is bad, matted and uneven' (*manda dogadogabi ko*) is another element of 'bad skin', as are any other defects of the wig. The state of the eyes and nose indicates the inner condition. Where this is poor the eyes may be said to be smoky (*de haguabi*), or dull (*do home*), or sunken (*de uli tegelehe*). The nose may be dry and scaly (*ngui kaia kaiabi*) or the forehead and bridge of the nose dry (*de ngui yope ko*). The actual physical changes to which these expressions are applied are in most cases considerably less marked than simple translation may suggest. Sometimes I had difficulty in identifying any change at all when such changes were seemingly obvious to Hulis. But I would not expect to find frogs in the throats of Englishmen, nor clouds in their eyes. The Huli terms are also metaphors, but they differ from many of our bodily metaphors for, instead of taking a quality of an object in the natural world and applying it to the body, the Huli are taking a quality of a person's body, and applying it to his social world.

A person's figure is also important. Those who diverge widely from the ideal are less likely to gain respect, and may be referred to by such terms as *guruhayale tombehe* (with the fat belly and spindly legs of an orb spider), or *ko ma gali* (with a neck so long and skinny that his head may topple off) or *haite* (with a belly so distended that it hangs down over his hips).

The implications of these allusions are again broader than the physical state alone, a common theme in these societies. Fortune (1932:136, 171) comments on the Dobuan identification of 'having' a bad person with 'being' a bad person (being deformed or incurably sick). The Huli feel that the sort of negative attributes I have described are in some sense the responsibility of the person afflicted. The extreme antithesis of the man with a 'good skin' is referred to variously as *ibatiri, dari, hunguli wiagada* and similar epithets. The name *ibatiri* can be translated as 'the rubbish on the surface of water'. It is variously applied to spirits and to men. The qualities that *ibatiri*, spirits or men, share is their lack of allegiance, and their being marginal actors either in spirit affairs or, if men, in social affairs. Such men may be physically unwell, often with ill-defined chronic complaints. They seldom speak at public discussions, contribute little in exchanges, are mainly preoccupied with their own subsistence work and are often unmarried or divorced. Another epithet, *hunguli wiagada*, means 'flying around eating *hungu* fruit' (a worthless inedible fruit). Such a person is discounted as a significant member of the parish in which he lives.

The young man who has newly emerged from *ibagiya* embodies the positive pole of the Huli view of health. He is beautiful, vigorous, knowledgeable, chaste and striving to establish himself. The negative pole is inhabited by an *ibatiri*, a shabby, sickly, impoverished recluse.

Illness

Poor health, in its broadest sense, does not necessarily imply illness. But illness is the most important aspect of it, carrying as it does the risk of incomplete recovery or even death. The continuity between illness and death is openly accepted by the Huli. The only general way to refer to illness is to use the verbs that also mean dying. Someone who feels ill from any cause, when asked how they are, may simply reply, '*homedo*' (I am dying). If they recover the next day this is not regarded as an indication that they were exaggerating the severity of their symptoms. While they may use such phrases as a means of gaining sympathy for lesions which are not seen as life threatening, in general this use of the words for dying to denote illness is quite different from our idioms of the sort 'I am dying of cold'. The morbid implication of the Huli usage is clear. But this usage also differs from the English 'he is dying', for the Huli see dying as a fluid state which need not necessarily result in decease. For them, dying is a vulnerable condition in continuity with demise, from which recovery is likely. These terms may be as ambiguous to the Huli as they sound to us. *Homaya*, he died, can be said of a corpse, or of someone who was very ill but is now all right. The Huli live in scattered settlements, so most people depend upon verbal reports for their knowledge of another's illness. They will not gather in large numbers at the house of a sick person until they are dead or near death. Women may hear that someone has died, *homaya*, set off keening to the house, and find that the person is really not very ill. In such circumstances the mourners would feel that there had been a misunderstanding, and the sick person be irritated at their haste.

I have established that there is a broad category of Huli experience that relates to our term 'illness'. This does not imply that the boundaries of this category of experience correspond with what constitutes illness for us. But the use of this term is not especially misleading in isolating this area for study. The actual boundaries of this area of experience will emerge from the details of their view and behaviour.

5

Morbidity, explanations and actions: quantitative perspectives

The nature and severity of the illnesses to which people are exposed may influence their view of illness and guide their responses to it. For example, where infant mortality rates are very high, illnesses in young children may lead to less complex responses than illnesses of similar gravity in adults. Conversely, the burden of illness is likely to differ according to age, sex, division of labour and, in highly differentiated societies, class and status. These differences may reflect societal influences upon illness. A simple example from the Huli is the difference between the skin lesions of men and of women that follow from the sorts of tasks that they perform. As a background to these and other discussions I will therefore present an analysis of the burden of illness to which Huli are exposed.

Hulis pay more attention to some complaints than others. The anthropologist is also likely to approach the array of illnesses selectively according to the focus of his or her study. To place both these aspects of selective attention in perspective, I will also present a breakdown of types of explanations of illness in all episodes of illness occurring in a sample population.

The Huli have available to them a wide range of alternative treatment strategies. These include simple home remedies, more intricate traditional cures, recourse to the facilities of the Department of Public Health, various forms of Christian faith-healing and inaction. Finally in this chapter I will present a breakdown of their choices of action in illness, and indicate some broad influences upon these choices.

The burden of illness

I have already indicated two obstacles to gaining representative data: the different significance given to some illnesses by the Huli, and my own theoretical concerns. An additional problem in assessing the burden of illness and responses to it in this geographical area is the residence pattern. Huli homes are scattered, and hidden one from the other. When they are ill people do not usually appear in public, so that knowledge of who is ill can depend upon chance meetings or gossip, particularly when the ill person is not a close

Table 3 *Age and sex distribution of the morbidity sample*

Age (years)	m	f	Total
0–4	89	56	145
5–11	100	99	199
12–19	77	95	172
20–39	95	126	221
40+	132	129	261
Total	493	505	998

associate. This residence pattern, and the potential invisibility of the sick that follows from it, was a third reason for my organising a formal morbidity study. Fourthly, I was also engaged in a study of the utilisation and functioning of health services, and for this it was as important to know who did not use these services as who did. This can be determined only through a community based study.

Most information on levels of illness in Papua New Guinea is derived from the records of treatment facilities. Such figures are known to be a poor reflection of actual morbidity, but often are all that is available. Studies from Papua New Guinea which include community based measures of morbidity include Feachem (1977), Lewis (1975), Maddocks (1978) and Sinnett (1975). Less systematic material is contained in Vines (1970). The morbidity study that I will present here is derived from the study of a final sample of 992 people living in Hambuali, and the four neighbouring parishes of Tigua, Dagima, Yumu and Linavin. The age and sex distribution of the study sample is shown in table 3.

Each person, or parent in the case of small children, was questioned fortnightly for one year about the symptoms that they had experienced during the preceding fortnight and, if they had suffered any symptoms, what they had done to alleviate them. These interviews were conducted by three literate Huli men, each of whom was a member of the parish where most of his respondents resided. These assistants worked under my close supervision. I often accompanied them on their rounds, and I followed up cases of illness where more detailed enquiries were indicated.

Unless I specify otherwise, I have expressed the morbidity rates as days experiencing the symptom/person/year. I devised this unit as it conveys the actual burden of illness. For example, if a particular age category has a morbidity score of seven for a certain symptom, this means that people of that age suffer that symptom for an average of one week per person per year each. A key methodological issue in a study of this sort concerns the problem of translating between the terms of scientific medicine and those of a folk

61

taxonomy of illness. Problems of this sort would arise in attempting to imply any simple correspondence between higher-order Huli diagnostic categories and Western diagnoses. In the main the categories selected here do not present such problems. Cough (*ko*), vomiting (*magu*), headache (*hagua*), sores (*dere*) and so on mean broadly the same to them as they mean to us. Only in two of the complaints initially selected did ambiguities arise. The Huli term *kamilami* refers to measles, but it is also applied to chicken pox, other rashes and also to thrush and other mouth sores. It was therefore excluded from the analysis. Fever is normally *poboyogo bira*, which also means 'he (or she) is hot'. This refers to fevers in children, where the child is hot to the touch and the parent is reporting, and those fevers in adults where patients themselves feel hot. But rigors are experienced as cold, and are described as such. Rigors are also described as *wabi warago* (illness from the lowlands). In the analysis, cases of *wabi warago* were treated as 'fever'.

Findings

Here I will detail symptoms, from the trivial to the most severe, and indicate their duration. My intention is to show the impact of illness of all sorts upon everyday life, and the differing spectrum of illness at different ages and in either sex. As I have already explained, I am including all instances of illness as this might be defined upon external medical grounds. In practice this presents few problems, as the Huli view of what is and what is not a symptom of illness differs little from ours. The significance that they may attach to various symptoms and their categorisation of them may differ markedly, but this need not affect this presentation of the burden of illness. In terms of the scheme of portraying their view of illness that I presented above (pp. 8–9), these findings are an expression of their illness descriptions, answers to the question, 'What is wrong?'

Broad characteristics of the population

I have included tables 4 to 7 to place the subsequent morbidity rates in their demographic perspective. These four tables are taken from Riley (1979). Table 4 shows the familiar population pyramid. Tables 5 and 6 show the high mortality of early life, followed by a good chance of survival once the age of five is reached. The birth rate shown in table 7 has changed little over the last three decades, but the mortality rate has. The resultant increase in population is largely due to the availability of effective treatments for infectious diseases.

Fig. 11 shows the number of days per year that people suffered any symptoms at all. This shows the susceptibility of the under-fives to illness, and a rate that falls during later childhood and adolescence. After twenty

Morbidity, explanations and actions

Table 4 *Distribution of the population in the east and central Tari Basin census divisions in* 1973

Age	Male	Female
0–4	768	801
5–9	742	830
10–14	640	652
15–19	671	622
20–24	610	499
25–29	408	437
30–34	292	357
35–39	307	410
40–44	303	361
45–49	290	305
50–54	203	263
55–59	163	147
60+	203	192

Table 5 *Birth and death rates per* 1,000 *per annum*

	rate per 1,000 population
Crude death rate	12.0
Neonatal mortality	26.6
Post-neonatal mortality	45.8
Infant mortality	72.3
1–4 age specific mortality	15.7

Table 6 *Life expectancy (years)*

	Male	Female
at birth	52.01	50.43
at 1 year	55.31	53.08
at 20 years	40.67	39.25
at 50 years	16.56	14.98

Table 7 *Fertility*

Crude birth rate	34.1 per 1,000/annum
Rate of natural population increase	2.19% per annum

63

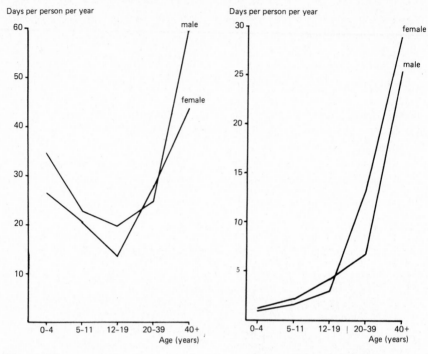

Fig. 11 All symptom days   Fig. 12 All aches and pains

years the amount of illness increases, to rise steeply after the age of forty. The effects of particular symptoms in producing these variations with age as well as the differing rates for males and females will emerge as we look at each sort of symptom in turn.

Aches and pains

I will begin with the various aches and pains that Hulis suffer. In fig. 12 I have grouped all symptoms of this sort, specifically: backache, joint pain, headache, body aches (*tingini nara*, 'it consumes the skin'), injuries (broken bones, twisted ankles and the like), and pain in the chest (with no concomitant respiratory illness). As we might expect, these problems are reported as affecting the under-fives only rarely. There is a gradual rise in their prevalence into middle life, and a very steep rise for the over-forties, where there is a mean rate for males and females of 27.0 days/person/year. Even in this composite category, a sex difference is apparent, most strikingly in the 20–39-year group, where men have a rate of 6.7 and women 13.1 days/person/year (p < 0.01; probabilities in this chapter are derived from t tests.)

Backache (fig. 13) shows a clear sex difference in later life. The rate for

64

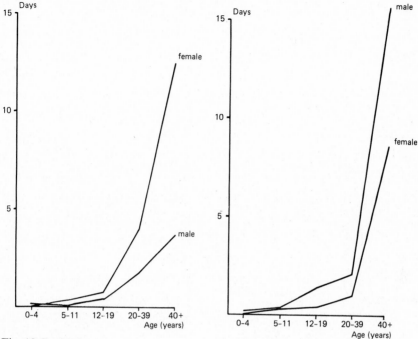

Fig. 13 Backache

Fig. 14 Joint pain

women in the 20–39-year group is more than double that of men (1.8 as against 4.0 days/person/year, p < 0.01), and in the over-forties it is more than threefold (3.7 for men and 12.3 days/person/year for women, p < 0.01). These differences are a clear reflection of the division of labour. The high rates for older women are the product of a lifetime of carrying heavy loads, and long hours spent in the characteristic stoop of their gardening position.

Joint pain (fig. 14) shows an even steeper rise with old age, but here the trends for men and women are reversed. In the over-forties men have a rate 15.7 and women 8.6 days/person/year (p < 0.01). Almost all this pain is in fact arthritic pain in the knees. This difference is explicable on two counts. The first is the differing mobility of men and women. Throughout their lives men walk long distances going about their affairs or just visiting friends and interesting events. Women are more tied to their homes. A lifetime of walking on often poor and treacherous tracks would predispose them to osteo-arthritis of the knees. Further, they are very reluctant to abandon their journeying through age, so that long walks on already arthritic knees aggravate symptoms. The second explanation is warfare. Arrow wounds in the joints were relatively common injuries. A man may still suffer the effects of such a wound decades after the battle.

65

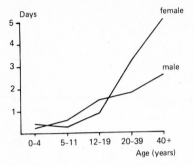

Fig. 15 Headache

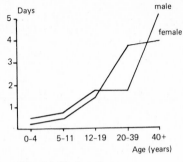

Fig. 16 Body aches

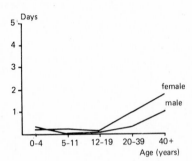

Fig. 17 Trauma

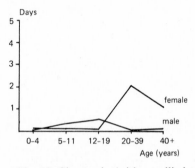

Fig. 18 Chest pain (with no allied
respiratory symptoms)

The differences in the rates for headache (fig. 15) I would also ascribe to
the division of labour, in that the weight of women's loads is born across the
crown of the head. But a further issue is involved here: relations between the
sexes. The higher rate for women between the ages of twenty and thirty-nine
for headache, body aches, trauma and chest pain ($p < 0.01$) is to a large extent
the product of beatings (figs. 16, 17, 18). Most of these would have been at
the hands of their husbands, but brothers, co-wives and other women would
also have contributed to the injuries that led to these symptoms. The blows
are often delivered with a stick or plank. The head and sides of the chest are
common targets. Attempts to ward off the blows lead not infrequently to a
broken forearm. The duration of some of the symptoms attributed to violence
can also be influenced by the progress of litigation aimed at securing
compensation for the injury (pp. 124–36).

Cutaneous lesions

Minor cutaneous lesions show the opposite trend with age (fig. 19), being
common in early life, and less so with maturity. The differences between the

66

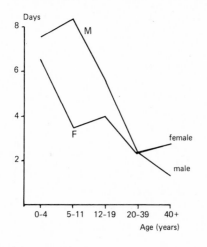

Fig. 19 All minor cutaneous lesions

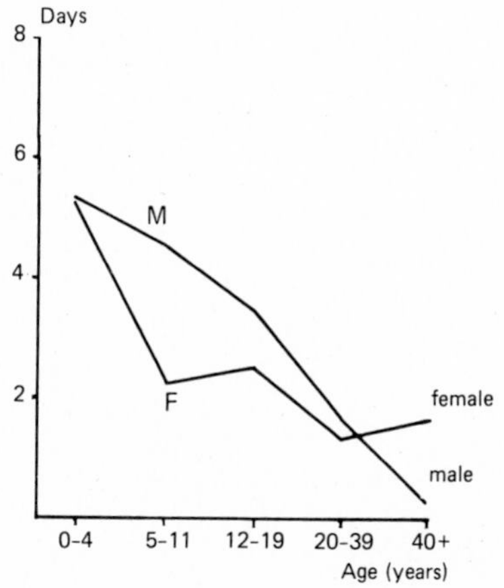

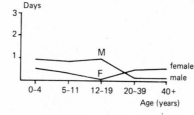

Fig. 20 Small sores

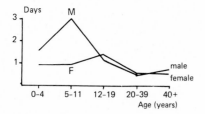

Fig. 21 Small cuts

Fig. 22 Small burns

sexes in the younger groups, ($p < 0.01$), is understandable in terms of the norms of behaviour for boys and girls. Particularly between toddlerhood and adolesence, boys run free, learn to use axes and bush knives, chase each other, fight, climb trees, roam in the forest and are generally free to please themselves. In contrast, girls stay with their mothers, help with the chores and are otherwise much constrained. There is no significant difference in the rates for small lesions in the under-fives for boys or girls. After five years, the rates for small sores (fig. 20) and for small cuts (fig. 21) shows marked differences ($p < 0.01$). Considering that Hulis lead their lives in such close proximity to fire, the prevalence of small burns is impressively small (fig. 22). In the cases of major skin lesions, these differences continue into later life (fig. 23). The generally higher rates for males of large sores (fig. 24, $p < 0.01$) and abscesses (fig. 25, $p < 0.01$) reflect the greater risk of injury from their tasks in the division of labour. This influence is particularly clear in the rates for large cuts (fig. 26, $p < 0.01$). Between the ages of twenty and forty most of a man's allotted tasks involve the use of an axe. He must supply himself and

67

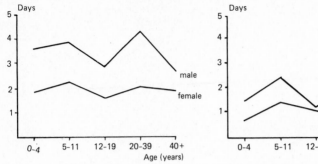

Fig. 23 All major cutaneous lesions

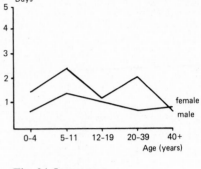

Fig. 24 Large sores

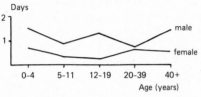

Fig. 25 Abscesses

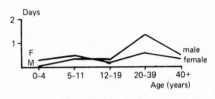

Fig. 26 Large cuts

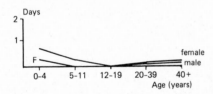

Fig. 27 Large burns

his family with firewood, build his own and his wife's house, build fences for their gardens and maintain them. Their skill as axe-men is reflected in a rate for large cuts of 1.45 days/man/year. When these cuts occur, a common site is on the dorsum of the foot which he uses to hold down the timber he is cutting. For women, a characteristic lesion is a series of small cuts on the fingers and sides of the palm from uprooting the coarse grass used in thatching.

Large burns occur infrequently in the under-fives, and very infrequently at other ages (fig. 27).

Respiratory symptoms

I will begin the more detailed analysis of life-threatening conditions by looking at serious respiratory illness (fig. 28), including lower respiratory

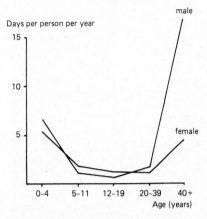

Fig. 28 Severe respiratory symptoms

infections, and in older subjects, symptoms of chronic obstructive airways disease as well as acute infections. Between the ages of five and forty such symptoms are infrequent. The under-fives are considerably more susceptible with a mean for males and females of 6.1 days/person/year. Over forty, the prevalence of such symptoms shows a marked difference between men and women. Males suffer an average of 17.6 days/person/year, and females 4.5 days/person/year (p < 0.01). Tobacco smoking is likely to be a factor here. Huli men are avid pipe-smokers, and inhale deeply whenever other activity does not preclude the preparation and lighting up of a pipe (fig. 29). Traditional lore was strict in the discouragement of women from smoking. To older men's disgust, some women are now beginning to smoke openly. If women do become as committed to smoking as men are we might expect the gap between men and women's experience of severe respiratory symptoms to narrow.

The prevalence of cough (fig. 30) shows a similar trend, though there is no increase for women over 40. The prevalence of the symptoms of upper respiratory infections (cough with fever, runny nose) is shown in fig. 31. These symptoms are commonest in the under-fives, and show no significant sex difference.

Gastro-enteritis

Fig. 32 shows the combined prevalences of diarrhoea, bloody diarrhoea and vomiting. The mean rate for males and females in the under-fives is 3.6 days/person/year, considerably greater than that found in any of the other age groups. This we would expect. But the difference between the rates in the under-fives between males and females (4.78 and 2.05 days/person/year respectively, p < 0.01) demands explanation. The difference derives mainly

69

Fig. 29 Bareagua with his pipe

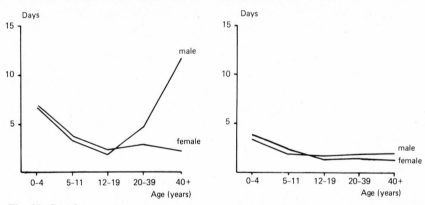

Fig. 30 Cough

Fig. 31 Upper respiratory symptoms

from the rates for diarrhoea (3.38 and 1.5 days/person/year respectively) shown in fig. 33. But the rates for dysentery (fig. 34) and vomiting (fig. 35) also contribute. There are two obvious explanations. First, it could represent a genuine difference in the number of days of diarrhoea suffered by boys as opposed to girls. This may be so, and in that case one would have to look for differences in the way that parents look after children of either sex, and for differences in the behaviour of little boys as against little girls. But we must remember that rates in the under-fives are derived entirely from patients'

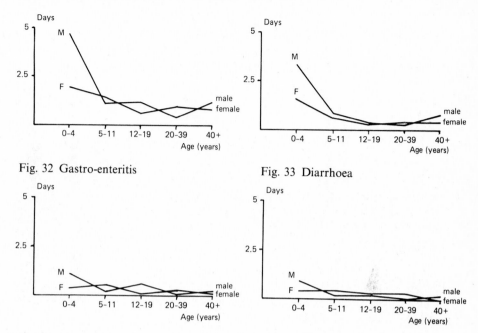

Fig. 32 Gastro-enteritis

Fig. 33 Diarrhoea

Fig. 34 Bloody diarrhoea

Fig. 35 Vomiting

reports, and are thus also a measure of the parents' concern. To qualify as a case of diarrhoea in this study the child had to have produced three watery stools in one day. This symptom is thus particularly sensitive to the care of the parents' observation. I would suggest that the higher rate for males over that of females in the under-fives is to a large extent the product of the higher valuation by parents of their sons over their daughters, which leads to a somewhat higher level of concern in life-threatening illnesses. I will present other evidence for this when I consider the actions taken in illness (p. 78).

Fevers

The distribution of fever with or without rigors is shown in fig. 36. Malaria is not a major problem in this area, but it is present. These cases of fever are therefore likely to be malarial, although blood slides were not collected in most cases. The difference between males and females in the under-fives ($p < 0.01$) may again stem from the differing levels of concern in the parents. The higher rates in males from adolescence to the age of forty ($p < 0.01$) is likely to follow from the higher mobility of males between these ages. They travel much more in the Southern Highlands Province, and so move to areas with more malarial transmission. A high proportion of them have travelled

71

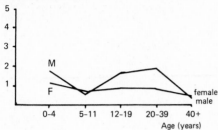

Fig. 36 Fevers

to other highlands areas, and also to the coast (49% of men from twenty to thirty-nine years had travelled outside the Southern Highlands, while only 5% of women had done so).

Explanations of illness

These rates of illness indicate the extent and medical nature of morbidity experienced by the Huli. The symptoms I have described may be interpreted by the Huli in a variety of ways. Their interpretations may vary from the symptoms being accepted as unexceptional features of living to their being viewed as specific retribution for improper acts. Explanations of this latter sort are the ones that tend to preoccupy anthropologists, though the findings I present in this section show that they may be applied only infrequently. This focus upon complex explanations is quite legitimate, as key facets of a culture may become apparent in such times of crisis. Much of my later discussion of Huli responses to illness is concerned with explanations of this sort. But it is also my intention to demonstrate how the Huli medical culture orders their more mundane experience of illness, and how they select between the various sorts of explanations and different treatment strategies available to them. In this section I will therefore place the various sorts of explanation in a quantitative perspective as background to the later detailed discussion of the nature and utilisation of these explanations of illness.

I have already outlined the problems entailed in ordering Huli concepts of illness for purposes of description and analysis. There is no single body of knowledge that relates solely to illnesses. Here I will present their illnesses in terms of the level of explanation implied in the diagnosis. Higher levels of explanation are likely to include lower, so that when the question Why? is answered, How? and What? will commonly be known. Each illness episode is here included in terms of the highest level of explanation only.

For six months (from July to December 1978) a sub-sample of the morbidity sample (the 417 respondents living in Hambuali parish) was

72

Table 8 *Episodes of illness according to level of explanation*

Question answered by the diagnosis	Diagnosis	Episodes
What?	Various symptoms (cough, aches, diarrhoea etc.)	237
	Skin lesions	117
	Syndromes – *homama*	65
	– *amali*	7
	– *warago*	21
	TOTAL	447 (81%)
How?	Old Age (*wahe*)	23
	Changes in the body fluids	7
	Worms (*ngoe*)	13
	Dirt (*dodo*)	8
	TOTAL	51 (9%)
Why?	Work	9
	Sleeping crookedly	6
	Effects of the sun	1
	Beating	21
	Arrow	8
	Female pollution	5
	Sorcery	1
	God/spirits	3
	TOTAL	54 (10%)

studied more intensively to determine the extent to which illness episodes were explained, and the frequencies of the various Huli explanations of illness. (I should stress that I studied the explanation of instances of illness in Hambuali and elsewhere throughout the periods of field work. This section of the study was designed to place that other less controlled material in a quantitative framework.) I recorded explanations or their absence in all episodes of illness, however trivial, for this sub-sample. This group suffered a total of 552 episodes of illness over the period. The explanations I include here represent the unequivocal opinions of patients, or parents in the case of children. Where higher-level explanations were tentative, I have included the lower-level explanations only. The breakdown of these findings is shown in table 8.

In 237 cases the sufferers or those caring for them simply offered a description of their symptoms, such as cough, diarrhoea, fever and so on. If pressed to discuss what led to this particular episode they might speculate about whether it could relate to this or that, or say that they did not know why it had occurred, or commonly would say *bamu*, 'for no reason'. A further 117 episodes were contributed by a variety of skin complaints such as sores, cuts, burns and boils. Many of these were attributed to particular episodes, such as stubbing a toe when walking. In a sense we could say therefore that these are explained at a higher level, but the explanation does not go beyond the immediate circumstances surrounding the development of the lesion. The syndrome names (*homama, amali, warago*, broadly corresponding to colds, chronic bronchitis and malaria respectively) are largely descriptive, though they may encompass some concepts that belong more properly at the next explanatory level. In total therefore, some 81% of Huli diagnoses are concerned largely with the nature of the lesion, rather than its causation.

To turn to diagnoses that answer the question of how the symptoms developed, 51 or 9% of illness episodes were diagnosed in this way. The Huli terms for these processes may imply particular symptoms, or the symptom may have to be specified separately. In this series diagnoses of this sort comprised old age, changes in the body fluids (hardening or loss of blood, and pooling of water in the body), activities of abdominal worms and the effects of dirt.

Clear statements of why the particular illness occurred are made in 54 of these episodes. Most Huli explanations of this sort are epistemologically straightforward, though their social implications may be complex. Diagnoses of this sort are mostly concerned with the direct physical effects of one's own actions, or assaults by others.

In only 9 cases, which represents less than 2% of the episodes of illness recorded here, did they invoke their more elaborate explanations. Of illness in adult men, 5 cases were ascribed to the damaging effects of female pollution. One case was attributed to sorcery (*nambis poisin*) and 3 cases were attributed to causes involving syntheses of Huli views concerning spirits, and Christian teaching.

These figures are based upon a small sample over only six months. But I also had less controlled access to a population of some 30,000 people, and so saw many other cases of illness where complex explanations were applied. I studied cases of illness in Hambuali throughout the period of field work. People from parishes other than Hambuali came to my house to tell me of their ills. I heard of ill people in other areas whom I then visited. And I saw ill people at aid posts and at Tari Health Centre. By these means I was able to further my knowledge of the application of their more complex schemes of explanation. These data from a small sample are intended to place the later findings into the perspective of the general response of Hulis to their ills. The small proportion of episodes where elaborate aetiological explanations were offered in part reflects the relative rarity of serious illness. But it also shows that much of the time Hulis wait for their symptoms to resolve without relating them to the more complex schemes of explanation available to them.

The choice of actions in illness

Actions taken in illness provide one index of the relationship between belief and behaviour. A wide range of sometimes conflicting strategies in illness is available to the Huli. During this period of rapid social change it is especially important to be able to determine their degree of commitment to these various types of response. The quantitative data presented here are intended as background to the later discussion of their differential abandonment of traditional approaches to illness and adoption of aspects of introduced concepts and practices. I will therefore examine the actions that people take to seek relief for themselves or their children from the symptoms described.

The data on the choice of action in illness presented in this chapter derives largely from the morbidity study. Where illness occurred, the choice of treatments and the number of days on which they were applied were recorded. I have expressed these findings in terms of the percentage of days of illness when a particular sort of treatment was applied. In addition, I undertook a number of other studies concerned with the utilisation and functioning of the various treatment facilities of the Department of Public Health. These data include details of in-patients at the Tari Health Centre (730 cases), out-patients at the Tari Health Centre (521 cases), attenders at Hambuali Aid Post (1,000 cases), and attenders at six other aid posts (1,722 cases). In this study I will draw on selected aspects of that research, but again these aspects are described in more detail in other publications.

The range of available actions

For the purposes of this statistical summary, I have grouped possible actions into six categories. The first is 'nil', that is, no action at all. The second I have called 'self-help'. This includes all traditional measures from changes in the diet of the ill person, to rubbing with nettles, to the use of bespelled water, extraction of spirit arrows or major healing cermonies. The third category of treatment is 'Christian healing', which includes private prayers as well as public services. Fourthly, 'aid post', which is self-explanatory. The fifth category, 'out-patients' involves a visit to the out-patients department at Tari Health Centre, and the sixth, 'in-patient' involves the patient's admission to Tari Health Centre.

The five positive actions (all actions apart from nil) are expressed as a percentage of the symptom days. For example, an aid post score of 25% for a particular illness means that in that illness people visited the aid post on one day in four while they had symptoms. The nil score is computed differently. It is derived from the mean of the number of days when symptoms were recorded and no action at all was taken during that fortnight. It is

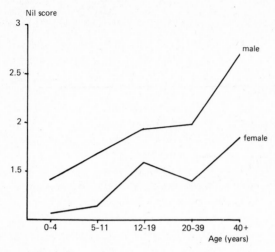

Fig. 37 Inaction

important to stress that is not numerically comparable to the other scores, nor is it arithmetically incremental as are the other scores.

Selection between the various actions
Nil
To obtain a nil score at all, in any particular fortnight, nothing at all must be done about the symptoms. The relationship between the willingness to do nothing, and the age and sex of the ill person is shown in fig. 37. This shows that broadly, the older the person, the more likely they are to do nothing about their symptoms, or have nothing done about them (p < 0.01). Males appear to do absolutely nothing more often than females at all ages, though this difference is not statistically significant. The nature of this relative inaction will emerge below when we consider the influence of particular symptoms.

Self-help
Turning to self-help (fig. 38), it is striking how infrequently Hulis make use of their traditional means of coping with illness. A little over twenty years ago all available treatments were of this sort. These methods have now been eclipsed by introduced measures. The graph shows that on only 1.2% of sick days are treatments of this sort applied in the case of the under-fives, as opposed to 7.5% for the over-forties. Older people are keen church-goers, but in general women are more committed than men. This is reflected in the use of traditional practices in 9.5% of sick days by men over forty, as against 5.5% of sick days for women (p < 0.01).

76

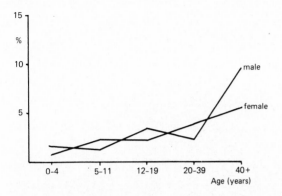

Fig. 38 Percentage of symptom days when self-help is used

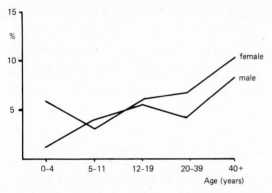

Fig. 39 Percentage of symptom days when Christian healing is used

Christian healing

One alternative to traditional measures is Christian healing. That women are more devout, and become committed to the church at an earlier age than men is reflected in the selection of this action in illness as shown in fig. 39, (p < 0.01). This action is also more acceptable than self-help in the case of younger people.

Aid post

Numerically the most important alternative to traditional measures is the aid post (fig. 40). Fig. 41 shows that approximately one-third of symptom days in the under-fives result in a visit to the aid post. This rate falls steadily with age, until the over-forties visit the aid post on one day out of every seven that they experience symptoms. In my presentation of the burden of illness, I suggested that the apparently higher prevalence of some potentially serious symptoms in the under-five group was at least in part the result of greater

Fig. 40 Waiting for treatment outside an aid post

parental concern when sons are severely ill than when daughters have similar complaints. A comparison of the measures taken in such illnesses in this age group is also suggestive of this. In potentially serious illnesses (lower respiratory infections and diarrhoea) boys under five years were taken to the aid post on 46.4% of the days that they had symptoms, while girls in this age group were taken on 35.9% of days (p < 0.01). Not to bring a child of this age with these symptoms for treatment at the aid post is generally regarded by Hulis as negligent, whatever other treatments are applied. I would suggest that the lesser readiness to bring girls for aid post treatment is indicative of a higher valuation of boys over girls.

The highest rates for aid post attendance in serious conditions are in the 5–11-year age group. The even greater readiness for parents to make use of aid post facilities in this age group probably stems from the fact that such symptoms are much rarer in children of this age, and are therefore even more alarming. After the age of twelve, the male rate of attendance for these conditions is consistently lower than the female rate (p < 0.01). This may be partly stoicism, but, particularly in the older ages, is to do with the greater number of days that men have symptoms, and the chronicity of the illnesses, particularly chronic obstructive airways disease, that affect them (see fig. 28).

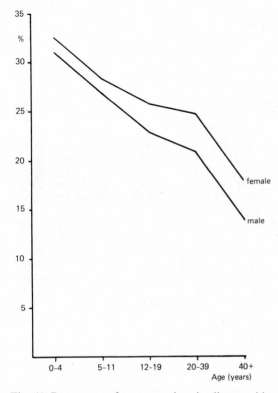

Fig. 41 Percentage of symptom days leading to aid post visits

Table 9 *Distance of peoples' homes from Tari Health Centre*

Distance	% of sample at this distance
Aid post equidistant	4.8
+ 1 hour	26.7
+ 2 hour	16.5
+ 3 hours	52.0

Tari Health Centre
The homes of a very small percentage of the people within this sample are equidistant from both Tari Health Centre and the aid post. For most people the health centre is a long way further (see table 9).

The distance is one of the factors which cause people to use the out-patients department at Tari Health Centre only infrequently (fig. 42). The overall attendance for all ages is 0.8% of symptoms days, varying from 1.6% for the

79

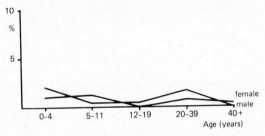

Fig. 42 Percentage of symptom days leading to out-patient visits

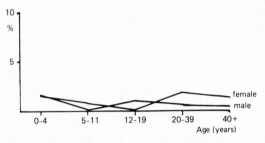

Fig. 43 Percentage of symptom days leading to in-patient treatment

under-fives, to 0.3% for the over-forties. People are admitted to the health centre on 1.0% of all symptom days (fig. 43).

These findings represent one approach to the problem of characterising Huli illness behaviour. First, I have defined the sphere of experience I am concerned with, and outlined its nature in broadly medical terms. We find that the frequencies of some symptoms differ in ways which are referable to aspects of the organisation of Huli society. Secondly, I have examined the frequencies with which they select different sorts of explanation, and shown that their more complex explanations are invoked only rarely. Thirdly, I have indicated the differential selection between the various sorts of treatment available to them. In general, we see the rejection of traditional cures and a preference for the recently introduced measures of Western medicine and Christian healing. In the next four chapters I will examine these trends in each of the main categories of explanation of illness.

80

6

Illness attributed to proximate causes

In this chapter I consider Huli diagnoses that are primarily descriptive, and those which refer to processes of physiology and pathology as these are understood by them. Diagnoses of this sort account for the vast majority of instances of illness. On the relatively uncommon occasions when they explain their ills according to the particular circumstances that led to the development of the illness, the process is also likely to be describable in terms of the bodily changes produced by the prior cause. I will begin by describing their broad view of bodily and psychological processes.

The Huli have a good anatomical knowledge and an extensive vocabulary relating to parts of the body. As we would expect, the focus of this knowledge relates directly to their concerns. Bodily appearance is highly significant to them, and their language possesses a large number of terms which allow them to discriminate finely between different areas of the skin and even different areas of the hair. Knowledge of internal anatomy is now applied only in the dissection of pigs, but formerly was necessary for surgery and post-mortems.

In general, they are not concerned to ascribe specific bodily functions to particular anatomical organs. The liver (*buni*) and lung (*gubalini*) may be said to house the *bu* (life force). But it is the roving *bu* that is of more interest, not the static tissues through which it may pass. The liver and lung are known to be important. Injuries to them may be fatal, and they may be said to support life (*buni ina yaga*, literally, 'the liver holds us'). This quality of being indispensable for existence is alluded to in metaphors of friendship and fraternal trust, as when one man says to another '*i i buni ore*' (literally, 'you are truly my liver'). But the organs themselves are accorded no discrete bodily functions. The kidneys and spleen are named (*lilini* and *ayuni* respectively), and known to be potentially fatal sites for wounds, but no particular bodily processes are related to them.

If asked, they will describe the passage of food through the different portions of the intestine, but find the discussion of such issues as the transformation of food to faeces dull and axiomatic. They have various words for parts of the intestine. For example, the terms *harabane* and *dugutabane* are applied to supposedly different parts of the small intestine. But the

81

attempt to establish a consensus as to which term applies to which section of the intestine reduces informants to irritation or apathy. Such discussions lead eventually to responses such as 'there is nothing of importance there, just faeces' (*mbiriale nawi tihangu pada*). It is the essence of thought and feeling which interests them, not the details of the bodily structure which the personality inhabits. When asked about the limbs they might say 'the arms and legs are just there, they have no thought' (*bamu gi ge kaba mini nawi*), or, 'they are just pain and blood' (*ibu tandaga dage darama hangu*).

The blood

Pain and blood are closely related for the Huli. The one word *darama* is used for two contrasting states of blood, the first normal and vital, the second pathological. There is a vague sense of blood moving in the blood vessels (*gungubuni*, a general term which includes tendons and nerves as well as blood vessels) but no formed concept of the circulation of the blood. Bright blood, flowing in its proper channels, is necessary for normal functioning. 'Our strength is based upon our blood' (*hongo daramame hariba*) expresses this idea.

When feeling weak, they may say 'the blood is not doing its work' (*darama biabe nabi*). Where a sick person is near death, one attendant may say to another 'see if his blood is still working' (*darama biabe birabe handa*). The 'work' referred to here is the loosely conceived task of maintaining life. A weakly state may lead to the comment 'there is no blood' (*darama nabere*). The lack of blood may be said to have followed from bleeding from a specific injury, or from menstrual loss. But more usually this is merely a descriptive statement indicating debility, and does not in itself suggest how that state came about.

Related to this ascription of weakness to the lack of vital blood is the more dire state of blood turning to water, for 'when the blood turns to water, a man's skin becomes bad' (*darama biagani ibane tagira ibiragala agali tingini ko haragani*). The specific relationship between such water and the blood is unclear. For example, a man who developed swellings in different parts of his body (which medically were abscesses following a septicaemia) said that they were water, but he was unsure whether they had developed from the blood, or just appeared for no reason (*darama ibu birabe be bamu bidabe manda nabido*). Whatever its origins, the settling of water in the body is a very serious sign. The statement 'there is water' (*iba beda*) suggests that the speaker expects a bad outcome. In such cases oedema or ascites may or may not be present.

Where blood escapes from its proper course it alters its character and leads to pain. A backache may be ascribed to the 'blood bursting' (*darama tongo leda*) out of its proper bounds, and 'settling' (*darama beda*) at the site of the

82

pain. A person in pain may say simply 'blood' (*darama*). Characteristically, the pain is one that began suddenly, after straining with a heavy load, for example. The image is that of a sudden pressure causing the tissues that confine the blood to rupture. The movements of a pain may be ascribed to movements of this bad blood. For example, of an abdominal pain and backache, 'when the blood had returned into my belly it burst, and so I am suffering' (*darama tiniha daibidagola tongo lowa homedo*). Once escaped, this blood may be said to harden and clot (*darama giambe*), and such a clot may lead to chronic pain.

Pooled blood may turn to pus (*angibu*). Pus and blood may be said to travel from one part of the body to another in ways that we would find anatomically impossible. For example, when chronic bronchitis is ascribed to an old injury, the pus, derived from the blood released by the original trauma, may be said to have travelled to the heart, where it hung 'like a fruit' until it burst (*tugu dayadagani*), and produced the copious phlegm of this condition.

I will now turn to the broader concepts that guide Huli interpretations of bodily and psychological processes. Life, consciousness, intellectual activity and moral sensibility result from the interplay between four principles: *bu*, *mini*, *manda* and *dinini*.

Drives

Bu is the most fundamental. It is requisite for life. It has the everyday meaning of 'breath', as in *bu hi he* (panting). The pulsation of the heart is its visible manifestation, and this will be pointed to in answer to the question 'where is *bu*?' But *bu* has no precise anatomical position. It is broadly sited in the region of the solar plexus, but it does not coincide with any particular internal organ. In the wider sense, *bu* is the life force, the drive which activates all other functions. It is also the source of the emotions and desire. In anger and other strong feeling it is said to rise into the throat and head, and fall back as the emotion subsides.

An affection of the *bu* has grave implications. In health the *bu* is seen as being unconstrained as its beat changes intensity and its position shifts with physical exertion or emotional experience. In severe illness the *bu* may become smothered. This state manifests itself as rapid or laboured breathing, which is referred to as *bu dambi* (literally 'covered *bu*'). For the Huli, dyspnoea in illness is understandably one of the most inauspicious signs, burdened as they are by a high frequency of fatal or incapacitating respiratory illness. When asked what is wrong with her sick child, a mother may reply simply, '*bu*' and an old man with chronic bronchitis may simply refer to his affliction as *bu*. In both cases they are referring to their perception of the pathological lesion as much as to the symptom of dyspnoea.

It may be said of someone *in extremis*, 'there is just a little *bu* left' (*bu emene nga*). Such a person would be expected to die, and may effectively be regarded as dead already, as expressed in the phrase 'He is dead. There is only *bu* left now' (*homaya buhangu nga*). The distinction here is similar to the one that we make between cerebral and cardiac death. Such a person is regarded as dead despite their continuing breathing and heartbeat, as they are felt to be irreversibly without *mini*.

The phrase 'there is no *mini*' (*mini nawi*) can in some circumstances properly be translated as 'unconscious'. But *mini* has a more specific meaning than the general term 'consciousness'. It refers to thoughts of immediate social significance. When talking of oneself, *mini* are thoughts that are emotionally charged, the conscious expression of emotions that derive from the *bu*. Hulis refer to worry as the experience of too many such thoughts, *mini dawa* (*dawa* is 'many'). When talking of others, *mini* are also thoughts of social significance, and particularly those that allow proper social responses. A normal child of, say, three years who is incompletely socialised can therefore be referred to as without *mini* (*mini nawi*), as can a man who is drunk, mad, furious or, for whatever reason, not behaving in a socially acceptable fashion. It seems that it is this feature of an unconscious person, their social unresponsiveness, that is primarily being commented upon in this use of the phrase *mini nawi*, rather than their unconsciousness *per se*.

A second term referring to cognition is *manda*, as in *manda bido* ('I know', or 'I understand'). *Manda* is reserved for memorised knowledge, comprehension, calculation and other forms of thinking without the immediate emotional and social significance of *mini*. *Manda nabi* (he is not thinking) is equally applicable to an unconscious person as *mini nawi*. But it is used only rarely.

These three principles are necessarily located within the body. The fourth principle, *dinini* (spirit) is not. During sleep it may wander, and the images of its journey are seen in dreams. In illness too it may detach itself from the body, or conversely illness may follow if the spirit becomes detached.

Discussion of the relationship between the emotions and illness, and of the influences of the spirit, lead to considerations which are not properly the subject of this chapter. I return to them later.

Environmental agents

I have outlined their conception of the main bodily processes. Here I consider a number of environmental influences and the sorts of illness they may produce.

Sticks, stones, blades of grass, old tin cans and the like are the most commonplace of these. Skin lesions are the commonest afflictions affecting the Huli, and if their origin is of interest at all, they may be ascribed to the agent that first broke the skin if this is known. The names they attach to these lesions reflect their size and quality. A sore (*dere*) becomes a *tiwa* (or *balari*) if it begins to erode the tissue at its base and to enlarge its diameter. Boils and abscesses are referred to as *moge*. Such lesions may be related to an injury of some sort, though occasionally maggots or cockroach bites may be blamed. Sores which are thought to arise within the body and then emerge through the body wall are regarded much more seriously. For example it was said of a child with several sores on its abdomen that 'they had come out from the stomach' (*dere tombeha howa bia tagi ka*). Sores in the throat are felt to be an especially bad sign.

The diets of Huli adults and children are guided more by taste and availability than by specific prescriptions and prohibitions such as are found in many Papua New Guinea societies. Food is in general held to be necessary for growth and proper development. But clinical states that would be explained medically as malnutrition are commonly ascribed to the sorts of causes I describe in later chapters, though parents may accept that food might help the child recover.

One food-related environmental influence that may be regarded as injurious is dirt. A child's diarrhoea may be ascribed to its having eaten earth (*dindi*) with its meal. But earth is only one possible type of dirt, which is referred to by the general term *dodo*. *Dodo* can be sweepings or any muck off the ground, but it also refers to the taint of female pollution which I shall consider in detail in the next chapter.

Another contamination that can be associated with food is worms (*ngoe*). Edible pitpit is held to be particularly likely to carry *ngoe*. In this context *ngoe* refers to *Ascaris lumbricoides*, the roundworm. The Huli feel that this is a very vigorous parasite, and attribute a number of symptoms to its activities. The most common symptom is abdominal pain, when they say the worm is 'eating the liver' (*buni nara*). The worms may also be said to be in competition for ingested food, as when 'the worms alone, they ate all the food' (*ngoe ibu hangu mo naraya tomo bibahende nayago*), or be thought to have sucked a person's blood (*ngoe ibu darama biago dulumu naraia*). Gurgling within the abdomen may be attributed to the worms (*ngoe gu lara*, literally 'the worms are gurgling').

Some foods are known to be harmful unless they are prepared properly. For example it is known that the mushroom *Russula emetica* will cause vomiting unless it is cooked thoroughly. Symptoms after a meal of these mushrooms are likely to be attributed to inadequate preparation. Other mushrooms are known to be poisonous under any circumstances, and so are avoided completely.

While most ingested foods are thought to pass rapidly through the gut, harmful fragments are said to stay (*pada*, literally 'sleep' or 'lie') there indefinitely, and so cause illness. For example, one child's abdominal pains and failure to thrive were ascribed to its having eaten a snail some years before. Traditionally, abdominal illness was not ascribed to the ingestion of pig, but the Huli have accepted the scientific explanation of enteritis necroticans to such as extent that they now very commonly attribute abdominal symptoms to pieces of pork 'lying' in the abdomen.

Other illnesses may be attributed to simple environmental influences. Excessive heat or cold may be held to be damaging, particularly to young children. Illness is attributed to such changes in a direct way, and not as part of a detailed scheme of complementary influences. If a child has been out in the rain and then develops a cough, the cough may be attributed to its having been too cold. When a child is left lying in the sun and subsequently develops dyspnoea its illness may be attributed to excessive heat.

Illness may also be ascribed to irritants. For example, the mother of a child with kwashiorkor ascribed his illness to dust from the blanket getting in his eyes. A case of otitis media was ascribed to soapy water getting into the child's ears.

Syndromes

When sets of symptoms concur regularly, we call the conditions syndromes. The Huli recognise three common syndromes: *wabi warago, homama* and *amali*. These broadly correspond to malaria, the common cold and chronic bronchitis respectively.

Wabi warago means literally 'the illness of the lowlands to the south'. The key symptoms are a subjective feeling of cold, and shivering. Young children are rarely given this diagnosis. Their illnesses are diagnosed for them by adults, and a subjective feeling of cold is therefore not relevant. Instead it is the heat of their skin that is remarked upon by those caring for them. In these cases *poboyogo* (hot) serves as a diagnosis. *Wabi warago* is associated by the Huli with lower altitudes, though cases commonly occur amongst those who have never left the Tari area. Malaria transmission occurs in all altitude zones inhabited by the Huli, and is very frequent at altitudes below 1,500 metres. Many cases of *wabi warago* are caused by malaria parasites, though other infections may of course cause these symptoms. The link with mosquito bites is now common knowledge, but formerly no specific causative mechanisms were acknowledged. In this illness, according to the particular circumstances, any of the causative agents I discuss later could be implicated.

Head colds are usually referred to as *homama*, but an additional element indicating this diagnosis is the timing of the illness. A runny nose is a usual symptom. A cough and headache may or may not be present. But a person with typical symptoms of *homama* may say that he does not have *homama* as it is not *homamangi* (the time for *homama*). Such illnesses usually spread rapidly from person to person, so one aspect of 'the time for *homama*' is that many people are suffering from it. 'The time for *homama*' (*homamangi*) is also related to seasonal changes. A common reference is to the time when the *dagiruba* tree (*Nothofagus grandis*) produces a new growth of leaves. During 'the time for *homama*' symptoms that would normally indicate a different diagnosis, shortness of breath for example, may be referred to as *homama*.

Amali is for the Huli one of the most feared conditions. This is a common complaint particularly in older men, and is held to be a very common cause of death. This is such an unwelcome condition that the usual terms, *amali*, or more simply *bu*, are euphemisms for the real term, which is *hagara*. To say the word *hagara* within the hearing of someone who may be suffering from it is both indiscreet and unkind. The main symptoms are cough, shortness of breath and often yellow sputum, which is called *anga* in distinction to *angibu* (pus). Most cases would be diagnosed as chronic bronchitis but many men with these same symptoms may say that they do not have *amali*. Some may say this to avoid the implications of the diagnosis, and in such cases others would privately disagree with their self-diagnosis. But if there is a specific alternative diagnosis, such as where the symptoms may be ascribed to an old arrow wound, there would be general agreement that this is not a case of *amali*. For one of the features of *amali* is that it is generally seen as idiopathic. Apart from its insidious nature and eventually fatal outcome, some of the dire implications of this condition stem from its being seen as potentially infectious. An *amali* sufferer should not share food, pipes or utensils, and this is a troubling restriction where such sharing is the norm. In most cases of *amali* no explanation of why this particular person should suffer are offered. Some say that it is hereditary, passing from father to son, but the distinction between nature and nurture here is not finely drawn. When they speak in general of the consequences of ritually or morally improper acts, *amali* (or *hagara*) is often cited as a likely penalty. In practice this is rarely so. In only one case that I saw was such an explanation offered.

The quality of Huli illness descriptions

The orderly presentation of these concepts may give a misleading impression of precision and restraint in Huli descriptions. In many cases this is the case, but the Huli are fond of flamboyance and allegory in their speech, qualities found also in their language of illness. I will attempt to correct that balance by indicating the tenor of some of their descriptions of illness.

Dramatic images are common. A woman who related her abdominal pain to a fall when she had banged her back said that she had 'fallen and broken her spine into pieces on a stone' (*erene toleni tuguda holo pilene*). A woman with stomach trouble said 'it is as if there is a piglet in there' (*nogo igini ale pada*). A man who had been banged on the eye said that his eyeball 'had been squashed, like a broken egg' (*de togo daya*). A man had abdominal pain as his 'guts had rotted' (*tini togo bini*). After a blow a man's head was 'smashed to pieces' (*embone kai biya*).

They often draw upon features of the natural world in their images of illness, and particularly the qualities of plants. For example, leprosy (usually *ge hamua*) may be known as *guraya* (the hoop pine, *Araucaria cunninghamii*): with its few branches it is reminiscent of the sufferer from advanced leprosy with his damaged limbs. An itchy rash may be called *haberolo* after the mushroom of that name (*Polyporus arcularius*). The texture of the mushroom's cap is similar to that of a scaley rash. A small deeply eroding sore may be known as *mandi pubu*, which means literally 'the grub that penetrates the *Acalypha insulana*', after an insect larva which burrows in that tree. A small abscess with a glary white centre may be called *hongo* (Job's tears, *Coix lachryma-jobi*).

Their descriptions often have an indeterminate quality, alluding to vague movements or obscure objects within the body. They may talk as if 'something' is there, without trying to define what 'it' is. For example, a man with abdominal pain pointed to his stomach wall and said 'it went there, rippling the skin' (using a term normally said of the ripples that an invisible fish may make in a pool, *ni niau laya*). Again of abdominal pain, 'There is something big there in my intestines, but who could see inside to tell what it is? No one' (*timbuni mbirame tiniha haya ka ai hendede*).

I have already pointed out that body fluids, especially pus, may be said to travel widely in the body, so that an old lesion in a leg, for example, may eventually lead to chest disease. In addition to movements of this sort, there are also allusions to movements within the body of indefined qualities. For example, 'Something came upwards, and when it had come up, she fainted' (*mbirale yiyu lama iragi haya ani buwa de mborere*). Arrow tips too are thought to grow, turn and wander freely within the body. Another common idiom is that the body is being consumed or eaten, as in *hale nara* (literally, it is eating the ear) for earache. On occasions this may conjure up the image of a spirit actually chewing on the ear, but in general these are simply idioms typical of the Huli style of expression. *Yandare*, used for pleuritic pain, means literally 'spear', carrying the graphic implication that a spirit has driven a spear through the chest wall. But it is my impression that the image in most cases does not convey this literal meaning, and when used conjures up the image of a spear wound no more than the phrase 'I have pins and needles' conjures up the image of actual needles for an Englishman.

Traditional treatments

The treatments that I consider here are those which are deemed to alleviate symptoms through their direct action upon the lesion, or direct effect upon the underlying pathological process. I am therefore excluding from this discussion those treatments which relate to their more elaborate schemata of explanation. The methods of healing which I describe comprise what Evans-Pritchard (1937) referred to as 'leechcraft'. In considering their traditional treatments and the adoption of Western treatments in this and later chapters, I am primarily concerned with the specificity of the treatments, and the extent to which they follow from their explanations of illness.

I will begin with their traditional treatments for the commonest problem: skin complaints. A number of plants are used as dressings for sores. The bark of the *tibabo* tree (*Platea excelsa*) is favoured. Some plants are said to promote healing: the leaves of *nogo iba loba loba* (*Adenostemma hirsutum*) are warmed and bound onto the sore; the sap of the *pai* tree (*Castonopsis acuminatissima*) is rubbed onto large ulcerating sores; the leaves of *polange* grass (*Paspalum conjugatum*) are squeezed over sores. The sap of the *hubi* tree is introduced into a new cut before the edges are opposed. The cut is then bound, and healing is said to occur rapidly. The saps of a number of plants are used to draw the pus from abscesses. These plants include the *embo* tree (*Homalanthus nervosus*), and the *poge* tree (*Ficus copiosa*). The sap of the ground creeper *gondo* (*Commelina* spp.) is applied to suppurating wounds as it is said to be both analgesic and to ensure the continuing drainage of the wound. The sap of the shrub *tombe* (*Euphorbia plumerioides*) is used to stun fish, but in this context it is applied to tropical ulcers to kill maggots. The flower of the grass *moge dene duguaga* (literally 'it removes the head of abscesses', *Bidens pilosa*) is twirled in the centre of an abscess to lance it and remove the pus.

The jelly that adheres to the root of *polange* grass is used to treat eye infections, or to remove particles from the eye. Diseased eyes are covered with red leaves, either a red cordyline (*payabu kayumba*), or the leaf of the *embo* tree, lest the sight be lost.

A number of nettles of varying strength (*nigi, Laportea* spp.) are used as counter-irritants to treat different aches and pains, especially joint pains, abdominal pain and chest pain. Hot or cold water is applied according to the preference of the patient. Hot water is commonly applied to painful backs, chests and joints. Wads of leaves are heated over the fire and applied to painful chests. Fevers may be treated with blanket steam baths. Dew is a favoured form of cold water. It is rubbed onto painful joints, or sprinkled all over those with a fever. It is tipped into the ears of those with earache, and drunk by those with chest pain.

A few plant substances are ingested for their specific therapeutic efficacy. Hot ginger (*palena*) or a hot bitter fruit (*pabu hoea, Bubbia* spp.) are said to cure worm infestation. *Talembaria*, a type of taro, is said to relieve persistent cough. The bark of the lowland tree *balima* (which unfortunately I was unable to identify) is said to be effective in *wabi warago*. In the treatment of diarrhoea, dry foods are favoured. Scorched taro or plantains are eaten, and nowadays store biscuits and boiled rice are thought to perform the same function. Some plants are held to possess specific anti-diarrhoeal properties. These include the leaves of the *kambali* (*Blumea arnakidophora*) and the fruit of the *poge* tree (*Ficus copiosa*). This fruit is also said to relieve vomiting.

Illness attributed to proximate causes

The thick red juice of the oil pandanus (*Pandanus connoideus*) is said to be good for those weakly through 'lack of blood' (*darama nabere*). Pork, especially the liver and blood-soaked greens, is also valued in these conditions. These practices are concordant with modern nutritional education which also stresses the value of soup for malnourished children. As a result of this teaching people make soup for themselves out of a chicken or whatever is available to them when they are feeling weak through illness.

Various inhalations are used. When suffering from head colds (*homama*) they throw some *malingi* leaves (*Cyathea aenifolia*) onto the embers and inhale the smoke. With cough and shortness of breath, leaves of the *lai* tree (*Dodenaea viscosa*) are used in the same way. Men with bad coughs may give up smoking.

A number of treatments involve physical manipulations. The simplest of these include the pulling out of the hairs on the arm or leg when these are affected by pins and needles (*gi/ge amburi*, which may be regarded as a serious sign). One treatment of backache caused by 'burst blood' (*darama tongolaya*) is for the patient to lie face down while the operator stands on the upper spine, and with his full weight slides down to the small of the back.

More elaborate treatments of problems relating to blood involve releasing that blood. These procedures are guided by the view that in terms of the movements of escaped blood, the body can be divided into three regions: the head, chest cavity and neck, abdominal cavity and spine. Escaped blood does not pass from one of these areas to another except in the most severe cases. The treatment of headache thus involves making a number of cuts at the hair line to release the blood that is causing the pain. This procedure is known as *are* after the quartz blade that is used for the operation.

The operation to remove blood from the chest is known as *kuabe* (rib cage). This operation is not performed now, though in former times the commonest indication for it was an arrow wound to the chest. Releasing the blood from such a wound is regarded as an emergency, so that a man who sustained a chest wound was likely to be carried to the side of the battlefield and operated upon immediately. The incision was made laterally over a lower intercostal space on the side of the wound. After cutting the skin with a quartz blade, the operator exposed the pleura by exploring with his finger, at which point a rush of air was expected (with the formation of a pneumothorax). When the incision was thought large enough, the operator and his assistants turned the patient over to tip as much blood as possible out of the wound, which was then bound with *tondo* bark cloth (*Broussonetia papyrifera*). In a series of twelve well-substantiated cases, patients who suffered the combined traumata of an arrow wound to the chest followed by this operation, it is surprising that only three men died.

Wounds to the lower chest and abdomen, and 'burst blood' in the spine, are treated differently. The operation here is known as *tigui*. Arrow wounds

90

are again an indication, and this operation is also regarded as an emergency procedure. A bad fall, say from a tree, a crushing blow or severe backache are also indications. In all these circumstances the blood is said to pool at the lower spine. It is drained by stabbing a thin bamboo knife beside the anus to a depth of some four inches. A free flow of red blood is held to be a good sign. If the blood flow is deemed insufficient the procedure is repeated the following day on the opposite side. The performance of *kuabe* and *tigui* is now thought to be illegal. The circumstances where *kuabe* would be indicated now rarely arise. But after a serious fall older people particularly may feel themselves to be at risk if *tigui* is not performed. I know of several cases where such people could find no practitioner willing to perform the operation for fear of prosecution, and so operated upon themselves by sitting on an arrow.

Other surgery is now no longer performed. But in former times specialists acquired reputations for their skill in the removal of arrows. These surgeons used probes of *hangapo* (a tree fern) to explore beneath their incisions to determine whether the arrow tip was removable or not. Other specialists were skilled in setting bones. A few men were skilled in the treatment of compound fractures of the long bones by internal fixation. A length of *mandara* wood (*Graptophyllum* spp.) was introduced into the medulla of the bone, and the limb splinted. Another procedure was to replace damaged areas of the skull with pieces of pig scapula.

Their surgery appears ambitious in comparison with other accounts from New Guinea, and their vigorous approach to bleeding is generally unusual (Ackerknecht 1947). This raises the question of why they performed these procedures, particularly those that were likely to make the patient's condition worse. It is not unusual for medical practices to be harmful: obvious examples are the bleeding and purging advocated by earlier generations of European physicians. The imposition of such measures by practitioners and the acceptance by their patients implies some commitment to the theory upon which they are based. In societies like the Huli we might expect them to reserve this degree of commitment for magical or religious theories, so what is striking about Huli surgery is that they were sufficiently committed to a theory of pathology to act upon it so forcefully. I do not wish to exaggerate the extent of their concern with physiological and pathological processes in illness, but a number of features of their knowledge and practice do contrast with the indeterminacy commented upon by ethnographers of other New Guinea societies (e.g. Lewis 1975:135–6; Barth 1975:142–3; Glick 1963:105–10). The size of the Huli population and the mobility permitted to individuals by their social organisation may have facilitated the growth of knowledge of this sort. Interested individuals may see or hear of a wide range of illnesses. Specialists can practise over a wide area. Knowledge of patterns of symptoms (such as the syndromes I described) and interest in pathological processes might be encouraged by such circumstances. A similar phenomenon is apparent on a larger scale where the rapid advance in Western knowledge of morbid anatomy and the natural history of disease coincided with the rise of charity hospitals in the late eighteenth and early ninteenth centuries. For the first time large numbers of patients were gathered together, so that doctors saw many cases of each type of disease. Previously each physician saw a few cases of most diseases only, so that only remarkable individuals like Sydenham became aware of any but the commonest sorts of disease types (Shryock 1948).

The treatments I am describing here are deemed by the Huli to act directly upon the patient's condition, and do not involve attempts to influence responsible spirits or men. Many healing spells may be seen as equivalent alternatives in some of the illnesses I have described. This matter-of-fact view of spells is expressed in the common observation that 'you white doctors use injections while we use spells'. Spells are referred to as *gamu*, but the meaning of *gamu* is wider than this, for it may also refer to the ritual of which the spell is but a part. One means of distinguishing the spell from the whole ritual is by referring to the spell as *gamugamu*. Of the conditions I have described in this chapter, the following may be treated by simple spells: *hagara* (*amali*), toothache, backache caused by *darama*, diarrhoea, vomiting, worms, arthritic knees and headache.

Modern treatments

As we saw above, treatments such as these have been largely eclipsed by introduced methods. This is particularly the case in conditions such as those I have been discussing.

For example, in cutaneous lesions we find that an aid post visit is the treatment of choice, and that major lesions merit more visits than minor ones (figs. 44 and 45). The distance they have to travel influences their use of Western medicine. The effect of distance in minor lesions is noticeable at the half-an-hour level, while for major lesions distances of up to one and a half hours do not seem to discourage a journey to the aid post. Other actions are unimportant in minor lesions, while with major skin lesions both self-help and Christian healing are used to a limited extent, and in the case of self-help particularly, more frequently when the person's home is more than half an hour away from the aid post (p < 0.01). Comparing aid post visits with these types of lesion according to the age and sex of the sufferer, we find that with major lesions the under-fives are brought most frequently (figs. 46 and 47). Children of either sex in the 5–11-year group and 12–19-year-old males appear to be the most careless about these lesions. Females between twelve and forty years take them more seriously (p < 0.01).

Similarly, sufferers of aches and pains again make most frequent use of the aid post for relief, but also make significant use of Christian and traditional

Illness attributed to proximate causes

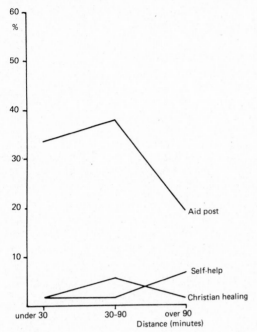

Fig. 44 Choice of action by distance from the aid post with major cutaneous lesions

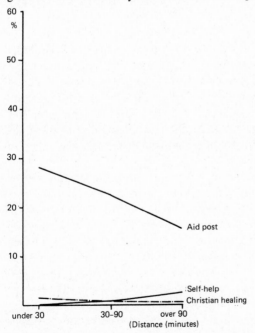

Fig. 45 Choice of action by distance from the aid post with minor cutaneous lesions

93

Illness attributed to proximate causes

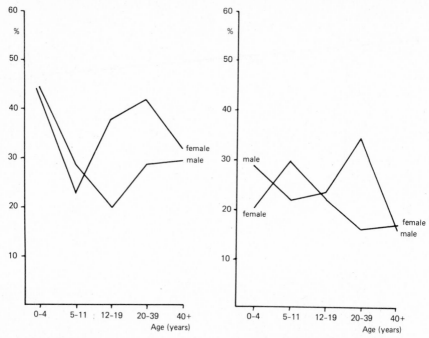

Fig. 46 Aid post visits by age with major cutaneous lesions

Fig. 47 Aid post visits by age with minor cutaneous lesions

methods of healing (fig. 48). The distance from the aid post has little influence on these rates overall. The mobility of most of these sufferers appears to be the significant factor in causing them to be unaffected by distance. If we look at the influence of distance according to age in these cases, we find that it is very great in the under-fives, small in the 5–11 age group, and non-existent in those over twelve years (fig. 49). It seems that parents do not think that aches and pains in their children are sufficient grounds to carry or accompany them to the aid post.

These trends are predictable from what we know of the Huli view of treatments of the sort I have been discussing. Their interpretations of these conditions do not extend to encompass issues of ritual or wider social importance. Their actions in these illnesses are based upon largely pragmatic considerations. Their adoption of one sort of treatment or another is guided by issues such as accessibility, cost and assessments of efficacy. The treatment of abdominal pain ascribed to worms by *ngoe iba* (worm water) from an aid post rather than by their own *pabu hoea* fruit does not involve any reinterpretation of either the cause of the condition or the aims of therapy (fig. 50). *Ko iba* (cough mixture) has largely replaced the inhalation of *malingi*

94

Illness attributed to proximate causes

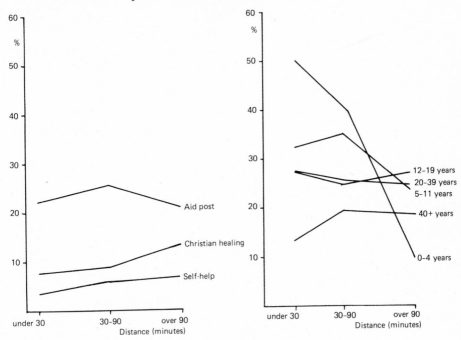

Fig. 48 Choice of action by distance with aches and pains

Fig. 49 Aid post visits by distance from the aid post with aches and pains

Fig. 50 An aid post orderly treating a child

95

smoke, bandages are preferred to bark dressings, linament is a popular alternative to nettles, reduction of fractures under anaesthetic is a valued service and so on. Much of their readiness to use introduced methods and abandon their traditional methods of treatment in these sorts of conditions can be seen in these terms.

7

Explanations relating to sexuality and growth

Fertility and the control of sexuality are central concerns in Huli religion. Their view of these issues guides much everyday behaviour, and intermittently becomes manifest in their interpretations of illness and responses to it. Here I will consider such cases of illness, but first it is necessary to introduce elements of their cosmology, the lore concerning proper conduct and the theoretical penalties for disregarding this lore.

In terms of my division of Huli illness descriptions according to the level of explanation that they represent, the diagnoses considered here range from the sort that I considered in chapter 6 (answering the question, how did this illness occur?) to those of the sort that I will turn to later which encompass the question, why? But the coherence of this aspect of Huli thought would make any attempt to divide these illnesses upon such grounds cumbersome and contrived.

I begin by presenting abbreviated versions of the three myths which illuminate much Huli behaviour and thought in this aspect of their lives. I then trace the individual's ideal developmental and sexual career from conception onwards, and discuss the hazards and means of avoiding them. Finally I analyse the cases of illness attributed to this sort of cause that I saw.

Mythological precedents
Tiame

Tiame would go to the forest and hunt possums (*tia*). She gathered many possums and cooked them with her own heat. She crouched over the mound of possums and cooked them. A young man would come, and she gave them to him, many cooked possums each time he came. The young man's brother, an *ibatiri* (a dirty witless fellow), saw his brother's possums, and wondered where he was getting so many. One day, when his brother was away, the *ibatiri* followed the tracks he had left, and he came to the place where the woman was. She said to him, 'What have you come for?' He said that he was looking for his brother. She said, 'I have not seen him, but are you hungry?' He said he was, so she said that she would go and catch possums. She came back with a huge quantity of possums. She started heaping them in an earth oven, and sent him off for water. She crouched over the mound, and the possums were cooked. He came back and wondered how they had been cooked as there was no fire.

She gave him some meat, and it was well cooked, falling off the bone. Then they went to sleep. In the night he saw a glowing fire in her arse. He went to her and copulated with her. And the fire went out. She said, 'Truly, now you are going to have to work hard. You will have to use a friction cane to light fires, and when you cook pig you will have to scorch the hair and have all the trouble of cooking it.'

In some versions of this myth, the woman is the first founding ancestor linked directly to the present population. In others she is isolated from the present. These variations need not concern us here. In this myth there is the allusion to a past era of effortless perfection. Other versions of this myth tell of axes cutting wood on their own, and pigs presenting themselves voluntarily to fall to a self-propelled stick. In this utopia the woman's heat is directed constructively to the cooking of food. But this heat, and its visible manifestation of glowing red genitals, arouse sexual desire in the witless man. By satisfying himself he extinguished the fire within her, and found that life could then be supported only by the burdensome toil that is mankind's lot today. On the positive side, however, this led to the emergence of the ancestors of the Huli.

Ni and Hana

I will include only the small section of this long myth which is specifically relevant to the discussion of the Huli view of the origin and significance of sexuality.

(The brother and sister, have come to Bebene Te, the site of one of the major ritual centres for the Huli. In this version of the myth they are referred to as Ni and Dagiwali. It is also common to add their patronymic, when the names become Hona-Ni and Hona-Hana.) Every morning and afternoon she went out. She went to Luya Tale Te (another sacred site about a mile from Bebene Te). He did not know what she was doing. He thought that she just went off to relieve herself. Once he went to Tale Te, and there he saw a Tale tree, and saw that the bark was rubbed off it. So he realised that she came to scratch her arse there. He found a piece of quartz (*are yogona*). He took it, and made sure that it was sharp. He took it to the Tale, and fixed it to the tree, making sure that some of its blade was protruding. He went home. The next morning she ran down to Tale Te, turned her arse to the tree and scratched. She cut herself deeply, and bled. She looked down and said 'What has happened?' Ni said, 'Eighth, eighth, bachelor (*ibagiya*) eighth, woman in her house eighth time, take food from her eighth, emerge from spirit houses eighth time, eighth, eighth.' (*halini halini igiri ibagiya halini wali wandia halini ai ina mule haliningi liduanda kebeanda tago hole haliningi halini halini*). This is what Ni said. Before his sister had had no vagina. But now he copulated with her. A dog came and saw. Ni thought that the dog would tell everyone what had happened and so he would have been shamed. So he twisted its tongue, which is why dogs can only howl. Ni and Dagiwali had two daughters.

There are numerous versions of this myth. The origins of the brother and sister, their names, their later progress and their relationship to the present population vary, but this central happening at Tale Te varies little between one authority and another. In its full form this myth ramifies into various aspects of major ritual, in particular the main fertility ritual cycle (*dindi gamu*), for which Tale Te is a central site. But it is not possible to enlarge upon other aspects here. The main features for the purposes of this argument are first the origin of sexuality and menstruation through man's ingenuity and trickery; and secondly the statement of the law concerning the avoidance of women by men for the first eight days of the menstrual cycle, and the time that men must avoid women after they have been inside spirit houses.

Ibagiya myth

(A young man living alone in the forest has received mysterious nightly help with a new garden. He waits by the track to see who is responsible, and ambushes the last girl in a long line of women. The girl changes through many forms in his grasp but he holds on. A girl again, she takes him and hides him in the house where she lives with her parents, brothers and sisters. He plays beautiful music on a mouth harp she has given him, and is discovered. He wants to take the girl home with him, and her parents agree to this). Her parents, brothers and sisters wrapped the girl up in a bundle and gave her to him. They said, 'You must put this bundle in a place in the deep forest, a secret place forbidden to others, and build a high fence around it. You must look after it, keep it with you all the time, and carry it wherever you go.' He went back to his own home. He was beautifully dressed, and looked very fine. He saw a big tree with a hollow in it. He thought that there was likely to be a possum in it, so he rushed off with his bow to catch it, leaving his bag on the ground. He climbed the tree, but found that the possum had gone. When he returned, where he had left his bag he found a fine girl, laughing and digging in the garden. He said to her, 'This is a place for bachelors only (*ibagiyanda*), how is it that you have come?' She did not answer, but carried on laughing and working. 'Did you not see the huge fence I have built around this place? No women come here, how is it that you have come?' Again she did not answer, but laughed and carried on digging. He became angry, took his bow, and shot her. She said, 'I told you to look after the bundle well, and you left it alone. Now you have shot me. Quickly, go and fetch some bamboos, some with marks on them, and some without.' He went to fetch his bag. He saw that there was a hole in it, and the bundle had gone. Before it had been heavy, but now it was light. When he had fetched the two sorts of bamboo, she said, 'Come quickly. Pull out this arrow, and then my blood will flow. Put the good blood (*daramabi bayale*) into the bamboo with marks. The bad and dirty blood (*daramabi awe ko dodohe*), put that in the bamboo with no marks.' She said, 'Take that dark blood in the bamboo with no marks, and bury it in that swamp.' He did what she said. 'The blood in the bamboos with marks, take that, bind it in bark-cloth, and hide it in the *ibagiyanda* for the bachelors to see *ibagiya* with (*ibagiya hondole ngelabe*).' He took those bamboos to the forest and hid them. When he came back, she said 'I will stay here. You must cut many strong trees, and make a fence around me.' This he did, and she told him to go to his house for seven days, and on the eighth to come and look at the bamboos.

He did as he was told, and on the eighth day he came back. When he looked inside the fence that he had made, he found many kinds of magic plant growing there. From her body above her waist, all the *ibagiya* plants had grown. From her body below her waist all the magic plants that are good for pigs had grown.

This myth ascribes the origin of the bachelor cult and the magical plants which are at its core to female blood, and expresses the distinction between 'good' and 'bad' blood which is central to the Huli understanding of sexuality. I return to these themes below, but first I will describe the Huli developmental career.

Conception to parenthood

The foetus is formed from the admixture of sperm and menstrual blood in the womb. These fluids mix and solidify, the sperm producing the skin and bones, the woman's blood producing the child's blood and *gungubuni* (blood vessels, nerves and tendons). Sexual intercourse should take place on the eleventh, twelfth, thirteenth and fourteenth days of the woman's menstrual cycle.

While sexual intercourse on less than four days is said to be insufficient to produce conception, to continue beyond four days is said to prevent conception. The sperm and blood are said to harden (literally clot), but if more sperm is placed in the womb while the clot is firming, this will break down again and the conception be lost.

The couple should therefore wait to see if conception has occurred. If she does menstruate again, they will wait until the eleventh day of her next period, and have sexual intercourse for four more days. If she does not menstruate, they must not have sex again during her pregnancy. The risk here is primarily to the mother, and increases as the pregnancy progresses. The theory is that a second conception will be still immature when the first is due for delivery. The second conception will therefore block the birth canal, and the mother will die of an obstructed labour. The husband would then be expected to compensate her relations for her death.

The relationship between sexual intercourse and conception is thus quite unequivocal in Huli thought. There are a number of terms for sexual intercourse, and these tend to distinguish between the 'legitimate' act between married couples for the purpose of producing a child, and 'illegitimate' sex, only for pleasure, whether within or outside marriage. The former is referred to as *waneigini honowida*, literally 'bearing a child', and the latter most commonly as *tanga*. There is some variation in ideas of the origin of sperm. Some say that it arises in the testes, and some that it arises at the junction of the base of the penis and the colon, a region that is important in Huli ideas of the pathology of pollution, and which is said also to be joined to the umbilicus. Even those who say that sperm arises at this conjunction acknowledge that the testes have an essential function, pointing out that castrated pigs cannot procreate, and say that the testes 'strengthen' the penis.

The gestation period is counted from the time of the first missed period, a period of eight months. The first four months of pregnancy are called 'the bad months' (*ege ko*). 'Bad' refers particularly to the danger of miscarriage, and during this time the woman is supposed to avoid hard work and heavy loads. If she does not restrict her activities her husband may say that she is trying to lose (literally 'throw away', *waha*), his child. The only means of attempting to bring about abortion known to Huli women is through disobeying this rule. During the second four months, the 'good months' (*ege bayale*), she is not so restricted. During pregnancy she covers her belly from modesty. During the later 'good' months, she would traditionally have gone to a fast flowing stream frequently to perform *honowale gamu* (spell for birth) to ensure a favourable presentation, an easy birth and a well child. The edible ground creeper *gondo* (*Commelina* spp.) is rubbed over the belly, and its name commonly cited in these spells. It is soft, pliant and when cooked in a bamboo its juice will spurt out.

Traditionally she gave birth in a secluded hut, though now most women prefer to go to one of the mission health centres. Women were expected to cope on their own. They feel shame (*taga*) to be seen giving birth, and would only summon help from another woman if they felt themselves to be in difficulty. They cut the cord some four inches from its insertion, pinching it medially to this point to prevent the flow of blood, and cutting upwards with a bamboo knife. A common complaint about modern birth practices is that the nurses cut the cord too short, and that this damages the abdominal organs in some unspecified way.

The lanugo hair was carefully scorched off soon after birth with a torch of dry grass. This is referred to as *irini heda haramali* (we scorch off the hair) where the word *irini* is normally applied to an animal's fur, while *iri* is used for human hair. The child is thus symbolically separated from its mother's womb and its foetal state.

The importance of the separation of the child, boy or girl, from its mother's sexual essence is underlined in the danger of *kuyanda*. If the child swallows the mother's blood, this blood is said to settle in the child's chest, and as the child grows, so the blood grows within it as an amorphous parasitic mass. This blood is the *kuyanda*. The knowledge that the child was born with blood in its mouth may be sufficient for the parents to summon a specialist to perform the ceremony to 'bind' the *kuyanda* (*kuyanda hubua biaga*) or, better still, the more elaborate rite to remove it (*kuyanda duguaga*).

Or they may come to suspect the presence of *kuyanda* within the child on the basis of the manifestations of this condition, and so decide to root it out. These signs include a lack of resilience and fitful growth. In the spells intended to cure this condition, the *kuyanda* is referred to variously as the leech (*gindi*) and the snail (*gangade*). Like the leech, the *kuyanda* is seen as a silent bloodsucker that causes no sensation to its host. And like both these creatures it is said to swell and contract, fluctuations that are expressed in the rate of growth of the child. Very rapid growth can therefore be seen to be as pathological as a failure to thrive. Another sign of the presence of *kuyanda* is an inordinate appetite, and a willingness to eat unsavoury morsels, such as old pig fat. An extension of this idea of uncontrollable greed in those so affected is the suspicion that a covetous glance at your food by someone with *kuyanda* can cause you illness. I will return to this when I consider *lingi* below. But the most serious risk for those who harbour *kuyanda* is that the *kuyanda* may burst, causing sudden death. Strong emotion can be damaging in a variety of ways (see pp. 136–44), bur for those with *kuyanda* such feelings are potentially fatal. Envy, anger, fright, desire and other emotions may present problems to all Hulis, but only in the presence of *kuyanda*, a taint arising from the birth flow, do these feelings become serious hazards.

Treatment of the umbilicus and placenta vary. A common course was to bury them at the base of a newly planted fruit tree, and for the fruit of that tree to be eaten subsequently only by the mother or child. Each time the mother places the child in its net bag she might spit a spell into her cupped hands, and rub the child with her saliva. An example of this spell, *wandarigini hongolo helo gamu* (spell for strengthening children) runs: 'the wild dogs have large young, the wild bamboo has great shoots, the banana has great fruits'; this is repeated for three types of banana (*tutu hongone nguengue, bindi hongone nguengue, hondua hongone nguengue, tigo hongone nguengue, giebi hongone nguengue*). Just as these animals and plants have sturdy young, so will this child thrive. On the eighth day, the *ma hiraga* (scorching taro) ceremony will be performed as I described briefly above (p. 54).

The father should not see the child for some two months. This is partly for his protection, but also the child would become weakly if exposed to a father who has been adulterous. In such circumstances they would say that the child was ill as *angua haya*, which means literally that '(the father) stepped over (the child)'. *Angua* is used in a number of other contexts, including the problems that follow from a woman 'stepping over' food and so contaminating it. But here it refers to the man having 'stepped over' his wife and gone elsewhere for sexual pleasure. The implication is that sexuality directed solely to satisfying desire is antithetical to reproduction, so that the adulterous father is dangerous to his new-born child.

The mother would introduce solid foods, banana and pig fat, from the fourth month or so but would not normally attempt to wean the child until she gave birth to another. Before a sibling was born another strengthening ceremony was performed (*ma ibira gamu*, 'spell for strengthening the neck', to make the child support itself both physically and metaphorically; this is also known as *mende honowale gamu*, 'spell for bearing another child').

In one version of this ceremony, the ritualist spits the spell into his hands, and clenches his fists around the bespelled spittle. With his fists still clenched, he throws the child into the air. A section of the spell runs, 'Trunk of the boy, trunk of the *hale* tree (*Syzygium* spp.), trunk of the boy....' (*huliya irane*, *ira wale irane, huliya irane).* The action of thrusting the child upwards, and the spell image of the larger forest trees, cause it to become sturdy enough to tolerate the birth of a sibling.

People say that the ideal is to wait until the youngest child is around four or five years old before another is conceived. They say that this was necessary in times of war, for the mother would only be able to carry one child if the home was attacked, and other children should be old enough to help with the escape and not hinder it. Children that are born with too little interval between them are referred to as '*iriyale*', weakly 'like a hair'. The parents of such families are mocked for their lack of self-control. Older people say that standards have fallen badly in the last two decades, so that babies are appearing annually with no regard to the lore. In actual fact, fertility histories suggest that there has been little change in spacing, so that *iriyale* were probably as common before as they are now.

Few demands are made of the child while it is still held to be 'without sense' (*mini nawi*). Around the fourth year when it starts to become capable of performing simple domestic tasks it will begin to be allocated chores, such as watching another child, taking a piglet to forage and the like.

Traditionally a boy would live with his mother until around puberty. For the next few years he would live with his father, helping with the chores, drawing water, gardening, looking after pigs, and the older men would instruct him informally in all sorts of knowledge, including that to do with growth, and the need to avoid women to achieve a good 'skin'. Older men, looking back on those days, say that in traditional times they really were very chaste and naive. While still living with his father or another male relation he began the formal care of his hair and skin. Each morning at dawn he went into the forest, washed his hair and body with dew, and said the spells that he had been taught. As his hair grew he teased and combed it out into the crescent shape of the *manda tene*, the everyday wig.

Eventually either he or his parents would probably decide that he should receive formal training in *ibagiya*, the bachelor cult, which centred upon special houses hidden in the forest of each clan territory. Each of these was run by a specialist in the lore, spells and techniques that help a young man care for his hair and his body, ensure his health and beauty, protect him from the causes of premature ageing, give him the power that causes others to be generous in their dealings with him, and that causes his pig herd to grow rapidly and without disease. The specialist was always a bachelor. Young men would select him as their teacher largely on the basis of his reputation and the efficacy of his spells. They would enter quite voluntarily, paying a large fee of pig and shell on admission. Almost all young men would elect to go through this training. When there was a new intake of novices, the teacher (*daloali*) would renovate the forest house with the help of men, still bachelors, whom he had previously trained. They would all move from their usual homes into this forest house (*ibagiyanda*) and stay there for four months or so, avoiding the sun, caring for and growing their hair and learning spells. They grew and made a special type of wig, the *manda hare* (literally 'red wig'), and the climax of the tuition was their admission on their last day and night to the central bachelor house, ringed by great fences, where they were tricked and bullied by the older bachelors, and shown the most important magic plants. They spent their last night singing the *ibagiya* spells, spells which are also statements of the lore. The next morning they would appear again in public, pale, gleaming and beautifully decorated. For the next couple of years the *ibagiyanda* would function as a sort of club for these young men. They would return for further instruction, going over parts of the spells that they had forgotten. They would help with a new batch of trainees, and just spend time there, enjoying what sounds like a very amicable atmosphere.

In the next few years most men would marry. A number of men would stay bachelors throughout their lives, but of these some defect was as common a cause as the wish for ritual purity. The specialists themselves would usually marry after some ten years of running an *ibagiyanda*.

An adolescent girl helped her mother with gardening and other chores. She was similarly chaste, but unlike the young men, she was taught no elaborate means of protecting her health. Most of the ritual knowledge she acquired at this age was concerned with courting magic, though she was introduced to the ideas concerning the dangers of her sexuality to men at marriage by a woman other than her own mother. A mother would be ashamed to talk of these matters to her daughter.

A more diffuse form of female pollution is represented by the danger of young children being 'scorched' (*guyu naya*) by the 'heat' emitted while she is menstruating by a sexually active young woman who has never been pregnant. To avoid this occurrence, girls must learn and practice a spell and ritual known as *hame gamu*. In this context *hame* refers to mixing in public, so that the young woman who has taken this precaution can move freely. The heat of such a woman can be fatal to children, but this spell is said to 'close the door (seal off) this fatal influence of her blood' (*hame gamume panga payaga daramame boli lowa*). Once she has become pregnant she loses this particular destructive power, and no longer uses the spell.

I have already mentioned marriage ritual (*ndi tingi*) and discussed its aim of ensuring prosperity for the couple. It is also concerned with the fertility of the woman, and the protection of her husband from her damaging influence. Traditionally in the case of a first marriage, the man's specific instruction on women's sexuality did not begin until the bride-price had been given, and his wife had moved into his mother's house. Neither the bride nor groom should sleep for the next four days and nights, and he would begin to learn the lore and spells that he needs to protect himself from her. On the fifth day, the couple were taken to a secluded area of their garden land by the specialist in this lore (*ndi tingi gamuyi*). There they dug a small garden mound, and the couple sat on opposite sides of the mound. The ritualist intoned a spell while both partners planted a leaf of ginger, or another magical plant.

This ceremony is primarily concerned with fertility. During the ensuing months the couple continued to live separately, and the husband learned a number of spells to protect himself from his wife's pollution. The following example indicates the purpose of these spells. It is from a *nogoba gamu*, given to a piece of pig fat which is then rubbed over the skin:

The stink stuck to me before, the taint stuck to me before, the matted filth its stink, the tar (the residue in a pipe for example) its stink, became stuck to me, the tar its stink, the smell of her anger, became stuck to me, its stink, the stink of her smoke, the stink of (her) heat, the stink of (her) steam, became stuck to me. (*Ngu nguni ala wayayada, dodo nguni ala wayayada, karo nguni, kalaro nguni, ala wayayada, kibi nguni, keba nguni, ala wayayada, ngu nguni, hagua nguni, pobo nguni, pobaye nguni, ala wayayada.*)

The spell goes on to talk of scraping this stink off the man's skin with grasses. Once he has learned these spells, he will perform them himself each time his wife menstruates. When their first garden has matured, or even after a second garden cycle, the rituals leading up to consummation are performed.

Sexual excess may ultimately be weakening and may result in premature ageing, for there is a concept that in his ejaculate a man is squandering fluids that are necessary for his vigour and beauty. But more important for Huli men is the danger of contracting a specific disease from sexual contact with women. Much of the lore surrounding marriage is intended to permit sexual relations without the risk of catching this disease.

Sexual intercourse is regarded as being highly dangerous to the man in three sets of circumstances. First, at any time in the menstrual cycle other than the eleventh to fourteenth days. The nearer to the first day of the period that sexual intercourse takes place the more dangerous it is. During the four days in the middle of the cycle it is not regarded as dangerous at all.

Secondly, a woman who has just given birth, or miscarried, is regarded as highly dangerous, more so than a normally menstruating woman. Sexual intercourse with such a woman was regarded traditionally as inevitably fatal unless the most powerful healing spells were used, and probably fatal whatever action was taken subsequently. For this reason a period of eight months' abstinence was prescribed after a birth or miscarriage. After eight months, if her periods have returned, intercourse on the proper four days is without danger.

The third type of woman dangerous to men is the woman approaching or beyond the menopause, who is described as *gabuni*, literally 'dry'. She is as damaging as a woman who has just given birth.

While these three sets of circumstances entail greater or lesser danger, the pathogenesis of pollution is the same in each. Women can be dangerous to men in other ways too: by stepping over a man's food for example, or by looking at him while she is menstruating. But in sexual intercourse at these times he is most intimately exposed to her destructive essence, her 'heat' (*pobo*). This heat travels to the conjunction of the base of the penis and the colon, the area said to be joined to the umbilicus. The effects of this heat, and the taint (*ngu*, literally 'stink') of the woman, include a blackening of the intestines, and their twisting and tangling. The umbilicus will also blacken. At this stage the sufferer will be aware mainly of abdominal pain, and perhaps black diarrhoea. The taint also travels up his spine, causing his neck to weaken and so his head to droop, as well as backache and headache. As the illness progresses his intestines will tangle so firmly round each other that they will knot and then the colon will burst. Symptoms are said to begin in months rather than days after exposure, and to result in death a few days after their onset unless proper measures are taken.

The Huli word *agali* can mean simply 'man'. But in the context of illness, *agali* refers to those illnesses in men deemed to be caused by contact with women. In such cases, when asked what is wrong with him (*agime homarebe*, literally 'of what are you dying?', thus, 'what caused your illness?') a man might reply, '*agalime homaro*' (literally, 'I am dying of man'), or simply '*agali*'. The other main idiom here is *walime bara* (literally 'by woman it strikes', thus, 'my illness is caused by woman').

Traditional healing of *agali*

A sick man will be asked continually to admit that he has exposed himself to *agali*. It is usually assumed that he has, however strenuous his denials, but it is not possible to perform healing ceremonies until he confesses his improper or foolish conduct.

Healing entails the symbolic manipulation of the disordered internal organs. It is specifically directed towards the extrusion of the woman's taint, the untangling of the intestines, their recovery from a putrid blackened state to their proper shiny pinkness, and more generally towards the sufferer's return to strength.

Agali gamu refers both to the specific spell which is the central point of the healing ceremony, and to the whole healing rite. *Tini gamu* may also be used, *tini* meaning 'intestines', the anatomical site of the lesion. Bespelled water is used in many other ceremonies, but the term *iba gamu* (*iba* is 'water') is assumed to refer to *agali gamu*. The more elaborate ceremonies, which are likely to include the sacrifice of a pig, can also be referred to as *agali gamu*, but it is more usual to refer to these by their specific names, for example, *nogo tini gamu* (literally 'pig intestine spell'), where bespelled pig's intestines are eaten, amongst other measures.

106

Explanations relating to sexuality and growth

The central element of most healing is the spell, and this is applied to the patient in conjunction with objects selected for their symbolic properties, particularly those relating to strength, durability and 'shine', for the shine of a person's skin is synonymous with health. In the simplest version of *agali gamu*, the *gamuyi* (literally 'holder of the *gamu*', thus in this context, healer) plugs the mouth of a water-filled bamboo with special leaves, blows his particular spell into the water, and then gives the water to the sick man to drink. Four bamboos are usually bespelled and drunk on each of four successive days.

I will illustrate these points by a brief description of *nogo tini gamu*, one of the more elaborate forms of *agali gamu*, which necessitates the killing of a pig.

The selection of a specialist in this particular sort of ceremony indicates an admission by the patient or the suspicion of his relatives that he has not followed the sexual code. The healer (*gamuyi*) may ask about the severity of the patient's exposure. A small pig is killed. The blood from its abdominal cavity is tipped into a dish made from a banana leaf. Leaves of various plants are placed in the blood: commonly *gigipaye* (*Dianella ensifolia*), *kangabu* (*Nothocnide mollisima*), *gondo* (*Commelina*), *tigibi* (*Oenanthe javanica*), *embereli* (*Setaria palmifolia*), *kanga* (*Elatostema blechnoides*), *baya* (*Holochalmys* spp. Fam. *Araceae*). These plants are all small herbs and grasses. The property that they share is their tenacity, for when uprooted they still tend to regrow, and the strength of their leaves. With a blood-soaked bundle of these leaves in each hand, the *gamuyi* crouches before the standing patient, his mouth close to the other's navel, and begins the spell. He slowly sweeps the bundles around his patient's abdomen, from the small of his back to his navel. When he reaches the navel, he presses the bundles inwards and vibrates them, an action referred to as 'planting' the leaves. The umbilicus is considered to be in continuity with the intestines. In severe cases the umbilicus too is said to become black. Through these manipulations the healer extrudes the taint, revitalises the blackened intestines and ensures their future resilience.

The spell is part chanted, part blown breathily on to the damaged navel. These spells call upon the indestructability or other properties of particular plants, and pass this strength to the diseased organs. For example:

Mugu hununu, walu hununu, mugu hununu, ngoe hawela hununu, pugua hugula hununu, hununu hununu, tombene hununu, endolobane hununu, tibani hununu, dugutabane hununu yabuni hununu, wi hununu, dalaga hununu, dalapari hununu, wapuya hununu...

Here *hununu* refers to regrowth after damage, particularly the scar tissue produced in some trees where they have been blazed, or where branches have been lopped. The trees named, *mugu* and *wali* (*Garcinia dulcis* (*Roxb.*) *Kurz*, and *Garcinia* spp. *Guttiferae*) are both said by Hulis to be particularly prolific in their production of such scar tissue. When stripped of their bark they also

107

secrete glary sap; similarly the patient's intestine is intended to become moist and pale, recovering from its black and dry state. The spell next summons the earthworm, *ngoe*, desirable in its similarity to a healthy intestine, and in its apparent immortality: cutting a worm in half leads to its increase rather than its death. *Pugua* and *hugu* are the taints themselves, menstrual blood and vaginal secretions. The damage these have done must heal. There follows a list of the most vulnerable organs, each to be regenerated in turn: the stomach, colon, perineum, small intestine, rectum and penis. The three snakes (*dalaga, dalapari* and *wapuya*) are named to 'claim' (the healer's interpretation as well as my own) particularly the properties of renewal. When its skin is dry and loose, for Hulis an indication of a moribund state, a snake sheds it to reveal a glossy tight skin beneath.

The next stage of the healing ceremony is the drinking of bespelled water. The water is in four bamboos, each plugged with special leaves, usually including those mentioned in the spell above. The imagery of the *iba gamu* (water spell) is of the same sort as that in the spells I have quoted from. The water is seen as having two functions. First, it carries the spell (which is blown into the top of each bamboo) to the site of the pathology. Its second beneficial effect is more mechanical. In *agali* the intestine is said to be tangled up, and thus becomes black, a concept reminiscent of the condition known to Western surgeons as volvulus. The flow of water into the intestine helps to straighten it out again. The quantities of water that are administered may be large: three, four or more litres are common quantities. Ideally *iba gamu* should be repeated on each of four consecutive days.

The third stage of the ceremony is the administration of the cooked bespelled intestines of the sacrificial pig. Finally the cooked pig is eaten, without ceremony, but with pleasure and much optimistic conversation on the part of the patient, the healer and the helpers.

This account of methods of healing *agali* underlines the following two points which are necessary to the understanding of *agali*: the pathology of *agali* is seen by Hulis as a specific anatomically sited process that can be expected to progress in a predictable fashion unless appropriate action is taken to halt it; traditional measures to combat *agali*, while they invoke influences implausible to Western medicine, are in Huli terms matters of fact, and designed to interrupt and reverse the pathology of the condition as it is understood.

Symbolic themes

The issue of male–female relations has been a central concern for New Guinea Highland ethnographers, a focus which reflects the concerns of the people themselves. The earlier simple correlations, such as Meggitt's (1964), suggested division of these societies according to the level of hostility towards affinal groups, have proved untenable by later work where relations between the sexes have been examined in more detail. Marilyn Strathern's (1972) study of Mount Hagen showed the complexity of the sex roles there. Other research has examined the place of sexual relations in terms of broader cosmological issues (e.g. Brown and Buchbinder 1976), and more recently in terms of the conceptualisation of gender (Gillison 1980, M. Strathern 1980). Here I must concentrate upon those aspects of the Huli view of sexuality which relate to their responses to illness. The account I have given of the ideal sexual career, the hazards sexuality entails and the myths which validate these beliefs reveals the antithesis in Huli thought between, on the one hand, the controlled begetting of children and their healthy development, and on the other abandoned incontinence. Before analysing actual cases of illness attributed to these causes, I will first summarise these themes.

The sexual properties of women for the Huli seem to be broadly divisible into two sorts: productive and destructive. In the mythological utopia of the asexual era, the woman's heat is at the service of men, as she produces and cooks limitless delicacies. In the *ibagiya* it is the woman's blood which generates the plants which are at the core of the bachelor cult. In the present she bears and nourishes children. But her heat can also cause fatal illnesses in men, and can scorch children to death. Her blood can grow into the parasitical leech, *kuyanda*, or may kill men and children directly.

Comparison of those occasions when women are deemed polluting with those when they are not suggests the basis for the ascription of positive and negative attributes to women's sexuality. Women are potentially dangerous to men at the following times: around the time of their menses; when they approach or pass the menopause; when they menstruate after coitus but before they have first conceived; and after they have given birth. The Huli regard the middle four days of the cycle as the only ones when a woman might conceive. The further from these four days in her cycle the woman is, the more dangerous she becomes. She is least likely to conceive during the time of the menstrual flow, and this blood is a lethal substance. But we cannot equate the danger of pollution with the presence of blood. In the case of the woman approaching the menopause, intercourse during the proper four days is potentially dangerous. And if she has passed the menopause the danger is greater still, despite the irrelevance of any concern about menstrual blood. The common feature in the circumstances discussed so far is that sexual intercourse at these times is unlikely, in the Huli view, to lead to conception. The 'heat' of a woman not engaged in reproducing is too great for a man to withstand. This heat becomes generalised in the case of the childless but sexually active young woman who may 'scorch' children when she menstruates. Nor is the woman who has recently given birth thought to be likely to conceive, so that intercourse with her is not for the purpose of reproduction. Conversely, the only time when sexual intercourse is deemed entirely safe is during the middle four days of the cycle of a young or fairly young woman. Such intercourse is also in the Huli view the most likely to lead to conception (that this corresponds with the medical view is incidental to the argument).

Actions driven by desire are likely to have grievous consequences. In the myth, the *ibatiri*'s desire led him to copulate with Tiame, and so destroy the Huli Eden. Uncontrolled desire is the force which exposes men most commonly to female pollution. They may ascribe this to the attractiveness of women, and so present themselves as victims. Or they may admit their own weakness. If a couple have intercourse while their child is small the woman should wash her breasts as the 'desire' (*hame*) that is stuck to them may damage the child when it suckles. An adulterous father has had sex for pleasure only and should therefore keep away from his baby. In the myth of Ni and Dagiwali, the sight of her flow aroused him, equating desire with the menstrual flow itself. In *kuyanda* the mother's blood grows into a tumour whose inordinate greed may reach out to sicken others.

Modern marriage and sexuality

I have been describing ideals and theoretical dangers. In practice their desire leads men to seek sexual satisfaction at times which would not lead to conception, and so are deemed dangerous. But in addition to dangers and restrictions, Huli lore includes a variety of protective spells and rites which are regarded as sufficient to neutralise all but the most dire exposure to female pollution. The acquisition of these is an important aspect of ritual training for marriage.

Much of what I have been describing is very much the ethnographic past, for, as we have seen, Huli society has undergone drastic changes in the last twenty years. The present situation is only understandable with this background, but now much of what I have been describing is practised very rarely, and then often in an attenuated form. Towards adolescence boys are very free, roaming in groups with other boys, eating food when they find it and sleeping where they choose. There are only three *ibagiya* houses in the whole Tari area that I know of that still function intermittently, so that only a very small proportion of boys now enter the bachelor cult. During 1977 and 1978 probably less than a score of young men passed through *ibagiya* training out of an eligible group of several thousand young men. In former times almost all young men would have attended. At the time of their lives when traditionally they would have been most pure they are now very free. They go to *dawanda* courting parties, which previously was strictly forbidden, wander around the roads watching or joining in card games, go to the different markets hoping to meet girl-friends and do little work. Traditionally they would have cared for pigs, and done their own garden work. While the picture of obedience that older men insist on as true for their own youth is exaggerated, it is certain that young men did not behave as they do now. The threat of war, murder, injury and sorcery were very real in those times, so that young men did not wander as they do today. The knowledge the older men possessed was essential to a young man's success, even to his survival, and that created a dependency that no longer exists. Young men now have the option of leaving the area completely if they find their lives to be tedious or oppressive; they may go to Mount Hagen or further afield to find work or to stay with friends or relatives.

Girls' lives have changed much less. They usually stay with their mothers until they marry as they always did. They are still closely watched, and reprimanded for any immodest behaviour. But with the new mobility they have considerably more opportunity to meet boys, especially at markets which are as much to do with courtship as with selling produce.

Some couples lead determinedly modern lives: the bride moves straight into the husband's house, and they consummate their marriage without delay. But it is more usual to make a cautious compromise between traditional and modern ideas. The bride will move in with her husband's mother or other female relations, and the couple will observe the basic restrictions, such as not having intercourse in the early part of the cycle, but they will not perform the rituals I have mentioned above. Older men will frown on all this, tell the young man that he will become ill, and comment to each other on how dry his skin is becoming, and how his eyes have lost their shine. If he does come down with any illness they will pressure him to accept bespelled water, and he will usually comply, though denying that he really believes in it. These changes are best understood through the analysis of actual cases of illness attributed to these causes.

Cases of *kuyanda*

Illness is ascribed unequivocally to *kuyanda* only rarely. This is surprising, as *kuyanda* is said to develop inevitably whenever an infant swallows some blood at birth, which must be a common occurrence. One reason for parents' reluctance to diagnose this condition in their children may be the unpleasant implications of the diagnosis. A person with *kuyanda* is a potential danger to others, for by subconsciously coveting food they can cause illness through *lingi* (see pp. 140–2). A second reason may be that a primary diagnosis of *kuyanda* must be made by women, who are in general committed church-goers. Whatever their private fears, they may be unwilling to admit belief in *kuyanda*, particularly as the only effective way to remove it is through the sort of ritual that is quite unacceptable to the church. This dilemma is expressed in the following case:

Case one (case histories are numbered consecutively for reference). A girl aged four months had had bouts of shortness of breath and coughing since birth. She was born at a mission midwifery centre, and had breathing difficulties at birth, requiring oxygen and other special treatment. The mother thinks that the child swallowed 'taint' (*dodo nayada*) at birth, and so has *kuyanda*. The mother has been baptised, and says that she must therefore do nothing but pray. Further, she thinks that the medicine she gets (penicillin) is not sufficiently strong to make the child completely better, as some of the *kuyanda* will remain. But her husband does not go to church, and she hopes that he will arrange for the *kuyanda* to be removed by traditional means.

In cases where parents are certain of the diagnosis, they may waver for years, assessing whether or not the child's condition is such that they should arrange for the *kuyanda* to be removed. For example:

Case two. A four-year-old girl is known to have swallowed blood at birth. The mother had hoped to reach the mission, but instead bore her en route beside the track. The woman helping her saw the blood in the baby's mouth. She is not regarded as a hardy child, though she has grown and developed normally. Her father says that when he is cross with her he notices that she sobs deeply and silently. He is careful not to strike her in case her *kuyanda* 'bursts'. He might arrange to have it removed, though the mother may not approve.

Other parents harbour vague suspicions that children that are not thriving or are just a little frail may harbour a *kuyanda*. This concern is quite common, but when it is just a suspicion and leads to no specific action it is only one tentative explanation among others, and cannot be regarded as a diagnosis. They may be reluctant to admit their suspicion for the reasons I have given, and in any case would be discouraged from submitting their child to traditional treatments by the disapproval of Christians. But even if they suspect *kuyanda* strongly and want it removed they might have difficulty in finding someone to perform the ceremony. Healers must satisfy the demands of their clients. If their diagnoses and treatments are not deemed appropriate they will not be consulted. But the availability of a specialist who can treat a certain illness may influence people's willingness to accept this diagnosis. This effect is apparent in a number of illnesses that I describe later, and is clear in *kuyanda*. In the Tari area one old woman specialised in the treatment of *kuyanda*. In pre-missionary times women were as important as men in healing, but this has changed to the extent that this was the only woman regularly practising traditional cures that I knew of. She found my interest in her activities threatening, assuming that I wished to put an end to her practising. Unfortunately I was therefore unable to study her work at first hand. But I was able to talk to those who had offered themselves for treatment. Her cure was particularly graphic as at the end of the procedure she produced the extracted *kuyanda* in the form of a small piece of bloody liver-like tissue. The importance of the availability of a healer in the certain diagnosis of this condition was demonstrated when a mother put forward her two children for treatment when the old woman was in the neighbourhood, though the mother had not previously discussed a diagnosis of *kuyanda*.

Cases of *guyu naya*

Older people often comment unfavourably on the promiscuity of the young, and the fact that they no longer learn the means to protect themselves and others from the dangers of sexuality. Women say that they no longer need *hame gamu* to prevent children becoming 'scorched', as they have gone into the church, and that is like a *gamu* (spell). The two cases I did see were both boys (though girls are said to be susceptible) under one year of age. They both had died after short illnesses where the significant symptoms in the diagnosis were abdominal swelling, and a dark colouration around the umbilicus (which was not obvious to me). They also had severe diarrhoea. The rectum of one of the boys was said to have 'come out' (*yabuni duguaya*, which can be used for rectal prolapse. In this case there was no obvious prolapse.) In neither case was any particular girl accused of being responsible, and none seemed to be under suspicion. The key issue in the diagnosis was the symptomatology, which is reminiscent of the changes that are expected in *agali*. The intensity of the polluting power of young women at such times and the extent to which it is antithetical to babies is shown by the attribution of two rapidly fatal illnesses to this cause.

Cases of *agali*

The aspect of pollution fears which most commonly finds expression in illness behaviour and discussions about illness is *agali*. Huli men frequently suspect *agali* as the cause of illness in others, but are reluctant to admit it for themselves. When a group of men are told that another man is ill, one of them is likely to make the downward jab of the middle finger that is the Huli version of the 'vee' sign. But here I will concentrate upon the cases I observed which were unequivocally regarded as *agali* by the sufferer. I observed fifteen such cases. I will first illustrate the common patterns by describing four of these.

Case three. A man of about fifty-five years developed a severe head cold and a chest pain that he described as something 'stuck' (*para ka*) to his epigastric area. He lost his usual rather debonair style. He sat hunched and depressed in his house, and came to resemble a decrepit old man. His concern was that he had had sexual intercourse with his young second wife two months after she had given birth. Other sorts of female pollution are dangerous, but that sort of exposure is regarded by some as necessarily lethal. One of the few confirmed non-Christians, he arranged for a healer to perform *nogo tini gamu* upon him, and also sacrificed a pig for the *dama* (spirit) with whom he had always maintained a relationship. When the *gamu* had been performed he became notably more confident. Before the ceremony he had asked me if I would give him an injection. But afterwards he did not mention that again, and recovered without other treatment.

My diagnosis was of a viral upper respiratory infection complicated by mild bronchitis. The implications of this illness were made alarming to him by the knowledge of his major exposure to female pollution. His symptoms were not exactly 'typical' of *agali*, but his exposure was such that he was certain of the diagnosis. The combination of the severity of his exposure, and his own traditionalist orientation, decided him to act quickly, and undergo one of the most potent forms of *agali gamu, nogo tini gamu*. This decision cost him two pigs, and required him to admit his foolhardy lack of self-control. But in his own view it restored his health.

Case four. A man of about forty-five who, when I first saw him, had been unwell for about two months. His illness had begun with a cough, and then he had become very weak (*ibira harudagane*, literally 'I fell down'). At that time he had abdominal discomfort (*tini tombe ogoha gedore*, literally 'my stomach and intestines were soft'), he vomited after he ate, had an unpleasant taste in his mouth and lost his appetite. He attended the Catholic Church regularly, though he had not been baptised, and at that stage of his illness he said that as a Christian he would not perform *agali gamu*. He had had sexual intercourse with his wife only seven days from the beginning of her cycle, was certain that he had *agali*, but felt it would be sinful to perform *agali gamu*. His other symptoms were severe pain in the lower sacrum (*ti wabene tandaga gibi*), and tingling in his arms and legs (*amburi biya*). The Catholics are more willing to permit ceremonies that are essentially transformations of traditional rites than are their Protestant counterparts. At this stage of his illness a Christian pig kill was held. Eight pigs were slaughtered, dedicated to the Christian God, and prayers were said for the sick man's recovery. Many of the prayers said on these occasions are almost identical to those invocations (*ambi*) which are addressed to the *dama* in traditional sacrifices. He was also accepting a number of medicines from the aid post orderly, including aspirin and penicillin injections. At that time he said that *iba gamu* and Western medicines were equally effective in *agali*. He doubted if Christian prayer alone was sufficient, but he was happy to try it alongside Western medicine.

Over the next few weeks his condition deteriorated. He became very weak, to the point where he was unable to sit up for more than a short period. Apart from this weakness, his main complaint was that his intestines were very noisy (*tiniha bi lolebira*, literally 'there is talking in my intestines'). He was given *iba gamu* (the simplest cure with bespelled water), then *nogo tini gamu* (using pig's blood and intestines) and finally *palena gamu* (another form of *agali gamu* where bespelled ginger is used). He had become severely constipated, and explained this in terms of his intestines being tangled, so obstructing the faeces. If that state had been allowed to continue, he felt that his intestines would ultimately have burst (*tini tongolebira*).

These cures made little difference to his condition. He had been ill for about three months now. He was very constipated (*ti ndibu*), and in a weakly state of inanition (*kutugu hara*). As he had not made a significant recovery following such a thorough programme of *agali gamu*, he decided that he had been suffering from some illness other than *agali*. His new theory was that the skin of some pork he had eaten just before he became ill had stuck in his gut, and that that was the cause of his illness.

I found his illness difficult to diagnose. I think it is most likely that he had a severe chest infection, and what he was suffering from subsequently were non-specific sequelae to that illness and his long period of inactivity. He refused to go to hospital, so I treated him symptomatically as best I could. It took several months for him to recover his full strength.

Explanations relating to sexuality and growth

The interpretations and strategies adopted over this long illness highlight the predicament of many Huli men of this age group and older. They are often the most devout Christians, but also are deeply imbued with the values which have only recently been displaced. This man's wish to avoid traditional remedies was eroded by his increasing conviction that without them he would die. It also underlines the coherence of the concept *agali*, and the confidence that men can have in the traditional remedies for it. When *agali gamu* did not result in a cure, they changed the diagnosis rather than their conviction in the efficacy of *agali gamu*.

Case five. A man of about forty: when I saw him he had been ill for four days suffering from severe abdominal pain (*tini tandaga timbuni ore*), headache (*hagua*), lower back pain (*erekuni tandaga*) and spurting diarrhoea (*ti putu lo baya*). He had had sexual intercourse with his wife on the first day of her period. She had told him that it was unsafe, but '*pobome mo luluya hayagola*': 'my heat made me insane' (so I did it). Since then he had been waiting to get ill. He recovered after one day. He ascribed this to the small dose of aspirin and kaolin he had taken. Though a Christian, he admitted that he would have done *agali gamu* if he had not recovered quickly.

Despite the graphic description of symptoms he did not seem to be very ill. The symptoms he described comprise the 'typical' form of *agali*. It seems likely that his extreme flouting of the rules led him to anticipate *agali*, and so give a different significance to his symptoms than he might otherwise have done.

Men who have exposed themselves to the risk of *agali* commonly present themselves at aid posts to take some treatment as a precaution, or for minor symptoms which otherwise they might have disregarded. Where the medical orderly is a sympathetic Huli, they might say 'give me some *agali* medicine' (*agali marasini ngi*). Otherwise they might just say that they have a bellyache. They usually receive a kaolin mixture, and regard this as beneficial. These incidents are commonplace, but as these men are generally responding to the threat of illness rather than actual symptoms, I have not included them in this series. I have included only one such case, as he had some minor symptoms, and was seriously concerned about his condition.

Case six. A man of about thirty-five: he had had sexual intercourse with his wife on the second day of her period. Two days later he said that '*dongone ibiraya*' (literally 'my skin has fallen down', used for a non-specific sense of being indisposed). He asked the medical orderly for medicine 'lest my rectum burst' (*yabuni tongo loli*). He was satisfied with some aspirin tablets, and by the next day was quite well.

The issue of whether or not a particular illness in oneself or in others is *agali* is a common preoccupation for Huli men. The fifteen cases which I am analysing here were given definite diagnoses. Before proceeding to discuss the features of those cases, I will give one example, from many, of the sorts of deliberations that can surround the rejection of the diagosis of *agali*.

Case seven. A man of about sixty had severe dysentery. His neighbour offered to perform *agali gamu* for him, but he refused, saying that he had nothing to do with women, so how could he have *agali*? Other men insisted that he accept the offer, but he was adamant. His clan brother suspected that he had accepted the services of one of the women who solicit older men on the road to market. The sick man admitted that he had been solicited, but was again adamant that he had rejected the woman. This only confirmed the others in their conviction that he was lying but was ashamed to admit his folly. He became angry, so they dropped the subject, saying that if he would rather die than admit something so unimportant that was his business. He was taken to hospital, but was treated in a way that he regarded as unsympathetic, so he ran away. He recovered at home with no specific remedies.

Determinants in the diagnosis and treatment of agali
Symptoms

Agali is primarily an illness of middle-aged and older men, as the age distribution in table 10 shows.

Table 10 *Age distribution of cases of 'agali'*

Age	Number of cases
c. 25 yrs	1
c. 35 yrs	4
c. 40 yrs	2
c. 45 yrs	3
c. 55 yrs	3
c. 60 yrs	2

The fifteen men reported a total of sixty-five dominant symptoms. These are shown in table 11. Twenty-seven of the symptoms reported relate to the abdomen (42%). We would expect this from Huli descriptions of *agali*. But other of the symptoms that constitute 'typical' *agali* are rather infrequent. As described above, an *agali* sufferer would be expected to suffer abdominal pain, with or without diarrhoea, backache, headache and a particularly Huli symptom which translates literally as 'broken neck'.

The number of what Huli men regard as typical symptoms occurring in each case, and the nature of these symptoms, is shown in table 12. Of the five symptoms named in theoretical descriptions as being typical of the condition, abdominal pain was reported in a large number of these cases (73%). Backache was also common (47%). The other three symptoms were reported in a third of cases or less. In two cases none of these symptoms was reported. The reported symptomatology, then, while at least partially consistent with Huli theoretical concepts, is evidently neither a sufficient nor even necessary criterion in the selection of the diagnosis *agali*.

But the diagnosis of *agali* does influence the stress that sufferers put upon different symptoms. This effect was illustrated in the third case described

Table 11 *Distribution of symptoms in cases of 'agali'*

Symptom	Number of cases
Abdominal pain	11
Diarrhoea	5
Constipation, abdominal swelling, vomiting, appetite loss	2 each
Borborygmi, foul belching, 'soft' belly	1 each
Headache	5
Backache	6
Neck 'broken' (pain and weakness so head hangs)	2
Weakness	6
Cough	5
Shortness of breath	3
General aches and pains	4
Chest pain	2
Abscesses, rigors, fever, eyeache, tingling limbs	1 each

Table 12 *Relationship between the number of 'typical' symptoms in each case of 'agali' and the nature of these symptoms*

Number of 'typical' symptoms	'Typical' symptoms					
	Abdominal pain	Diarrhoea	Backache	Headache	Neck broken	Total
0						2
1	4		1			5
2	1		1			1
3	5	3	3	3	1	5
4	1	2	2	2	1	2
5						0
Total symptoms	11	5	7	5	2	

above. A broader indication of this comes from comparing the symptoms that these men reported with my clinical diagnoses. My diagnoses are shown in table 13.

If we compare this list with the symptom list (table 11) the most striking feature is the preponderance of abdominal pain in what are primarily respiratory illnesses. Abdominal pain is reported by Western sufferers of respiratory illnesses, but the stress upon abdominal pain here is likely to be a product of these sufferers' explanation of their condition.

Table 13 *Clinical diagnoses of cases of 'agali'*

Lower respiratory infections	8 cases
Septicaemia with multiple abscesses	1 case
Peptic ulcer	1 case
Mild influenza	1 case
Malaria	1 case
Non-specific diarrhoea	1 case
Constipation	1 case
Primarily fear of *agali*	1 case (case four)

Table 14 *Types of exposure*

Intercourse at wrong time of normal period	9 cases
Intercourse with woman regarded as 'dry'	5 cases
Intercourse too soon after childbirth	1 case

Table 15 *Relationship of type of exposure to age*

Age	under 35 yrs	35–50 yrs	over 50 yrs
Normal period, wrong time	5	2	2
'Dry' woman	0	3	2
After childbirth	0	0	1

Aetiology

In all fifteen cases the sufferers were certain that they had exposed themselves to female pollution. The degree of exposure varied, but none were in any doubt that they had exposed themselves to pollution. The different sorts of exposure described earlier were variously represented, as shown in table 14. The relationship of cause to the man's age, shown in table 15, indicates the different sorts of risk that men may be exposed to at different stages of their lives.

For men under thirty-five years the most common risk is intercourse with their own wives at a time in the menstrual cycle deemed unsafe. Men over thirty-five suffer the additional hazards of intercourse with a woman approaching or past the end of her reproductive years. Men of all ages could be exposed to the danger of intercourse too soon after the birth of a child. The only case of this sort known to me happened to be in a man of sixty with a young second wife.

Table 16 *Relationship between the number of 'typical' symptoms in each case and the severity of the sufferer's exposure to the causes of 'agali'*

	Exposure to *agali*			
Number of 'typical' symptoms	No exposure	Exposure long ago	Severe exposure	Extreme exposure
0			1	1
1			4	1
2			1	
3		1	2	2
4			1	1
5				

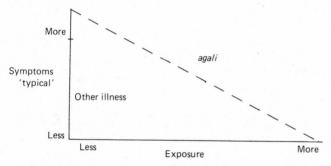

Fig. 51 Symptoms and exposure to pollution in the diagnosis of *agali*

Diagnosis

The diagnosis of *agali*, therefore, depends primarily upon exposure to female pollution. 'Perfect' symptoms in themselves are insufficient if there has been no exposure to risk. In the case of extreme exposure to the risk of *agali* it may be diagnosed in the absence of any major symptoms, as in the case of the man who had had intercourse on the second day of his wife's mentrual period, assumed that he had *agali*, and took Western treatment 'lest his rectum burst'. Most cases are between these two extremes of perfect symptoms with minimal exposure, and no symptoms with maximal exposure. The interplay between these two determinants of the diagnosis *agali* is illustrated in table 16. I have divided 'exposure' into four categories, from none to maximal exposure. The cases are further divided according to the number of 'typical' symptoms that they reported. The interaction between perceived cause and expected symptomatology is expressed schematically in fig. 51.

Explanations relating to sexuality and growth

Table 17 *Relationship between the performance 'gamu' and the severity of exposure*

Exposure	moderate	severe	extreme
gamu performed	1	7	1
gamu not performed	0	2	4

Table 18 *Relationship between performance of 'gamu' and type of symptom*

Number of 'typical' symptoms	0 1 2 3 4 5
gamu performed	0 5 1 3 0 0
gamu not performed	2 0 0 2 2 0

Choice of treatment

The selection of this diagnosis influences the choices that are made in deciding when and how to act to alleviate the illness. I have already pointed out that *agali* is one of the few conditions where Hulis still have recourse to traditional cures. Of these fifteen cases, *agali gamu* was performed in nine (60%). In most other cases the percentage performing traditional cures that involve spells or sacrifices would be zero, so this is striking in itself. But how do those who underwent *agali gamu* differ from those who did not? Severe exposure does not lead to the performance of *gamu*. If anything, there appears to be a negative correlation, as seen in table 17. The experience of more 'typical' symptoms also has, if anything, a negative correlation (table 18). These two features are important only in selecting the diagnosis. The decision to perform *agali gamu* appears to be influenced more by the severity and chronicity of the condition. This relationship is shown in fig. 52, and schematically in fig. 53.

Christians tend to say that they would not perform *agali gamu* under any circumstances. Men often said to me 'in the old days we suffered from *agali*, performed *gamu* and recovered. Today too we suffer from *agali*. Medicine may help, but if it is insufficient, then we just wait and die.' From these fifteen cases it seems that most men have their threshold of conviction in the modern influences upon *agali*. They can also be subject to a lot of pressure from their fellows. One man, who decided that his lower respiratory infection was not in fact caused by *agali*, so it is not included in this series, awoke to find a clansman administering *agali gamu* to him. He says that he pushed him away, saying that he did not believe in that devil-worship.

In the graph (fig. 52) it can be seen that in one case *agali gamu* was performed in a short illness which was not very severe. That case illustrates

Explanations relating to sexuality and growth

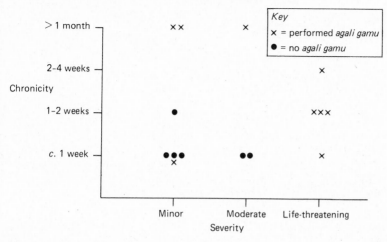

Fig. 52 Chronicity and severity of the illness as these influence the performance of
agali gamu

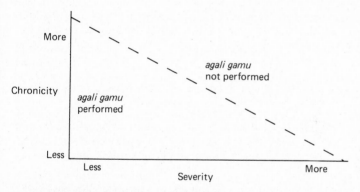

Fig. 53 Schematic representation of fig. 52

such pressures, but it also indicates another aspect of the *agali* complex which
I can only touch on here: its place in social control. That case concerns a
young man, newly married, who was suspected by his affines, with whom he
lived, of improperly early sexual intercourse with his wife. His symptoms were
not severe, but he was put under considerable pressure to confess his misdeed.
He refused to confess, but he agreed to drink the bespelled water. He said
that he gave in just to humour the healer, still maintaining that he had not
acted improperly. The birth of a child some seven months later showed that
he had not been restrained, and probably had felt that he was at risk. So it
is likely that he had taken the old men's warnings, that if he did not accept
agali gamu he would die, more seriously than he had admitted.

Hulis use Western treatments readily in most illnesses. In this series of cases,

121

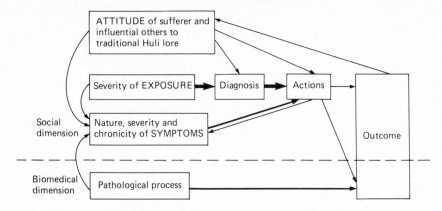

Fig. 54 Factors influencing the diagnosis, treatment and outcome of *agali*

Western treatments were not used in only two cases. In one of these cases (case one above), the sufferer recovered after *agali gamu*, and so saw no purpose in seeking other treatment. He almost certainly would have done so if he had noticed no improvement. In the other, the patient died five days after the onset of his illness (the only case to die in this series).

Case eight. A man of about forty years, he had had intercourse with his wife who was about the same age, and so *gabuni* (dry). *Agali gamu* was administered on two consecutive days, but on the third day his condition had deteriorated so much that the healer declined to give the treatment, saying that the man's exposure was obviously too extreme, and that he would certainly die. I did not hear of his illness until the fifth day, and when I saw him he was in a terminal state of broncho-pneumonia. He died that day.

Neither of these men were Christians, in fact they were the only two in this series who never went to church. This set their first choice of treatment, which was traditional, but they would have used Western treatments, in the first case if recovery had not been so prompt, and in the second if the condition had not proved so rapidly fatal.

Christian healing was used in four of these cases. In most other sorts of illness, prayers to God and Western medicine replace traditional measures in ways which Hulis find acceptable or positively advantageous. The low proportion of sufferers from *agali*, an illness regarded as potentially serious, using Christian healing reflects the particular incompatability between traditional and Christian approaches in this condition.

These various influences upon the acceptance of the diagnosis of *agali*, and upon the choice of action taken subsequently, are summarised in fig. 54. For the diagnosis to be accepted, the patient must not have rejected the Huli concepts concerned absolutely, nor resist them for the whole course of his illness. In general we find that in the face of actual illness, the diagnosis is likely to be accepted where other conditions are satisfied.

Agali is not diagnosed without prior specific exposure to female pollution through sexual intercourse at a time deemed dangerous. Both these elements can influence the symptomatology, causing the sufferer to stress symptoms regarded as typical of *agali*, but the symptoms are in most cases clear concomitants of a pathological process known to Western medicine. Exposure to female pollution is a necessary basis for diagnosis, but while it must be satisfied, other issues come to bear in greater or lesser proportion to lead to the diagnosis. The nature of the symptoms has some influence, as does the attitude of the sufferer and those around him, though this latter influence is difficult to quantify.

Once the diagnosis has been accepted, the choice of action, whether inaction, use of Western medicine, Huli cure, Christian healing or a combination of these, will depend particularly upon the severity and chronicity of the symptoms. The alacrity with which Huli treatments are applied also depends upon the attitudes of those concerned. Western treatments are freely used, but Christian healing is used less commonly than it is in other illnesses of similar severity.

The actions taken may influence the outcome, either through the specific therapeutic effect of Western treatments used (such as the administration of penicillin in chest infections) or any specific benefits of traditional measures (the only example I can suggest here is the benefit of drinking large quantities of water in cases of enteritis or in dehydration from general inanition), or the non-specific 'placebo' benefits of any measures. The outcome was influenced tragically by the choice of action in the one patient who died.

8

Illness grounded in social relations

Many of the illnesses I have already described can be seen as expressions of the social order. The sorts of injuries and the common positions of sores follow from the division of labour and other activities which relate to social roles. Illnesses that are explained in terms of Huli concepts of sexuality and development are thought to follow from flouting the norms surrounding marriage, and are seen as evidence for the necessity of these rules. The harmful activities of spirits and God that I consider in the next chapter can be seen as an extension of human affairs, and the ascription of illnesses to causes of this sort is often an expression of the relationships between the individuals concerned. But in this chapter I will present cases of illness which arise most directly from social relations. First, I consider cases of illness attributed to assault; secondly, problems that arise from the emotions; and finally cases of illness attributed to sorcery.

Illnesses attributed to assault

The implications of any injury have a variable relationship with the lesion as it may be defined biologically. Consider two cases. In the first a woman returning from her own garden, slips on a muddy bank, falls and cracks her back against a low branch. In the second, a woman complains to her husband that he is a good-for-nothing, and he strikes her across the back with a heavy stick. Both injuries may have entailed comparable force delivered by objects of similar resilience to identical tissues, and so would be indistinguishable pathologically. But the significance of these events may differ markedly to the sufferers, and it is this, the social connotation, which may influence the expression and outcome of the illness more than the pathological nature of the lesion. Hulis commonly give forensic aspects of injury precedence over simple medical responses, so that the progress of litigation and retribution become the major influences upon the course of an illness. Here I will analyse the various elements that combine in the attribution of cases of illness to causes of this sort, and the ways in which this diagnosis influences the course and outcome.

124

Hulis are subject to a variety of aches, pains and cutaneous lesions attributable to trauma. These traumata may be sudden and severe, such as an axe to the foot while chopping wood, or minor though sustained, like the damage to the spine that follows years of stooping to weed gardens. The analysis of the burden of illness shows that the prevalence of such symptoms differs according to age and sex in ways which are generally attributable to the division of labour and other aspects of the social order. The Huli too generally relate these discomforts to their way of life, accept them as such and treat them symptomatically when they become troublesome. But lesions that are attributable to the actions of other people may be treated quite differently. The nature and distribution of such lesions can also be related to norms and styles of behaviour. Examples include the frequency of knee pain in older men (see fig. 14) which relates to their past role in warfare, and for various pains in adult women (see figs. 15, 16, 17, 18) which arise largely from beatings. The relationship between the trauma and the lesion may be immediate and clear-cut, as in this case:

Case nine. A man brought an oil pandanus fruit home, and cooked it. His wife wanted to take some to a friend and take their son with her. The husband insisted that the child should stay with him, and they quarrelled over the child, pulling him one way, then the other. The child fell while the woman was tugging his arm, and that caused the man to lose his temper. He took a stick, and struck her forearm, breaking the bones. She was taken to the health centre where an X-ray was taken that was used as evidence for the severity of the injury in later discussions of compensation. The husband's clan gave twenty-three pigs to her clan, and she was permitted to keep one large sow. All parties were satisfied with the settlement, and the marriage continued amicably.

Irascibility is a common Huli trait, but the blows that are delivered when tempers are lost may be taken very seriously indeed. In many cases the relationship between the injury, illness and retribution is straightforward, making it unnecessary to describe such cases in detail. A man with an arrow wound to his lung, a woman with a fractured arm, a man who has been run down by a motor cycle or a woman struck in the back with the blunt side of an axe; such patients attribute their symptoms to the injury, as we would. In general, they would expect compensation from the individual they hold responsible.

But in other cases the significance attached to the injury follows from Huli concepts of bodily function. I have described their sense of fragility, the ease with which the spirit may depart the body, their use of florid language to describe bodily ills and how readily they come to suspect that an ill person may be dying. These aspects of the Huli view of illness are commonly seen in response to injury. For example:

Case ten. A woman of about thirty years was helping her cross-cousin (*hanini*) with a 'business party' (these are events where the host individual or group builds an enclosure and kills pigs. Those attending pay an entrance fee, and pay for the pork they eat. In the night there is a courting party and sometimes a string band.) Her task was to fry and sell pancakes. Her *hanini* thought she was putting too much flour in the pancakes for the price she was charging, and then became annoyed that she was joking with a group of men. He called her over to give him the money she had received, but she resented his brusque summons, and threw the money in his face. He was holding a pair of wooden tongs for removing cooking stones from the fire. He struck her twice across the abdomen, and twice on the neck. She became faint and collapsed. Women gathered around, tipped water on her, and held her hair (*mandari minaya*) to stop her spirit escaping. They said she was dying (*homara*). It was held to be significant that he had struck her across the side of the belly, damaging her womb (*waneigini anda*). They debated whether to take her to the health centre, but no one advocated this course of action very forcefully. Instead, women cradled her in their laps, splashing water on her head and rubbing the area where she had been struck with nettles. Her cross-cousin took little notice, maintaining that she was putting it on (*mo hondo hara*, literally 'deceiving'). The next morning she was much recovered, though very angry and talking of compensation. But she did not press her claim as she would be ashamed (*taga*) to ask for compensation from her cousin.

The flexibility of their ideas concerning the working of the body allows them to propose direct links between injuries and a variety of symptoms. Such links are usually mediated by movements of blood and pus. For example:

Case eleven. A man of about sixty years was engaged in a protracted dispute with a man whose sow had been serviced by the old man's boar, but this man had failed to pay the usual fee. Discussions about this payment became heated, ending in violence. In the fracas, one of his opponents lifted the old man across his shoulder, and threw him to the ground. He felt pain in this chest afterwards, but then recovered. A year later he developed dysentery. He related this to the injury to his chest, saying that the pressure on his chest had caused blood to settle, and later this blood had travelled down to cause his dysentery.

It is not usual to explain dysentery in terms of the *darama* (blood) of trauma, though in this instance the explanation was held to be plausible. It was also highly expedient, as the dispute was still current and the old man's adversary was also sick with an illness that he in turn ascribed to the blow he had received in the same fight. The case also introduced the idea that the implications of a blow may not emerge immediately. Indeed, the passage of many years between the blow and the illness does not exclude this diagnosis:

Case twelve. A middle-aged woman was very ill with chronic obstructive airways disease. On several occasions the rumour went around that she had died, and people gathered at her house to mourn, but each time she recovered. Her symptoms were of a feeling 'like a fire' in her head (*embone ira dagua bida*), a headache that 'moved' (*ema biya*), 'crackling' in her head which 'came down' into her neck (*ngidi ngudi lalu ibira ibira piyada*) making her throat dry, and stopping her eating. She was also very short of breath (*buhẽ timbuni timbuni*). She explained her illness as the product of a blow to the head with a door plank she had received from her husband some twenty-five years before. After the blow, she said that splinters had appeared in her mouth. Now 'it' (referring to some indeterminate pathological process) had gone down to her throat (*dende be ha daliara*) and made her short of breath. She had been to the health

126

centre for treatment on several occasions, but she was no longer willing to go as they always refused to take an X-ray of her head, where she felt the trouble mainly was. She felt that the X-ray would confirm her view of the illness, and would also be useful evidence in the discussions concerning compensation. Even without this evidence, the attribution of her illness to her husband's blow was accepted by his clan, and they gave her clan sixteen pigs as compensation. They felt that it was preferable to pay this compensation while she was still alive, as this would forestall any greater claims after her death.

Her stress upon headache as the key symptom in this respiratory illness could well have been influenced by her view of the aetiology, and her wish for compensation. These are important concerns in all such cases, and in some can dominate to the exclusion of other aspects of the illness, as in this case:

Case thirteen. A man's elder brother died, and he wanted to take his brother's wife as a second wife for himself. He ignored his own wife, spending his time with his dead brother's wife, helping to tend her garden, and eating with her. While they were eating, his first wife came at this second wife with a stick. The first wife was too slow, and herself received some blows to the neck with a stick. After that she was always complaining that her neck and chest hurt, and that she should receive compensation (*homaro abi dano bule ibabe*, 'I am dying, come to give compensation.') Her husband's group thought that she was exaggerating her suffering to get compensation, but they eventually agreed to give her five pigs to forestall any large claim which might follow her eventual death. This was some ten years after she had been struck. Before the case was settled she was often to be seen stooped and rubbing her belly and she visited the aid post frequently for treatment. Once the compensation had been paid she soon became quite well. This confirmed the belief of those that had paid her compensation that she had been lying (*kẽ haya*).

General features of the diagnosis
Age and sex distribution
The preponderance of women amongst the fifty-seven cases of this sort that I observed between 1977 and 1979 (table 19) is the product both of the degree of violence to which they are exposed, and of their response to this violence. There is a clear difference between the sexes in the sort of injuries to which they attribute illness. This is shown in table 20.

Men fought, and occasionally still fight, with bows and arrows. Violence to women, whether perpetrated by other women or by men, most commonly consists of blows with sticks. But we cannot presume that these differences in the rates of attribution of illness to violence reflect the pattern of violence. Many men received arrow wounds before pacification to which they could now attribute their illnesses. Fist-fights between men are not uncommon, particularly at 'business parties' where alcohol is available. The preponderance of women amongst these cases in part reflects the level of injury to which they are exposed, but it is also a product of the circumstances which leads to this violence. These cases concern violence which has a particular social significance to the sufferer.

Table 19 *Age and sex distribution in cases of illness attributed to wilfully inflicted injury*

Age	Sex m	f
0–4	1	1
5–9	1	1
10–19	1	1
20–29	2	12
30–39	3	9
40–49	3	8
50–59	5	5
60+	3	1
Total	19	38

Table 20 *Types of injury*

Types of injury	Sex m	f
Arrow wound	14	1
Blow(s) with a stick	2	21
Punches, slaps and kicks	2	9
Blow(s) with an axe or spade	–	4
Blow(s) with a stone	–	2
Bite	–	1
Road accident	1	–
Total	19	38

The broad difference between the sexes here is that the violence to which illness is attributed by women is largely grounded in interpersonal relations with her own close kin, particularly with her husband. In contrast, the men have suffered largely at the hands of those with whom they do not usually associate (table 21). In thirteen cases the injuries were arrow wounds received in warfare, and are thus the product of inter-group rather than interpersonal conflict. The six cases in males that I have listed as 'others' in table 21 comprise three cases where the injuries were caused by people previously unknown to the sufferer (a European motor cyclist, a drunken man attacking people at random and a mad woman), one case of an accidental arrow wound at the hands of a friend, a boy kicked in a school squabble, and only one case where the protagonists were both well known to each other, and engaged in a personal dispute (case eleven above). Of the thirty-nine female cases, only

Table 21 *Relationship between assailant and patient*

Relationship of assailant	Sex of sufferer	
	m	f
Enemy during war	13	1
Spouse		16
Co-wife		3
Brother's wife		2
Son		3
Brother		2
Mother's brother		1
Cross-cousin		1
Others	6	9

Table 22 *Medical relationship between the illness and the injury to which it is ascribed*

Medical view of aetiology	Cases	
	m	f
Direct consequence of recent injury	5	11
Delayed consequence of past injury	6	5
Illness not specifically related to recent injury	1	9
Illness not specifically related to past injury	7	13

three of the assailants were previously not well known to the victim: one an enemy during a raid, and two drunkards attacking people at random.

Relationship between the injury and the subsequent illness

Here I will examine the characteristics of these illnesses as they might be defined medically. My concern is to determine the relationship between the Huli view of aetiology in these illnesses and the medical view, and to indicate ways in which their interpretations of these illnesses may influence the significance attached to them. Some sort of trauma occurred in all these cases. First, I detail the relationship between that trauma and the subsequent illness, both in terms of the time that elapsed between them, and in terms of their connectedness according to the view of scientific medicine (table 22).

'Recent' includes injuries received within a month of the onset of the illness. 'Past' refers to any period longer than this. In many cases the injuries were received decades before the illness became severe. Illnesses directly referable to recent injuries both in Huli and medical terms include sequelae to arrow wounds in men, and fractures and bruising in women. Delayed consequences of past injuries include backache and arthritis which are the chronic aftermath of such traumata.

The illnesses which medically were not specifically related to the recent injuries to which they were ascribed comprised, in males, a case of dysentery, and in females, four acute infections (one with influenza, one with bronchitis and two with malaria), two cases of dysentery, one of cystitis and two cases of hysterical collapse. The illnesses which were medically not specifically related to the past injuries to which they were ascribed were, in males, one each of chronic obstructive airways disease, dysentery, enteritis necroticans, impotence, nephrotic syndrome, mongolism and Parkinson's disease. In females, such illnesses comprised four cases of chronic obstructive airways disease, five of debility, two of influenza, an abscess and a case of polyarthritis.

Several points emerge from this. Just under one half of these illnesses are medically referable to the injuries in terms of which they were explained. Those that are not explicable in terms of the injury show a wide range of diagnoses. The symptoms of chronic obstructive airways disease are explicable in the Huli view in terms of movements of pus, which 'bursts', giving sputum, and 'covers the *bu*', giving shortness of breath (p. 83). Where this illness is ascribed to past trauma it is differentiated from *amali*, and is not as feared.

In cases ascribed to beatings, patients stress the pain where they were beaten as a dominant symptom in the illness. The discomforts of malaria or influenza are interpreted in the light of the injury the patient has received. If there has been no injury, it is likely that they would have described these illnesses as *wabi warago* (malaria, p. 86), and *homama* (usually upper respiratory infections, p. 87) respectively. Dysentery is explicable in terms of movements of blood after a blow. Some of these illnesses are painful (cystitis, enteritis necroticans and polyarthritis) and were loosely related to the previous pain of an injury to that part.

Arrow wounds are of course dramatic events. Those to the abdomen were held responsible for the cases of impotence and nephrotic syndrome, and those to the neck, for Parkinson's disease. The case of mongolism and a case of bronchitis in a baby girl were each ascribed to the intra-uterine trauma of blows to the mothers' abdomens. The cases of collapse were held to be both grave and plausible despite relatively minor blows in accordance with the Huli view of human frailty. The cases of debility were ascribed in a general way to the beatings these women had received.

Both men and women may ascribe their illnesses to injury when the illness is severe and they have suffered some serious injury at whatever time in the past. But the ascription of less serious illnesses to injury is also interesting.

Illness grounded in social relations

Here we find that women have a marked tendency to ascribe relatively minor illnesses to injury. This is the case with those illnesses that follow fairly recently after the injury. Of female cases, 24% are of this sort, but only 5% of male.

Responses to such illnesses

Sufferers of these illnesses may seek symptomatic relief through the aspirins that are available at aid posts, or they may accept whatever medical or surgical treatments are offered at the health centre. But a major preoccupation in these illnesses is to resolve their social implications. When asked what is wrong with them, people who explain their illnesses in terms of injury give full accounts of the background to the fight, the number of blows they received with what weapon, but will volunteer little about the symptoms they have. In addition, they will commonly describe the state of negotiations for compensation. In the following example, a man has been admitted to the health centre for treatment for what medically was osteomyelitis, and unrelated to his old arrow wound.

Case fourteen. (I will quote a transcription of his response to my enquiring what was wrong with him.) There was a war long ago, and I was hit in the left ankle by an arrow. I was just helping the man who was responsible for the war (*wai tene*). When I had come to hospital I told this man that I had helped him before, and so he should give me money to buy a blanket to bring to hospital. But he would not, and he would not pay my fare on a truck, so I walked here. I helped him in his war, and he would not help me. You must give me a letter for me to show him when I take him to court. I want eight pigs compensation from him.

This man is concerned primarily with the unresolved matter of compensation for the injury to which he ascribes his illness. In some cases, such as case thirteen above, we could say that the illness constitutes little more than a ruse to gain compensation for an injury. In that particular case many people felt the woman was consciously lying about her condition for this reason. Where this process is subconscious we talk of 'hysterical overlay' or 'compensation neurosis'. This is likely to be a component of many of the cases included here. But while the Huli differentiate those who are 'tricking' (*mo hondo haga*) or 'lying' (*kẽ haga*) from those who are straightforwardly ill as a result of their injuries, they do not resort to theories of subconscious motivation in relating the state of the illness to the progress of litigation. For them, the social and physical components of these illnesses are inextricably linked, so that payment of compensation may be equated with treatment of the illness. Compensation is said to influence the physical lesion directly. For example, symptoms ascribed to an old arrow wound are said to be caused by the arrow 'growing' (*anda haga*) and 'moving' (*ema biaga*). When compensation has been given, the arrow is said no longer to grow or move (*timu anda nahaga*

131

Fig. 55 The judicial mode of therapy: compensation for a past injury

ema nabulebira). A woman asking for compensation said that 'when you get paid, your illness disappears' (*yolo miragola o tigi bi bereba haga*. Another woman said that she did not want much compensation, but was asking for just one pig to see if that would make her better (she was suffering from cor pulmonale). The full payment of compensation can be held to constitute a cure for that illness, so that any further problems will be seen as the product of a different illness (*warago mende*).

The wish for compensation is the norm in such cases (fig. 55). People say that this activity has got out of hand in recent years, that in the past people would have been satisfied with fifteen pigs where now they wanted sixty and that women now demand payment where previously no action would have been taken. The wish for compensation for injuries has probably not increased, but with pacification and now the village courts it is easier to press small claims. On the other hand, Christian influence is now becoming effective in discouraging people from seeking compensation. Most of the missions say that it is not Christian to demand compensation. Committed Christians accept this ruling, but others find themselves in a conflict of interests, as in this case:

Case fifteen. A woman of about sixty years had been beaten over the head with a stick by her brother's wife about twenty-five years before. Her own husband had died, and when she came back to live with her brother, his wife was jealous of the pigs and food he gave his sister. She now has shortness of breath (from emphysema). However, she

132

is certain she has no other illness, like *amali*, but is suffering from the blow to the head (*tigi tara ndo walime bene*, 'not another illness, beaten by the woman'). She says that if she got just one pig she would get a bit better (*tigi emene karulape holebira*), that she is baptised, so does not want full compensation. But the church leader said that even asking for one pig would cause her soul to 'go into the fire', so she did not pursue it.

Of these fifty-seven cases, in fourteen there was no intention of seeking compensation. Seven of these made their decision on Christian grounds, whether from their own conviction, or following the advice of church leaders. The other seven made no claim as they would have been 'ashamed' (*taga*) to claim compensation from the close kin responsible for their injuries.

An important consideration which leads to the settlement of claims is that after the sick person dies, their kin can be expected to claim considerably greater damages than would have been acceptable during their life. Once a claim is settled in life it is usually unacceptable to reopen negotiations after the person has died. Seventeen of these cases (29%) were settled to the satisfaction of all parties. The remaining twenty-six people were either engaged in discussions initiated with the intention of securing damages, or were waiting to assess the gravity of their illnesses. These discussions can become protracted for a number of reasons. In some cases the assailant or his clan may dispute that the blow was responsible for the illness. For example, in one of these cases a woman who had been struck by her husband in the back with an axe some thirty years before attributed her shortness of breath and cough to the blow. He disputed this, maintaining that she had *amali*. In some cases the parties reach agreement in principle, but the person held responsible procrastinates indefinitely over actually paying the damages.

These cases represent the most explicit extension of the medical system into other areas of social organisation. Whatever the particular changes in the sufferer's body, what concerns them is the assault to which the illness is attributed, and the resolution of the social ramifications of the condition.

The frequencies of particular relationships between patients and their assailants reflects both the sorts of relationship in which violence commonly occurs, as well as the significance attached to the physical trauma that results. We saw that men's assailants were most commonly adversaries in warfare with whom they had no previous close relationship. Women's most frequent assailants in these cases are their husbands. Some of these illnesses are straightforward products of a blow. A man strikes his wife's forearm with a stick, audibly breaking the bones, and leaving the arm visibly deformed. The bones are set, and the woman's kin receive damages for the harm done to her ('we gave you her skin but not her bones'). The blow is an expression of the tension between spouses within this marriage. The enmity between the parties, including their kin, is resolved by a presentation of wealth, according to the Huli ethos of exchange as a means of dispute settlement. We can distinguish these events in the social sphere from those occurring within her body, where union takes place between the properly opposed fragments regardless of the outcome of the damages suit.

But in most of these cases it is not possible to make such a clear analytical distinction between the disease process on the one hand and on the other the social events which preceded and followed from the disease. The presence of illness may constitute evidence of a legitimate grievance, and the resolution of the conflict represent treatment of the illness. In the case of women, such illnesses can be seen as a strategy, whether conscious or not, whereby they can draw attention to their grievances, and achieve an equitable resolution. I would suggest that the different patterns of such illnesses in men and women reflect differences in legal status as much as they reflect the different patterns of violence to which men and women are exposed. Men have other means of pursuing their ends, while women are in general expected to comply with the wishes of their fathers, brothers and husbands. The lack of incorporation with the husband's group is expressed in the idea that her kin have given him her flesh (*mbirini*) only, not her bones (*kuni*). This idiom also relates to the idea of agnatic origin, for it is bones which are said to derive from the sperm, and flesh from menstrual blood. In damaging a woman, her husband is potentially exceeding his rights over her. An illness accepted as the product of a beating may lead to her receiving the support of her kin in her grievance against her husband. If the suit is successful, the payment of pigs that he must make to her kin represents an acknowledgement of the impropriety of his treatment of her. Amongst people who have such a finely tuned sense of equivalence in their dealings with each other, the imbalance of an unrequited injury is a major source of distress.

Women who are the subject of violence do not necessarily wish for compensation. Even if they react vehemently at the time of the assault, often collapsing and indicating in other ways the severity of the attack, they may later be unwilling to initiate the process which may lead to the payment of compensation. This is expressed as 'shame' (*taga*) at asking for retribution from someone with whom they are closely associated. (The Christian motive for forgoing compensation need not concern us here.) The women who forswore compensation through *taga* were attacked by men in the following relationships to them: two by brothers, two by sons and one each by her cross-cousin and her husband. Compensation claims against consanguineal kin are thus rare. Besides their impropriety, expressed as a feeling of 'shame', large claims between close kin are avoided as there can be no clear division between the parties according to relationship with the protagonists. This problem becomes unavoidable only where death occurs. The case where a woman did not want compensation for an illness she attributed to a beating at the hands of her husband was interesting in that they normally had a conspicuously harmonious relationship, which she evidently did not want to put at risk by initiating the potentially divisive process of claiming against him.

The implications of the ascription of illness to injury centre on the Huli concept of responsibility, and the events that follow from the attribution of responsibility. The likelihood of illness and claims for compensation following from his beating his wife are real deterrents to a Huli husband. He is also careful not to lead her by his ill-treatment to damage herself, as in this case:

Case sixteen. A man and his two wives were all living within the same homestead, though in separate houses. There were frequent arguments between the co-wives. The husband usually sided with his first wife, and beat the second. One morning an argument began over the harvesting of greens. The second wife saw the first taking greens from her garden, and objected. Their husband arrived and struck the second wife. Later in the morning this wife went to the husband's house to get a K5 note she had given him for safe keeping. (Kina: £1.00 = K1.50.) He found her, and accused her of also stealing K20 of his from the house. The first wife joined in, saying that he was not a man to accuse groundlessly, and that she had the money in her bag. The accused woman handed over the bag, saying that the money was not there, but it might be in her hand. With that, she took an axe, chopped off her right index finger, and threw it at the first wife. The injured woman returned to her natal parish. Her relations took the position that had her husband accused her correctly, then there was nothing more to be said. But as it seemed that he had accused her wrongly, he was responsible for the injury, and must compensate them with fifteen pigs, of which she could keep one sow 'for the pain' (*tandaganaga*). She said that she would go back to him if he compensated her, otherwise she wanted a divorce. A year later she was still living at her natal parish and the affair was unresolved.

It is not common for women to mutilate themselves in this way. In all I saw four similar cases. But the knowledge that they may do so can restrain men in disputes with women. An even greater threat is suicide. Whatever the personal consequences, a woman's suicide is a serious blow to her husband's clan if it appears to follow from his ill-treatment. He is held as responsible as if he had murdered her. Suicide is primarily a female act. Of the twenty-six completed suicides known to me, twenty-two were women. Where women's means of gaining redress are limited, suicide represents a desperate means of retribution, for they can be confident that major compensation will be given, as in this case:

Case seventeen. Her brother's pig damaged a woman's garden. She sent her daughter to return the pig, and tell her brother what had happened. The brother's wife was at home, and she became angry, accusing the child of trying to steal the pig. When the child's mother heard this, she went to her brother's wife, and told her not to insult her daughter, but save her accusations for her. The argument became heated, and at one point the brother's wife insulted the sister, calling her old and grey-haired (she was about fifty) and saying that she was 'without shame' (*dagua he taga nahe*). She was very offended at these insults, and went off home. She was found the next day, having hanged herself from a pig rope. She had twisted some grey hairs into the noose as a sign (*yobage*) of the grounds of her suicide. Her brother's wife was held responsible, and her clan paid compensation of ninety pigs to the woman's clan.

Illness grounded in social relations

A wife is enabled through compensation to gain redress and balance in an otherwise imbalanced relationship. Such claims may follow inevitably from the actions of the husband, where he breaks her arm in a quarrel, for example. Or the wife's behaviour may lead to redress, through acceptance of the interpretation that an illness follows from ill-treatment. Such means of redress may be quite conscious. The extreme and final form of such action is the suicide of the aggrieved wife which leads to very large claims for compensation from her kin.

Illness and the emotions

Hulis often speak of the emotions as if these are autonomous forces within the individual. The effects of strong emotions may be regarded as being beyond the control of the individual harbouring them. Any implications of the emotional state, including illness, may be explained in terms of the emotion itself rather than any intention to cause harm on the part of the person experiencing it. Liability for the effects of emotional states may be assigned to the person held responsible for eliciting strong feeling in another. I will examine these aspects of the Huli view of the emotions as this is revealed in illnesses attributed to fright (*gi*), sorrow (*dara*), desire (*hame*), anger (*keba*) and spite (*madane*). I have already described their view that these emotions, as well as happiness (*turu*), arise from the *bu*, the life force. The individual experiences emotional states as a rising and falling of the *bu* within the body. This intimate association between emotions and the basic drive is one factor in the relationship between illness and the emotions. Another is the effect of strong emotion, particularly fright, upon the spirit.

Fright

Illness is attributed to fright in many cultures (e.g. Rubel 1964 on *susto* in Latin America and Kleinman 1980 on *ching* in Taiwan). Hulis see life as a fragile state, and its fluctuations are paralleled by the ebb and flow of the spirit (*dinini*). In illness the *dinini* may detach itself from the body, or conversely illness may follow if the spirit becomes detached. It may be said of a sickly person 'his spirit has gone; just an empty skin is left' (*dinini pu wahene bamu andanehangu nga*). Particularly in children the spirit is skittish. It is easily frightened out of the body, leaving the person weakened and at risk. The rite known as *angawai* may be performed to recall the spirit into the body. It is thought to leave through the anterior fontanelle in babies, and the same area in adults. *Angawai* involves ministrations to this area, and the hair over this part of the crown may be held when someone is thought to be dying. This prevents the spirit leaving, thus allowing the person to recover. Fright (*gi*) is particularly dangerous in children. The word for startle, *mogo lara*, carries

136

the implication that the spirit has fled the body. Illness and death can be ascribed to this cause, and the individual responsible for the fright held liable for compensation payments. I will first illustrate the common features of illnesses ascribed to fright by describing one case:

Case eighteen. A man gave his second wife some money (K6). His first wife objected to her co-wife being favoured in this way, and a quarrel developed. Both the husband and second wife struck her while she was holding her baby of nine months. The next day the baby developed diarrhoea, followed by fever and shortness of breath. He became severely ill (with pneumonia), and was admitted to Tari Health Centre. The mother said that the child had started with fright (*mogo laya*) when she had been struck, and so his spirit had fled his body. He recovered, and there were no repercussions.

I saw a total of ten cases of illness ascribed to this cause. They all occurred in children under the age of three years, seven of whom were under one year of age, the period when the attachment of the spirit to the body is particularly tenuous.

The characteristic feature of these illnesses is that the child was caused to start, and soon afterwards became ill. Such an experience is essential for this diagnosis to be selected. But the nature of the illness may also be important. All these illnesses were acute and severe. Six were cases of lower respiratory infections, referred to by their mothers as '*bu*', three of diarrhoea (two with blood), and one who became unconscious:

Case nineteen. A boy of three became feverish, and then increasingly sleepy. His limbs shook briefly (*duru laya*) and he became quite unconscious. His mother thought that he had started (*mogo laya*) in church that morning, and attributed his illness to this. They held a prayer meeting at which they killed some chickens, and sprinkled holy water around their house. The child improved a little, but they were still concerned. They took him to Tari Health Centre, where he was treated for cerebral malaria. He recovered.

This illness was ascribed to *mogo laya* though nothing dramatic had occurred to frighten the child. The key symptom here is the fit. In three of these ten cases the mothers knew of no particular events which had precipitated their children's illnesses. Besides the case I have just described, one mother thought that her son of ten months may have been dropped when she had left him to be looked after by other children, though the children denied this. Another thought that her daughter of seven months may have been frightened by a dream. But one of these three children shook (*duru laya*) and the other two had convulsions (*nogo, bibi,* or *biango bibi*). There is thus an interaction between ideas concerning the concepts of causation of this illness and expectations of what constitutes its typical expression. This is comparable to the interaction between the various elements which were shown to be determinants in the diagnosis of *agali*, and can be illustrated in a similar diagram (fig. 56).

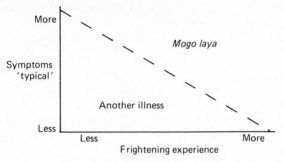

Fig. 56 Symptomatology and preceding experience in the diagnosis of *mogo laya*

The believed fragility of children, the tenuous attachment of their souls, is one expression of the incorporation of the startle reaction into a Huli theory of pathogenesis. A second concerns the nature of the symptoms of this illness. The Moro reflex, with its jerky movements of rapid abduction and extension of the arms with opening of the hands, and the startle response which replaces it by the fourth month, have some similarities with convulsions and rigors. When children have these symptoms parents may suspect that the child has been startled. I would suggest that these neurophysiological responses provide some phenomenological basis for this diagnostic category. It is interesting to note that convulsions may be a feature of fright illness in children elsewhere. The symptoms of the Chinese fright illness *haák-ts'an* described by Topley (1970) include crying, a raised temperature and irritability, but it is also characterised by convulsive jerks. Hong Kong mothers also fear that fright will cause the child's soul to leave the body. Like Huli mothers they are particularly careful to protect their children from this threat for the first hundred days of life, and it may be worth noting that the Moro reflex is lost after this period. However, the symptomatology in *mogo laya* is only one feature amongst the others I will go on to examine, and convulsions are not pathognomonic of this condition. All convulsions are not attributed to fright, and those diagnosed as suffering from *mogo laya* may not have convulsions. The key feature of the diagnosis is the belief that the soul has departed the body.

These illnesses may have legal consequences similar to those I have discussed in relation to illnesses ascribed to assaults. Whoever is held to be responsible for startling the child may be liable for compensation. We must therefore consider the possibility that the ascription of these illnesses to fright may be influenced by such implications of the diagnosis. If we look at the relationship between the mother and the person whose actions frightened her child, we find that in four cases the husband is held responsible. These followed quarrels between the spouses, three of which ended with the husband striking his wife while she was holding the child that subsequently became sick, and one where the husband set fire to his wife's house. She escaped with her daughter, but the fright she suffered caused the child to become ill. As with illnesses ascribed directly to assaults, this preponderance of violence against wives by husbands in the causation of these children's illnesses reflects the patterns of disturbance in Huli society. But the ascription of illness to such incidents should also be seen as a means of redress by wives in an unequal relationship with their husbands. Had any of these four children died, the mother's clan could be expected to demand compensation from the father. In fact, the only child with this diagnosis who did die was one of those who had no clear history of a shock (the baby girl whose mother thought she may have been frightened in a dream). There was therefore no ascription of blame, and no legal repercussions.

All ten of these children were brought to health department facilities for treatment. In addition, Christian services were held for five of them. As is usually the case in young children, none of them was treated by traditional means, which here would have meant *angawai*, the returning and attaching of the spirit to the body.

By adulthood the spirit is less easily dislodged. Where fright has serious ill-effects that person is presumed to be especially vulnerable for an additional reason. Any particular sensitivity to fright is held to indicate that such a person must harbour *kuyunda* (see pp. 101, 111–13). Though not a case of illness, the following incident and its interpretation illustrate this view.

Case twenty. A young man and the girl he was courting (his *lawini*, 'betrothed') were walking through the forest with some other people of their own age. It was a gay outing, and for fun the young man secretly cut ahead of the others to surprise them further down the track. He jumped out at his *lawini* who was so terrified that she fainted. She soon recovered, and the incident was treated as a joke. But when he told his mother about it later she advised him not to marry the girl, as she probably had *kuyanda*. If he beat her or worried her the *kuyanda* might burst (*tuguda holebira*) causing her to die. He would then have to compensate her clan. He took her advice, and broke off the engagement.

None of the cases of illness that I saw which were ascribed to fright that was clearly attributable to an individual's actions resulted in death. Discussions concerning compensation were initiated in some of the cases where someone was held to be culpable, but these were dropped when the sick child recovered. To show that the threat of compensation demands in such cases is real, I will describe an incident that occurred some ten years before.

Case twenty-one. A group of adolescent boys shared a house. One of them was always afraid to go out at night. When there were chores to be done, such as fetching more firewood, he always refused to leave the house. They planned a trick for him. One of the boys stayed out one night, and covered himself with phosphorescent fungus (*ira manda*). The others told the nervous boy that there was some cooked pig for him, but they had left it in a shelter outside. The thought of pork caused him to overcome his fear of the dark, and he went out. While he was looking for the pork, the fluorescent boy came towards him, picked him up, and carried him towards the forest. The victim of the prank collapsed. He was later found to be dead. 'His *kuyanda* peeled open, and he died' (*kuyanda lagala homene*), though he had not been suspected of having *kuyanda* previously. All the boys in the house were held responsible for his death. Compensation of 120 pigs was paid to the dead boy's clan.

Desire

The word *hame* can most generally be translated as 'desire'. This may be a simple desire for food, but extends to stronger feelings including cupidity, lust and yearning. The commonest circumstances where *hame* leads to illness is where one person covets the food of another. The combination of a hungry glance and the act of swallowing are sufficient to cause illness in the person whose food it is. This is known as *lingi*, which means literally 'give me what is there'.

Case twenty-two. A man's mother and first wife prepared the afternoon meal without the help of the second wife, who had gone off to market. When she came back she was hungry, but her mother-in-law would not give her any food as she had not helped with the cooking. The next day the first wife's three-year-old son developed fever, vomiting and diarrhoea. His mother assumed that her co-wife had glanced at him hungrily while he was eating, and so caused *lingi*. She was angry with her mother-in-law for denying the woman food, but not with the woman to whose covetous glance she ascribed her son's illness. The child was given medical treatment, and the *lingi* was also removed by traditional means (*lingi duguaga*). The child recovered.

Lingi is accepted with unusual equanimity. In contrast to most conditions which are in some sense attributable to the actions of others, there is little interest in apportioning blame, and in no case was there any litigation. *Hame* is regarded as an inevitable response to the sight of food, so that the individual is not seen as culpable for any ill effects that follow from it. One woman said 'How could we take anyone to court when we all have eyes?' Inasmuch as *lingi* entails an offence, this may be seen more as improper niggardliness on the part of the owner of the food than any malicious intent in the person whose vain swallowing led to the illness.

As with fright, desire has its most dire effects in association with *kuyanda*. The *kuyanda* within a person's chest is itself attributed with an insatiable appetite. The glance of such a person is particularly likely to lead to *lingi*. Some say that *lingi* can be caused only by those with *kuyanda*, but opinions differ on this point.

Case twenty-three. A six-year-old girl became ill with diarrhoea and abdominal pain. The day before the girl's mother had noticed another girl, the sixteen-year-old daughter of her husband's brother, watching her own daughter while she ate a banana. She assumed that this had caused *lingi*. The mother had not heard the details of the other girl's birth, and so did not know whether she had swallowed blood, but she suspected that she had *kuyanda*, as many children seemed to get ill when she was around.

140

Illness grounded in social relations

I saw twelve cases of illness which were ascribed to *lingi*. All were in children. Five of these were under one year, three aged two years, two aged three, and one each of four and six years. The theoretical description of *lingi* is of an abdominal illness. The covetousness (*hame*) of the person coveting the food is projected at the moment they swallow into the belly of the child with the food, giving diarrhoea and abdominal pain. The cases here generally conform to this picture. Diarrhoea with or without vomiting was the dominant symptom in ten of these children. The other component in this diagnosis is the suspicion or certainty that the child was the object of a covetous glance. The two children whose illnesses were not 'typical' of *lingi* (they both had *bu*, clinically pneumonia) had been the objects of clearly observed covetous glances, illustrating the same relationship between symptomatology and concepts of causation that we have seen in other illnesses where a particular symptomatology is expected.

The source of *lingi*, the individual coveting the food, was not specified in four of these cases. One child's mother thought that her son's illness was self-induced.

Case twenty-four. It is usual to begin to offer suitable foods at about four months. When her son of two months developed diarrhoea and vomiting his mother felt that he had been watching her eat, and desired her food so much that he had swallowed, and made himself ill.

The remaining seven cases were all attributed to the cupidity of women. Theoretical statements concerning *lingi* do not specify that it can only be caused by women, but amongst the instances that came to my notice men's covetousness was not suspected once. This conforms with the negative attribution of women as desirous creatures. Their own acceptance of the view that they have the capacity to harm is indicated by the fact that in *lingi* women suspect only other women. Men's opinions were relatively unimportant in these cases. Most of the women suspected were unrelated to the mothers of the sick child (*tara*, 'others'). For example:

Case twenty-five. A three-year-old girl developed abdominal pain and swelling (*lumbi hada tagi*, literally 'her umbilicus became untied and came outside'). The day before they had been at a funeral feast (*nogo homane*). They had eaten pork, and the girl had been covered in pig fat. On the road home they had passed some women from another parish who had joked about the greasy state of the girl. When she became ill, her mother assumed that one of these women had thought of the pork that the girl had eaten, wanted some herself, and swallowed. So the girl had been affected by *lingi*.

The three women who were relations of the mother of a sick child comprised a co-wife, a father's brother's wife, and a husband's brother's daughter. This indicates little about such relationships, only that these women happened to be present when others were eating, though they were not included in the meal.

141

Illness grounded in social relations

Gastro-intestinal illness is common in young children (see fig. 32), and covetousness too is a common feeling. This raises the question of why I only saw twelve cases of *lingi*. In fact I think that *lingi* is diagnosed more commonly than this suggests, but as there is no redress against the person felt to be responsible, people do not voice their suspicions publicly. This could lead to dissension with no benefit. It was only by chance that I heard that the mother whose daughter's illness I described above ascribed it to *lingi* (case twenty-three). She had come to me for treatment, and as I knew her quite well I asked her in some detail about her daughter's illness. During this discussion I had asked her directly about *lingi*, and she said that *lingi* was not the cause. Later I happened to overhear her telling her sister about the circumstances that had led to the illness. When I admitted hearing this, she laughed, and said that she had not wanted to air her suspicions in case it led to trouble.

Also, more women might admit their suspicions of *lingi* if they were still practicing the traditionally specific means of treatment (*lingi duguaga*). This is a very simple and widely known cure, where the healer recites a spell, then pulls out some hairs from the top-knot of the child with his teeth. This was applied in three of these cases. But the commonest treatment for gastro-intestinal illnesses in children is Western medicine, and to receive this the mothers need not admit to their suspicions as to the cause of the child's diarrhoea. In all twelve of these cases Western medicine was used. Four of the mothers also held prayer meetings.

Sorrow

The Huli term which includes sorrow and grief amongst its referents is *dara*. *Daraba* ('how sad') is a common observation following illness or death. But it is also used in a light-hearted way as a comment upon anything touching or poignant. For example, the news that a five-year-old girl wanted to kill her only pig for another child's birthday party was met by cries of '*daraba*'. The facial expression which accompanies this comment combines pathos and amusement: eyes half shut, nose wrinkled and mouth smiling, as if tasting a piquant dish. The sorrow (*dara*) of bereavement may be painful, but *dara* usually does no harm. Illness amongst survivors may instead be interpreted in terms of the pathological effects of their yearning for the deceased. This yearning is again known as *hame*, an overwhelming desire for the return of the dead person, and for the help and sustenance that they offered while they were alive.

Case twenty-six. A woman of about thirty fainted, and her relations were very concerned about her condition. Her sister had been buried two days before. When she recovered she said that she had been yearning for her sister, and fell unconscious (*hame lowa oda pe haya*). They said that if she had *kuyanda*, her *hame* could have killed her.

142

Illness grounded in social relations

Case twenty-seven. A man of about sixty came to me for medicine to 'hold his skin' (*tingini yani helo*). His wife had just died, and they had been very attached to each other (*gubalini haga*, literally 'she stays in my lung', an image of affection and trust). His main complaint was of sleeplessness.

One aspect of this man's concern was the fear that his wife's spirit might return to claim him. Traditionally, he would have performed a rite to protect himself from this (such as *dalo ira hangaga*), but as a Christian he was forbidden to do so. In addition his yearning (*hame*) for his dead wife could also harm him. Interestingly, this ill-effect of conjugal bereavement is statistically demonstrable. Huli widowers show an increased mortality rate in the first year after bereavement (Frankel and Smith, 1982).

Anger and spite

Anger (*keba*) is principally implicated in the sorts of illnesses involving self-destructive behaviour that I have already referred to, particularly self-inflicted wounds and suicide. *Keba* can also cause a *kuyanda* to burst, but I heard of only one case where a woman's collapse was ascribed to this. Her *kuyanda* was 'bound' (*hubua haya*) and she recovered.

Those who feel let down by others experience the emotion of *madane*. If a man promises to come to a court hearing to support the case of another, then fails to turn up, the man he has let down will feel *madane*. An aggrieved man experiencing *madane* may then retaliate surreptitiously. This can lead to illness. For example, in one of the cases of *nambis poisin* that I describe below (case thirty-one) the sorcerer's motive was *madane*. But *madane* is not said to have any direct effect upon the person experiencing it. And any effects it has upon others are indirect, being mediated by some clandestine act. Sorcery may be suspected, but this is very rare. More usually the person who acts from *madane* acts more directly, by sprinkling broken glass on a path used by the person who has failed him, for example, or secretly slashing the tyres of a car which did not stop to give him a lift. The fear of the possible implications of *madane*, like the fear of *lingi*, can influence people to act more generously to others than they may otherwise wish.

Explicit links such as I have described between personal feelings and the moral order appear to be widespread in New Guinea Highlands cultures (e.g. Newman 1964:261–2). Melpa concepts of this sort have been analysed in the most detail (A. J. Strathern 1968, 1977, 1981; M. Strathern 1968, 1972). The Melpa *noman*, 'individual capacity, will, intention, desire, motivation, understanding, social consciousness and human sociality' (A. J. Strathern 1981), is very similar to the Huli *mini*. The *noman* may experience *popokl*, a serious kind of anger, which can lead to sickness and even to death. But in Mount Hagen this ill effect of the state of the *noman* is mediated by ancestral ghosts. The ghosts 'look into the person's *noman* and, seeing the *popokl*,

143

intervene through pity for him' (M. Strathern 1968:557). The sickness elicits sympathy, and may cause the person whose actions are responsible for the *popokl* to relent. But when *popokl* is taken to extremes death may result, indicating ghostly disapproval of excessive egocentricity.

The Huli too are concerned by the dangers of unchecked individualism, and also have limited means of discouraging the pursuit of self-interest. But the penalties for egocentricity that I have discussed are not mediated by ghosts or spirits: they act directly. An extreme example of such direct harm is *tawaneme baya*. When someone is already sick from whatever cause they can die suddenly if anyone they have wronged comes into their presence. The wronged person is characteristically unaware that they have been abused, though they speculate about the offence (usually adultery or theft) after such a death. The patient is 'struck down by heat' (*poboneme baya* or *tawaneme baya*). This is said to happen directly, though a similar outcome can follow from the displeasure of the spirit Datagaliwabe (see pp. 154, 184).

These spontaneous penalties for impropriety contrast with the ghostly interest in their descendants' conduct found in Mount Hagen. Huli shades and spirits are thought to influence the living (see chapter 9) but they rarely intervene spontaneously in people's affairs to ensure proper conduct. This contrast with Mount Hagen may relate to the greater mobility of Hulis between parishes, and to their more pedantic interpretation of descent. The *mi* (mystical divination-substance) of a Mount Hagen tribe is an 'overarching symbol of identity' (A. J. Strathern 1972), and is 'intimately related to the ultimate origins of its tribe and so to its tribesmen's unity and singularity, founded upon the supposed fact of their common origins' (ibid:40–1). The *mi* is invoked in oaths, and perjury punished by death. This influence of the *mi* is supported by the ghosts, who ensure that the *mi* is not taken lightly.

Huli parishes are defined in terms of their founding ancestors, but with their deep genealogies and greater willingness to accept non-cognates, protagonists in a dispute would be subject to the putative influence of different sets of ghosts. The parish ancestors are important in causing generalised benefits or harm to parish members, but in interpersonal disputes excessive egocentricity may lead directly to harm and even death, without the intervention of the spirits.

Sorcery

A number of techniques for wilfully harming others by indirect means are known to the Huli. The most potent is to enter into a covenant with a spirit (*dama*), and to select victims for the spirit to kill. *Dama* Toro is pre-eminent as the destroyer of the enemies of men who have enlisted his support, but other spirits may also perform this service. I will return to such compacts when I consider the relationship between men and spirits below. Other types of indirect wilful harm, those that do not involve spirits, are known generically as *tomia*, and it is these that I will consider here. Most of these techniques are said to originate from the surrounding cultural groups. This is also the case with Toro, which is a Duna spirit and more dangerous than Huli spirits. I will first outline the main forms of *tomia* before considering their place in modern illness behaviour.

Hambu sorcery is said to originate with the Duguba peoples to the south. The sorcerer positions himself so that his unwitting victim is in the direction of the setting sun. He concentrates his gaze towards his victim, and whispers the *hambu* spell. In this spell he names each part of his victim's body, beginning at the toenail and ending at the head. After each body part he says 'I crush it' (*biala baro*) or 'I smash it to pieces' (*tuguda baro*). At each part he also snaps a piece off the end of a small twig that he holds hidden in his hand. The victim should then sicken quickly, suffering pain in his 'damaged' bones and eventual death, unless the *hambu* sorcery is removed.

Geria sorcery is also said to stem from the Duguba peoples. The sorcerer bespells a lizard, and hangs it over his fire to smoke. As it dries out so his victim will languish. If he breaks up the dried carcass and throws it into the fire, the victim will die. A sorcerer who wishes to spare his declining victim immerses the lizard in water. Men unable to muster the bride-price for a woman they desire were said to cause her to sicken with *geria* sorcery, so that she would not be sought by other men. When he had accumulated sufficient pigs, he released the *geria* by placing the lizard in water.

Besides *dama* Toro, the Duna people to the west are the source of *daburuli* sorcery, the only traditional type of leavings sorcery that I heard described. It is also known as Duna *tomia*. The characteristic feature of those who had been attacked by this means was the swelling of the part most closely associated with the leavings: the hand if peelings were taken, the lips if pandanus shells, the belly if faeces had been taken and so on.

From Obena (the Enga to the north) comes *yaborolo* sorcery. The sorcerer spiked pig fat onto a reed, wrapped this into a bundle with phosphorescent fungus and a ginger-like plant brought from the north, and threw the bundle into the fire, calling his enemy's name.

The word *tomia* can also be used specifically to refer to the main form of indirect wilful killing that is not said to have arisen elsewhere. The toxic agent in *tomia* of this specifically Huli sort is menstrual blood. This could be administered to the victim in one of two ways. In the first, the man wishing to kill surreptitiously selected an attractive young clanswoman and paid her to seduce his enemy on the first day of her menstrual period. Alternatively, he commissioned her to place blood from the first day of her period onto a leaf, and put the leaf in a bamboo. He allowed this to dry in his house, and later, handling the material with great care, he contaminated his victim's food or drinking vessel. This method entails no spells or other ritual acts. Just 'the smell of blood causes the man to die' (*puga ngubi biagome agali homolebira*). When they heard that the victim was dead, the clan of the man who had worked *tomia* staged a *mali* dance. The syncopated drumming of the two lines of dancers carries long distances. The dead man's relations were thus informed who was claiming responsibility for his death. Men say that in former times they were careful not to leave their drinking gourds about, and that one of them would always stay to guard an oven while food was cooking, lest an enemy performed *tomia*. But now there is little evidence of such vigilance.

With the exception of *hambu*, the techniques I have mentioned so far (including Toro) were not invoked in any case of illness that came to my notice. I will consider cases of *hambu* before describing the type of sorcery that has largely replaced former diagnoses of this sort.

Cases of hambu sorcery

I saw four cases where *hambu* was diagnosed: a man of about thirty-five years, and three women aged twenty-five, twenty and sixteen years.

Case twenty-eight. A woman of twenty-five went to Tari market to sell a pig. She returned home in the afternoon, and that night she developed aches all over, headache and a fever. She lived near a traditionalist who told her that someone had performed *hambu* on her while she was at market, and that it would be better if she let him perform the ceremony to remove it (*hambu duguaga*). She complied, and recovered.

All four cases shared several key features. First, their illnesses came on quickly, and involved pains throughout the body, severe headache and fever. (Three were probably cases of influenza, and the other had a blood slide positive for malaria.)

Secondly, the illnesses developed soon after those affected had been away from home, or while they were away. Three of them had been to markets, and assumed that they had been singled out by some unspecified enemy for *hambu* attack. The fourth was the wife of an administration employee who was working on the Papuan Plateau. *Hambu* is thought to derive from the Duguba, so when she became ill her husband assumed she had been attacked by one of the Duguba (in this case Etoro) people amongst whom they were living.

Thirdly, these cases show the importance of specialist practitioners in ascribing traditional diagnoses, and causing the illnesses so diagnosed to be treated by traditional means. In three of these cases the sufferers were close associates of men who knew how to perform the ritual removal of *hambu* sorcery (*hambu duguaga*), and who had stayed outside the church. All three patients agreed to undergo treatment, though they were Christians. In the fourth case, the woman who contracted her illness whilst living amongst the Etoro, the diagnosis was selected partly on the basis of her symptoms, but primarily through Huli assumptions concerning Duguba skills in a type of sorcery which was thought to have originated with them. Her husband tried unsuccessfully to obtain a healer to remove the *hambu*. She was so ill that she was taken to the health centre. Her illness was later given a Christian interpretation, and I shall return to it below (case forty-seven).

Modern forms of sorcery

Whatever their former concern for enemy sorcery, they now suspect the traditional types of sorcery in very few cases of illness. Instead there is growing concern about a new sort of sorcery which they refer to as *nambis poisin*. The Huli use the pidgin word *nambis* (coast) to refer to anywhere outside the Huli area where they may go to find work. The *nambis* thus begins at Mendi, the provincial capital, and extends via Mount Hagen to all parts of the mainland and islands. *Poisin* is the pidgin word for sorcery. The Huli fear some cultural groups more than others for their prowess as sorcerers. The people of Kagua and Samurai have particularly bad reputations. But whatever differences there may be amongst all the various *nambis* peoples, the Huli conceive of *nambis poisin* as a discrete entity. Its key feature is object intrusion. Traditionally, men were not thought to be capable of effecting this, although object intrusion was a traditionally known cause of illness arising from attacks by *dama* Ibatiri. This spirit characteristically inhabited pools of water in the forest, and anyone going near a forest pool ran the risk of being shot with one of Ibatiri's arrows (*tawa timu*). The resulting illness was usually discomforting rather than fatal. Cure entailed the removal of the arrow (*tawa timu duguaga*), which I will discuss in more detail when I consider the influence of spirits below. In this ceremony, Ibatiri's arrows were drawn into bundles of red leaves (*baraba, Begonia media*) where they were visible as small pieces of twig, charcoal, stone or grass.

Now men are also thought to be capable of causing illness by projecting material into the body. Sorcerers may be from *nambis* themselves. Or they may be Hulis who have bought these new techniques while away working. *Nambis poisin* may be treated by a ceremony that is indistinguishable from the traditional ceremony to remove *tawa timu* (fig. 57), or otherwise by new techniques. The matter that they remove may be similar to that which is held to constitute Ibatiri's arrow, or it may include modern materials such as glass, nails and wire. *Nambis poisin* is now included in the general term for sorcery, *tomia*.

Cases of nambis poisin

I saw eight cases of illness where this diagnosis was applied unequivocally. Two of these cases relate specifically to the life of Huli labourers away at *nambis*.

Fig. 57 Removing *nambis poisin*

Case twenty-nine. A forty-year-old man had worked on a tea plantation near Mount Hagen until about three months before he became ill, primarily with weakness. While at the plantation he had had an argument with a man from Kagua. The foreman often told him to work harder, and then the Kagua man started to urge him on as well. This angered him, as the man from Kagua was also only a labourer. The Huli clouted the other with the handle of his spade. Other Hulis warned him at the time that his adversary might take revenge through *poisin*. When he became ill he assumed that this was the cause. He went to Tari Health Centre, where he was treated for malaria and anaemia, but he decided to have the *poisin* removed as well. He found a Huli who removed the *poisin* using the same rite as in *tawa timu duguaga*. In one of the bundles they found a cow's tooth. The patient was satisfied that this was the *poisin*.

The following case indicates the level of distrust that may exist between men from different parts of the country.

Case thirty. A man of about fifty became ill while picking tea near Mount Hagen. He felt pain under his ribs, and assumed that he was the victim of *nambis poisin* at the hands of a Kagua man. A Chimbu man had a good reputation as a healer, so he paid him K10 to remove the *poisin*. He gave a spell, and sucked over the site of the pain through holes he had made in taro and cordyline leaves. He removed some twigs and some grey hairs. The man recovered. He returned home, but when his symptoms recurred he felt that the Chimbu healer had tricked him. He had heard that such men heal you, but that as you are leaving their presence they project more *poisin* so that you must return at a later date and pay them again.

Enmities between Hulis can now lead to suspicion of *nambis poisin*, as in this case:

Case thirty-one. A man of about sixty developed a polyarthritis. He was concerned that a man with whom he had quarrelled had either performed *nambis poisin*, or had paid some other Huli who had learned the technique to do it for him. His condition improved with health centre treatment, so he did not arrange for the *poisin* to be removed. Nor did he make his suspicions public.

This was the only case I saw where one Huli suspected a particular Huli individual of wilfully inflicting harm by indirect means. As was the case with *hambu*, on the other occasions where *nambis poisin* was diagnosed no individual sorcerer was suspected. All five remaining cases were in women. Also as with *hambu* sorcery, the diagnosis of *nambis poisin* can be influenced strongly by the opinions and special skills of people with whom the patient associates:

Case thirty-two. A thirty-year-old woman had been ill for some ten months with abdominal pain, weakness and backache. She spent several weeks in Tari Health Centre. She was given blood transfusions and other treatments, but when she returned home she still had abdominal pain. A distant kinsman had spent some time working at Kavieng, where he had learned to remove *poisin*. When he saw her he told her mother that her chest looked sunken, which was a sign that she had *poisin* (*galukini liayaya tomia nga*). He agreed to remove it, for which he charged K24.

Case thirty-three. Another woman in the parish section of the woman whose case I have just described was also suffering from abdominal pain and swelling. Her brother saw the treatment that the first woman received, and told her that she might have *poisin* too. She asked the same healer to treat her.

People have little experience with this diagnosis, and they therefore take particular note of the opinions of the specialists able to treat it. One woman underwent five different treatments for *poisin*, again with abdominal pain, before the healer declared that all the *poisin* had been removed. He had removed glass, wire, stones, fragments of china and hair from her abdomen. When her symptoms persisted he examined her and declared that she was free of *poisin*, but there was 'something else there still' (*mbiriale wiaabo*).

The direction of sorcery accusations may reveal lines of enmity that are structural to the society in question. In the Huli case it is striking that it is exceedingly rare for victims to specify the suspected source of the sorcery that is harming them. Further, traditional patterns of sorcery accusation are breaking down, to be replaced by suspicions of novel techniques perpetrated by outsiders.

9

Spirits and God

The spirits, now including the Holy Spirit (*dinini holi*), may influence any aspect of life. Illness may be seen as evidence of their disfavour, so that whatever other measures are taken, patients or those caring for them may attempt to appease the spiritual agent suspected of being responsible. In this chapter I will consider illnesses explained in this way. Such explanations may constitute the only cause of cases of illness, or they may coexist with any of the explanations that I have discussed thus far. They represent the highest level of explanation of illness, answering the question, Why did I become ill?, and often the questions, Why me? and Why now?.

Classes of *dama*

Spirits are known as *dama*. Amongst the profusion of *dama* a number of different sorts can be distinguished according to their origins and their relationships with men. A general characteristic of *dama* is their ability to harm by bringing disease, death or other misfortune. But they may also be persuaded to serve people's interests, and in some cases it may be their task to do so.

The original founding ancestors are generically known as Kebali, though the 'true name' (*mini tene*) of the Kebali of each clan or group of clans may differ according to their origin myths. Kebali can harm men, producing disease in individuals or generalised misfortune such as famine, epidemics or rout in war. But Kebali is regarded as amenable, so that such reverses may be remedied by rebuilding a dilapidated *kebanda* (temple dedicated to Kebali) and performing sacrifices there. While Kebali can cause harm, this may be seen as a justified response to his or her being neglected. In general, Kebali is said to 'hold our skins' (*inane dongone yani hole*), and 'look after us' (*haru haga*). The name Kebali can be used to refer to a single founding ancestor, or collectively to all the ancestors of the clan. The senior officiant in the *kebanda* ritual may also be known as Kebali.

Beyond a varying number of generations from the present, the *dinini* (shades) of the ancestors may be said to become *dama*. Kebali, the founding

150

ancestor, may also be referred to as a *dama*. But it is also said that he is 'not a *dama*, but truly is a man' (*dama ndo agali ore*). The *kebanda* ceremony is said to be not for *dama* but for 'the spirits of men' (*agali dinininaga*), or for 'our fathers' (*aba*). The distinction here concerns two aspects of those spirits that are universally and incontrovertibly regarded as *dama*: their separate origin from that of men, and a disposition dominated by capricious greed. Such *dama* are often referred to generically as *dama* Heolabe, though some authorities regard Heolabe as only one *dama* amongst others.

Most of these quintessential *dama*, the profusion of spirits typically hostile or indifferent to the affairs of men, are said to have emerged separately from the ancestors of the human population. Some of the major *dama* of the Heolabe sort may play their parts in origin myths, but their activities are usually tangential to the figures that founded the Huli. Most *dama* have no individual origin stories and are distinguished only by their names. It is said that this horde of *dama* impinged little upon the affairs of men until relatively recently, during the last few generations. It is said that they were confined within the major sacred site of Gelo Te, but that since they escaped (*tagira ibini*, literally 'came outside') their predation on the Huli has caused an upsurge of disease and death. Some say that this assault by a mass of lesser *dama* began only in the last fifty years or so. They specify a particular case where a female diviner, a Duna woman, ascribed a man's illness to such a *dama*. He recovered when pork was sacrificed to the responsible *dama*. Since then numerous lesser *dama*, many coming from Duna, have attacked the Huli, causing considerable cost both in human suffering and pigs lost in sacrifices. This novel predation by a horde of lesser *dama* may reflect increasing disease levels that occurred at around the time of contact (see pp. 27–8).

The word *dinini* refers both to the souls of the living and the shades of the dead. It is the individual's immaterial essence which may vacate the body temporarily in sleep or illness, and permanently at the moment of death. A shade may return to harm the living in a number of circumstances. It may attack those who caused its death. It may return in jealousy to attack a spouse who remarries. Or it may return through longing (*hame*) for someone it was close to in life, securing his company by causing his death. The ritual, *ira giambe hangaga*, is intended to protect those vulnerable to the attack of a shade for any of these reasons. Some months after death most shades are said to have reached *humbirini andaga*, the place of the dead, situated somewhere to the south. This is loosely conceived as a place without pleasure or pain. The shades retain their individuality but once there they cannot return to influence the affairs of the living.

Only key figures retain individual significance long after their death. These are usually senior agnates of each generation who also possessed the knowledge and control of major ritual, particularly the *kebanda* ceremonies and the *tege* cycle. These major rituals were directed both to the ancestors and to *dama* of the Heolabe sort (I must stress that the ancestors can also be referred to as *dama*). This division of spiritual labour is made quite explicit in these rituals. In *tege*, separate sacrifices were made to the ancestors, whose skulls were decorated with paint, and to the *dama*, some of which were represented by spirit stones. In the centre of the *kebanda* only ceremonies for Kebali and other ancestors were performed. But sacrifices for *dama* were performed outside the *kebanda* proper, as '*dama* come to visit' when they sacrifice for Kebali, and 'stay with' Kebali (*dama mandagi haga*).

We can therefore distinguish three broad categories of *dama*. First, spirits of the founding ancestors, such as Kebali, whose individual exploits are described in origin myths, which can be related genealogically to the present population in *dindi malu*, and which in comparison with the other sorts of *dama* can be said to be 'not *dama*, but men'. Such *dama* are generally seen as supportive, and when they act against men's interests this may be regarded as an understandable, though of course unwelcome, response to neglect.

I must make special mention here of Ni. He is an important figure in origin myths (for example in the Tale Te myth I referred to on page 98), but few Huli clans say that they are actually descended from him. He is unambiguously a *dama* and not a 'man'. But he is also seen as a potentially nurturing spirit, like Kebali. The *tege* cycle is largely directed towards Ni (amongst other *dama* and ancestor spirits). Many of the spirit stones that are decorated at these ceremonies are known as 'Ni's eggs' (Ni *habane*). Ni also means the sun. The Ni myth ends with Ni going up into the sky with his sister Hana (the moon). But the *dama* of these names are not identified with their corresponding heavenly bodies. When sacrificing to Ni, they do not address their dedication to the sun. *Dama* Ni is conceived like other *dama* as a proximate but imperceptible presence.

Secondly, there are major *dama* of the Heolabe sort whose mythological origins may be known, but their ancestry is separate from that of men. Major ritual may include sacrifice to them, and men may attempt to enlist their support, but in general they are seen as predatory and treacherous.

Thirdly, there is the welter of lesser *dama* of ill-defined origin which are concerned only to do harm to men if they impinge on them at all. The army of spirits of this latter sort is referred to as if it has a hydra-like quality: where one spirit is identified through divination (*halaga*) and propitiated, more may rise to take its place.

Relations between *dama* and men

Relations between the Huli and *dama* are, like their relations with each other, based upon reciprocity. The key interchange in dealings with a particular *dama* is usually an oblation of pork (*nogo ambi*) which is thrown onto the fire accompanied by a plea for assistance or relief from attack. This may be

Fig. 58 An oblation of pork to propitiate an attacking spirit

referred to as repaying a 'debt' (*dano*), or is offered in exchange for relief, as in the common plea accompanying the offering of *nogo ambi*: 'I am giving you pork; make me better' (*nogo ngerogo dabi habe*) (fig. 58). The grounds for holding the ceremony and the participants' expectations of its outcome vary according to the characteristics of the *dama* that is being propitiated. Sacrifices to spirits such as Kebali may be intended solely to cure a single case of illness which is attributed to attack by Kebali. But they may also be intended to secure more generalised benefits, such as fertility of the soil and of people, or success in war.

Dama such as Heolabe are seen as largely destructive, and are propitiated more to prevent their doing harm than in expectation of their offering assistance. But some men maintain covenants with individual *dama* of this sort. In return for generous supplies of pork the *dama* protects the man's health and brings success in his affairs, benefits which now include luck in

153

gambling. In addition the *dama* could be sent to kill his enemies. A man who maintains such a compact (*damaheba beda*, 'he sits with a *dama*') runs the risk of his *dama* turning against him, for such *dama* are dangerously capricious. Sacrifices to minor *dama* are performed solely to persuade the *dama* to refrain from its attack.

In addition to these *dama* which are more or less amenable to human influence is the aloof figure of Datagaliwabe. Unlike other *dama* he is concerned with moral transgressions between kinsmen. He is said to punish these with immediate harshness, and no intercession can save his victims. The paradigmatic account of Datagaliwabe's intervention concerned a young man, an *ibagiya*, who committed incest with two of his sisters, and was later killed by lightning. It is my impression that death was ascribed to Datagaliwabe very rarely. This dramatic case was the only death explained unequivocally in this way that came to my notice. Moral transgressions can lead to death directly through *tawaneme baya*, where a sick person may suddenly die if someone whom he has previously wronged comes into his presence. The patient dies of 'heat' (*poboneme*). In such cases people are undecided whether Datagaliwabe is implicated or not. But the concept of Datagaliwabe has become very important to modern Hulis, as his qualities dominate in the Huli conception of the Christian God. In former times it seems that Datagaliwabe offered little serious threat. His name was invoked to frighten naughty children, and very occasionally death was ascribed to him following the most serious breaches of the moral code. The consequences of people's acts depended more upon the response of those affected than upon the appraisal of those acts against a universal code of behaviour. The influence of Christianity has introduced the concept of a universalistic morality. Like Datagaliwabe, God punishes breaches of the moral code directly. But the moral code in which he is interested covers many actions about which there were previously no universal prescriptions. For example, God may bring illness if you steal. Traditionally, stealing from a brother was usually regarded as improper, but to steal from a group which had failed in its exchange obligations could be a proper act. The range of offences which are deemed to engender God's active displeasure in the form of illness arises from a synthesis of the particular preoccupations of the missionaries and the characteristic concerns of the Huli themselves.

Another effect of the ascendancy of Christian influence is a shift in the understanding of the word *dama*. Many *dama* were regarded traditionally as entirely destructive, but others were felt to be sympathetic to the interests of men. Some ceremonies were thought to be nothing to do with *dama* at all: marriage rites (*ndi tingi*) and the rituals in the bachelor cult (*ibagiya*), for example. But in the missionaries' and pastors' view, most traditional observances are directed to Satan. Most traditional rites are now said by Christians to be for *dama* (Satan) when they may have nothing to do with *dama* (spirits).

Also, the distinctions I have made between *dama* that may be nurturing and those that are inevitably destructive is discarded when all *dama* become evil spirits in necessary conflict with God. However, there are clear similarities between Huli ideas of *dama* attack and Christian views of demon possession.

Dama attack

Rather than continue in generalities, I describe below cases of illness which illustrate the key features of such explanations, and which introduce the current controversies that now surround this sort of diagnosis.

The hazards of continuing relationships with spirits

Case thirty-four. The sick man was about sixty years old. His illness began with backache (*darama*). Over a few weeks he became weaker, and had to give up his current task of building a new fence around a garden. He started walking with a stick, and then retired to his fireside. He assumed that his *dama* was responsible. He is the 'owner' of the *dama* Kebali (*dama anduane*). He says of Kebali that 'my ancestors held him, and they gave him to me'. As Kebali's *dama anduane* he had a central role in the major *kebanda* fertility ritual when this was still practiced. He had neglected to sacrifice to Kebali for a long time, and assumed that the *dama* had struck him down with a spear (*yandare*) in response to his neglect. The members of his parish were particularly fervent Christians. He was the only man in his clan actively to repudiate the church, and was under considerable pressure to join. When he became ill the Christians said that if he abandoned his *dama*, God would cure him. He decided to comply, and was told by the local pastors to kill a pig, and the congregation would hold a feast to cure his illness and celebrate his conversion. He killed three big pigs, and sent for the pastors. They held a service at his house, and the next day he was to go to the church. That night he thought he heard someone call his name. He went out of his house to see who it was, but, seeing no one, he decided that Kebali had come to kill him in anger now that he would receive no more sacrifices. He collapsed. His family were alarmed at his condition, and carried him to Tari Health Centre.

He was found to be anaemic, but no specific cause for that or his backache was found. He was happy to receive medical treatment. He felt that if it caused him to recover that would prove that he was not threatened by Kebali after all. He said that he would have liked to ask someone at home to sacrifice a pig for him, but that there was no longer anyone to help him as they had all gone into the church, adding that if the medicine did not cure him that he had 'come to die in the hands of the whites' (*honabinaga gini homole ibini*). His anaemia was treated, and he was discharged, which puzzled him as he did not feel that he had recovered. He reckoned that they were fed up with him for pulling the intravenous drip out of his arm while he was still confused, and so were sending him away. He went to stay with a kinsman from a neighbouring parish to be near the aid post, for he wished to continue with medical treatments. This kinsman was one of the few remaining traditional practitioners in the area. After a few days they decided that the medicine was insufficient, and that his *dama* was responsible. The kinsman performed a type of divination (*biangonga*) to identify the *dama*. He confirmed that it was Kebali, specifying the agnatic ancestor spirit of the victim's clan. They decided to perform the *kebanda* ritual (Frankel 1979a). The ritualist told the patient to rebuild the shelter at his neglected *kebanda* (sacred site for Kebali) and to prepare the materials for the ritual: tree oil (*mbagua*), red paint (*hare*) and ropes of cowrie shells (*dange*). When he had completed these preparations the old man began to recover from his illness, which they took to indicate that Kebali had called off his attack once he had seen their intention of honouring him. He kept his plans secret for fear that the Christians would insult him.

They had to call in another ritualist as the wife of the first had given birth three months before, rendering him ritually unclean, a state known as *honde taribu*. *Honde taribu* ends some eight months after the birth. They had to wait a further month as the second ritualist was also *honde taribu* from a child born seven months before. The day before they performed the *kebanda* ceremony they sacrificed a pig to a number of *dama*, including *dama* Heolabe, to dissuade these from attempting to spoil the *kebanda* ritual and reduce the benefits that should flow from it.

When it was time for the ritual proper, the *dama anduane* (the owner of the *dama*: the man who had been ill) brought the stone which is said to be Kebali from its secret place in the forest. This was a roughly cuboidal piece of sandstone some eighteen inches long. When not participating in the *kebanda* ritual this stone must be kept where no one, and particularly no woman, may 'step over it' (*angua holebira*). The ritual site, hidden within a thicket of pit-pit, was divided into two sections, the 'inside' (*tamuha*) and 'outside' (*tagira*). The stone was placed 'inside', and only the ritually pure were permitted there. The ceremony began 'outside'. While the ritual was directed primarily to Kebali, other *dama* may be attracted by the sacrifice, and must be satisfied too lest they disrupt the ceremony or harm the patient through spite (*madane*). The first sacrifice was to Hona-Hanawali, a female *dama* (or in some versions a group of female *dama*) loosely conceived as the counterpart of the important male *dama*. The pig for Hona-Hanawali was killed 'outside' with a bespelled stick. His being *honde taribu* did not exclude the first ritualist from this part of the ritual.

(I will include here excerpts from a transcription of the dialogue during this sacrifice. The pig has been killed by a blow to the head with a bespelled stick. The blood is dripping into the earth oven, which is filled with leaves upon which cowries have been placed. The *dama* are being addressed):

Patient: I kill this pig to give to Hona-Hanawali.
Ritualist: I'll do the talking as you are talking too softly. The red paint, oil, cowries, taro, *habia* (*Schefflera* spp.), and ginger I have put over there for *dama* Kebali to eat. Here I am killing (a pig) to give to Hanawali. Make this man better. I am giving you your pig and cowries.
Patient: Hanawali, I am killing this pig and giving it to you. There is one over there for Kebali. Lest you are jealous I am giving you this pig. Eat it. Pull out the arrows (*timu*) that are in my back. Make me better today. Make me recover and live long. Lest you are jealous of Kebali's pig, I am giving you this so eat it.

The patient and the second ritualist then went 'inside' to sacrifice to Kebali. The patient expressed his transaction with Kebali in the same terms that would be used in an exchange between men: 'he demanded oil and red pigment from me, and I am doing (what he wants) today' (*mbagua harela dano biyida lowa o ayu berogoni*, where *dano biyida* is the term for demanding prestations in exchanges). When they were in the most sacred part of the *kebanda* they referred to Kebali by his true name (*mini tene*) which in this case was Hunabe. When they had killed the pig, the patient addressed him as follows: 'Since long ago we have been together, Hunabe, and you always open my door, come inside, and strike me down. Hanawali has eaten, you must not be jealous, you will eat now, I have brought your food now. Hunabe, you are the mediator (*hanuni*, literally 'middle', said of men who settle disputes), so take out my arrow. Finish my illness tonight. I have brought cowries, pigment and pig. Hanawali has eaten, so you eat now...We have been together for a long time. Eat now and take the arrow out of my back. Make me like a young man again. Make me as strong as stone or trees. I am giving this to you, so you must give pig to me, make my pigs good. Pigs of mine that are sick, make them big and well.'

When the pigs were cooked, the patient threw pieces of pork into Hanawali's fire as an oblation to her: 'I give this to you Hanawali. Your husband is eating over there...Make my skin good. Brighten up this fire and eat well Hanawali.

The patient and ritualist returned to annoint Kebali's stone with red pigment, tree oil and pig fat. The ritualist recited *kebe gamu*, the spell for Kebe, while rubbing the stone. This completed they threw the oblation for Kebali into the fire. The ritualist told the patient to name all his father's *dama* (*i hame dama*). This he did, beginning with the names of the agnatic ancestors of his clan, telling them to 'carry us in your arms' (*gime bihende mo yai ha*). He then named the sun, Hona-Ni, and 'all my fathers' (*i hame bihende*), and finally 'this for Hunabe, you must take out the arrow that is in me today'.

This case highlights a number of features of traditional healing for *dama* attack, as well as modern influences upon the response to illnesses explained in this way. Those who wish to propitiate *dama* by sacrifice are under considerable pressure not to do so. *Dama* attack may be diagnosed by Christians, but the only response acceptable to most people is prayer or exorcism. Even where individuals are willing to tolerate the insults and mockery that they attract if they are known to perform a sacrifice, it can be difficult to find specialists to help with the ceremony, as few are now practising. This man's resolve and his success in finding assistance are both rare nowadays.

The statements these men made to the *dama* and the atmosphere surrounding the ceremony indicate the nature of men's relationships with *dama*. In other circumstances they would not address *dama* so boldly. But when they are presenting the things that the *dama* desires, particularly pork, tree oil, pigment and cowries, they are forthright and cajoling in their demand that the figurative arrow that he has placed in the sick man's back should now be removed. The element of exchange is clear both in the language used, and in the tone adopted. As they have been so generous, they demand more than relief for this illness. They also ask Kebali to confer other benefits, of strength and wealth. Their dealings with Kebali are complicated by the envy and greed of other *dama*. These must also be propitiated lest they ruin the ceremony through pernicious jealousy or spite (*madane*).

Fig. 59 The *ogoanda* at Tale Te

Similar problems beset one of the most active traditionalists who was attempting to stage part of a *dindi gamu* ritual.

Case thirty-five. A man aged about sixty had a painful swollen knee (a septic arthritis). The sacred grove, Tale Te, where Hanawali had cut herself while scratching against the Tale tree (p. 98) was on his land, and with the help of the few non-Christians in the area, all old men, he was attempting to continue with the ritual cycle that centred upon that site. Some six months before his knee became painful he had built an *ogoanda* (a tall conical form of temple) at Tale Te, and staged a large sacrifice there (fig. 59; Frankel 1979b). The central sacrifice was for Hona-Ni and Hona-Hana, the brother and sister in the myth (fig. 60). But they also killed pigs for *dama* unrelated to that creation story. When his knee became painful he decided that as he had neglected *dama* Kuarimago at that sacrifice, this *dama* was now attacking him. Kuarimago is said to have come from the north, from the Enga. He is said to dwell in the ashes of the hearth, and his attacks are characteristically sharp and sudden. An acute intense pain in the knee is typical of an attack by Kuarimago. Treatment is by *nogo golo*, a rite also said to be of Enga origin. The diagnosis may also have been prompted in this case by the fact that a close associate of the sick man was an expert in *nogo golo*. *Nogo golo* differs from other treatments of *dama* attack in that Kuarimago is tricked and then driven off, rather than propitiated. A pig is killed, and the fresh blood that runs from its snout is allowed to flow into a hole in the ashes where Kuarimago hides. A small fire is then lit over the ashes, and the pig's ear is roasted. This smell and the accompanying spell lure out the *dama*. He is attracted further by tree oil (*mbagua*) that is poured over the fire to make it blaze. At this moment the ritualist thrusts a small tripod with sharpened points (*wanga*) into the fire, extinguishing it, and stabbing repeatedly into the ashes. Kuarimago, stabbed in the eye while looking for a victim, flees.

Fig. 60 Hulia-Hewabe addressing the spirits during a sacrifice at Tale Te

They performed *nogo golo* (Frankel 1979c). What I referred to as the hydra-like quality of *dama* attack is illustrated in this ceremony. After the ritualist had stabbed the ashes with the *wanga* he said that he could feel the 'heat' of another *dama*. He pushed the *wanga* into the ashes again, and said that it would not go in as another *dama* was 'blocking the road'. They performed *nogo golo* again, and were satisfied that no *dama* were left.

This case again illustrates the complexities involved in maintaining advantageous relations with *dama*. The suppliant must identify the particular *dama* affecting his condition to induce it to release its hold, and perhaps assist him more positively. But he must also anticipate the implications of his actions for the relations between the *dama* themselves. In this case the general benefits that should have followed from the *ogoanda* ritual were subverted by the jealousy of the neglected Kuarimago. Kuarimago was held to be responsible for this illness partly on the evidence of the symptoms. That one

159

of the patient's associates was expert in the treatment of Kuarimago's attacks was also a factor. During the *nogo golo* ceremony another unidentified *dama* was felt to be present, attracted by the smell of oil and scorching pork. If the patient's symptoms had not subsequently resolved they would have suspected other *dama*, but he recovered sufficiently for them to be satisfied that they had found the cause of his illness.

The hazards of initiating a ritual cycle

Some rites are stages in a continual ritual cycle culminating in the major ritual of *tege*. The earlier minor ceremonies that are seen as leading up to *tege* comprise *himugu ere hiraga*, then *himugu hangaga*, followed by *deba paliaga*, then *ega kamia hangaga* and finally *tege*. The cycle then begins again. Months or years may pass between each of these rites. If a long period is allowed to lapse between one ceremony and the next, misfortune may be ascribed to the *dama* or the ancestors becoming irritated at having to wait so long to be fed and honoured again. This was the case here:

Case thirty-six. The patient in this case was a man aged about fifty-five who had developed pain in his face and especially around his eyes (probably from sinusitis). The sick man was a 'master of the *dama*' (*dama anduane*) and was unusual in that he stayed outside the church and continued his observances. It was some two years since he had performed *himugu hangaga*, and he ascribed his illness to his having delayed so long before performing the next ritual in the cycle, *deba paliaga*. While the ritual procedures for these ceremonies are clearly defined in the relevant lore (*mana*), the identity of the particular *dama* to which the rites are directed is a matter for the 'master of *dama*' to determine. The expert who is called to perform *deba paliaga*, for example, does not even have to know the names of the *dama* which his ceremony is intended to propitiate. This cycle of ceremonies is generally dedicated to Ni and Hana, other *dama*, as well as to ancestors. The characteristic element of *deba paliaga* is the recitation of the spell (*deba palialu gamu*) while squeezing pig fat over a small arch of twigs. The arch is about six inches high, and is made of a twig each of *habono* (*Ardisia* spp.), *mandi* (*Acalypha insulana*), *walu* (*Garcinia* spp.) and *pagu* (*Syzygium vesteegii*). The twigs are bound together with *neberapu*, a liane (*Cissus* spp.). In this case the ceremony was directed to the *dama* Hona-Ni and Lidu. When the oblations were thrown into the fire, the ritualist said to each *dama* 'You have consumed his eye (*de nari*), but make him better now.' The patient soon recovered, and said he intended to stage the next ritual in the cycle, *ega kamia hangaga*, before very long.

As I pointed out in my discussion of Huli illness descriptions, many of their apparently graphic terms do not carry the literal meaning that translation may imply. An earache will be described as *hale nara* (it consumes the ear) even though the sufferer may have no thought of a *dama* actually chewing at his flesh. But these terms are not invariably debased. In this case, the man was suffering from *de nara* ('it consumes the eye'). When he addressed the *dama*, the ritualist used the second person, *de nari* (you have consumed his eye).

The performance of *ega kamia hangaga* that I saw was staged by a man in a similar situation (Frankel 1979d). He had performed the ritual *deba paliaga* some years before, and ascribed a number of misfortunes to the fact that *ega kamia hangaga*, the next ritual in the cycle, was overdue. His wife and children had suffered frequent illness, his pigs kept escaping and he had failed to obtain a young bride. These rituals are small compared with the full performance of the culminating ritual of this cycle, *tege*, which involves the killing of many pigs and the cooperation of large numbers of people. It is unlikely that these men, or any other Huli, will succeed in staging a full *tege* again, in order to complete their ritual cycles. The ascendancy of Christianity is such that few people would cooperate. One man known to me did intend to stage the full *tege* ritual in 1978, but he was forced to abandon his plans under the pressure of constant insults from the Christian majority. The only *tege* known to me in recent times occurred in 1983 when two elderly brothers insisted, against considerable opposition from Christians, that it was imperative that they should at least attempt a *tege* before they died. The event was a sad reflection of the sort of massive gatherings described by Glasse (1965:44–5). The only assistance they could muster was from the son of one of them, who took pity on them against his better judgement, and from two young boys who lived with them. One of the old men explained their obduracy like this:

We were five brothers, and we held this *dama*. When famine or war came, none of us died, for this *dama* helped us and cared for us. My brother once was shot in the lung with an arrow, but he didn't die. The *dama* helped to remove the arrow, and he survived. Now only two of us brothers are left. Everyone is pressing us to forget all this and go into the church. Many men just threw their sacred stones (*Ni habane*, literally 'Ni's eggs') into the river or burnt them. But we could not discard this man who lives with us (*agali ina harimago*, where the 'man' is their *dama*). Soon we are to die. To go without marking our parting from him would not be proper. When we have staged *tege* (literally 'killed *tege*', *tege bo mini*) and he has consumed pork, cowries and tree oil, then we can say farewell.

Spirit arrows

Arrows from the *dama* Ibatiri are thought to cause discomfort rather than death. I have already referred to the continuity between traditional ideas of this sort of *dama* attack (known as *tawa timu*) and the new diagnosis of *nambis poisin*. *Nambis poisin* is commonly treated by the rite that was traditionally used to remove Ibatiri's arrows (*tawa timu duguaga*). *Nambis poisin* is now a more common diagnosis than *tawa timu*, but the traditional diagnosis is still used. Six cases came to my notice. They all suffered from acute pain of various sorts, and were not very ill. An important pointer to the diagnosis was that they had been near forest pools or streams soon before their symptoms began. These are the places where *ibatiri* spirits are found, and they may shoot at anyone who passes by. Four of these cases were treated by *tawa dimu duguaga*, the traditional rite I have described above in my discussion of *nambis poisin* (p. 147 and Frankel 1979e). Such a high rate of traditional healing for conditions that are not in themselves potentially fatal is now unusual. Two features of this cure may make it more acceptable than other traditional remedies. It does not involve sacrifice to *dama*, as it entails the extraction of objects rather then propitiation, and it is now associated with the modern condition of *nambis poisin*.

Spirit attack as a 'second spear'

Case thirty-seven. A very old man, of perhaps eighty years, suffered an exacerbation of his chronic bronchitis. He ascribed this to an arrow wound in the loin which he had received some forty years before. He was certain that the arrow was responsible and not *amali*, as in *amali* he would have been stricken earlier in life, and he would cough up *anga* (yellow sputum) and not the copious pus (*angibu*) that he was producing. The pus around the arrow had 'burst' (*angibu tugu dayadagoni*) and he was coughing it up. He had never pressed a claim for compensation, and now the other protagonists were dead. However, his case belongs here as, besides ascribing his symptoms to an arrow, he also felt that a *dama* was responsible, saying that 'the *dama* and the arrow went into me together' (*dama timula doba i kabeneha anda peda*). Despite some opposition from his Christian son, he decided to sacrifice a pig as 'when I am dying, if I kill a pig I recover again' (*homenego nogo bowa heyu bido*). He said that he is 'held in his father's hand' (*i abanaga gini ko*). His father 'gave' him the two *dama* who would care for him if he sacrificed to them. With another man's help he killed a pig, and when it was cooked threw oblations into the fire (*nogo ambi*), addressed his father (*aba*), and by implication all his agnatic forbears, as well as his *dama*. His helper told him 'your father (*hame*) is sitting there watching you, give him some pork' and threw some pork into the fire, saying 'make him better now'. The old man added 'I don't forget you. I am giving you pig, so eat and make me better.' He then told the *dama* to eat, and to cause him to recover. His helper continued, addressing the *dama*: 'I am ashamed (*taga*) to call your names, but the old man there, I am sorry for him. Help him and make him better.' But his condition continued to deteriorate, and he died three days after the sacrifice. His death was ascribed to the arrow.

This explanation is reminiscent of the Zande's 'second spear' (Evans-Pritchard 1937: 74). *Dama* attack is often referred to as a spear (*yandare*), and an attacking *dama* may be asked to remove his spear or arrow (*timu*). But the Huli conception differs from the Zande in that the first and second spears (in this case the arrow the old man received in a battle, and the *dama* that has also attacked him) are parallel explanations, either of which could have dire consequences. The Zande say that a physical injury would not normally fester unless the 'second spear' of witchcraft were active. For the Huli the 'first spear', in this case an arrow wound received many years before, may be regarded as a complete explanation for severe illness and death. Though here the old man felt that *dama* were also implicated, as they had entered him alongside the arrow.

The man with *agali* whose illness I described above (case three, p. 113) also suspected that he was being attacked by *dama*. He was certain that he had *agali*, but felt that *dama* had placed an 'arrow' in him which they would remove if he paid his debt (*dano*) to them in pork. He therefore killed two pigs, one for the treatment of *agali* (*nogo tini gamu*), the other to sacrifice to the *dama*. The ritualist was not particularly interested to know which *dama* he was sacrificing for, knowing only that one of the pigs was for *dama* Heolabe. The patient suspected four different *dama*, though he had performed no specific divinatory rite. They killed the pigs with blows over the snout with a bespelled stick, and the patient addressed the *dama* as follows, 'Make me better. Let me live long. Where you belong, go back there. Make my pig herd increase, and make me better.' The ritualist added, 'Make him better, make him better, give him water today', asking the *dama* to increase the efficacy of the bespelled water with which he was preparing to treat the female pollution.

As in the previous case, *dama* are suspected in conjunction with another disease process, here female pollution. These two disease processes are equally grave, and are treated separately. At the sacrifice, the patient asks the *dama* for more general assistance than just the relief of his illness.

Case thirty-eight. An old man developed rigors and a severe pain in his back. He went to the health centre where he was treated for malaria. His back was X-rayed, but no cause for his backache was found. He ascribed the backache to a blow across the back over twenty years before, and wanted to use the X-ray as evidence in a claim for compensation. While in hospital he had a dream where a man made a request for pork. He interpreted this as a demand from the *dama* that had caused him to become ill. He was a non-Christian, and after his discharge sacrificed a pig to the *dama* Yelowe, 'a relation of Ni', to whom he had always sacrificed. After that he was much better. Two months later he was still suffering from occasional slight fevers, so he decided to perform another sacrifice. He had intended killing only two pigs, one each for Ni and Hanawali. But a friend of his had a dream where he saw an archer trying to shoot him. This signified that *dama* Pariwayali, otherwise known as Dandayi, the bowman, should also be propitiated, and he killed a third pig.

He had been satisfied with the single ascription of his pain to a past blow. But his dream caused him to suspect that *dama* were involved. He assumed that the particular *dama* with which he had associated in the past were responsible, and sacrificed to them. Later he sacrificed again, and in his choice of *dama* to propitiate he was open to suggestions from his associates. When they talk about sacrifices ritualists imply that the individual *dama* to be propitiated are expressly defined. In practice this is often not the case. I have been at sacrifices where the view of each participant differed as to the list of minor *dama* to which the ritual was dedicated. The ritualist himself may recount different lists of minor *dama* at different stages of a ceremony, and insist later that he has been consistent throughout. The major *dama*, such as Kebali and Ni, would not be confused in this way. But many of the others are hazy figures that exist as little more than names.

Christian interpretations of and responses to illness

Instances of the sort I have described where the diagnosis of *dama* attack is unequivocal and the illness is treated by traditional means specific to the diagnosis are now rare. The word *dama* is used commonly in discussing illness, but the meaning and implications of this term have been shifted by Christian usage. I have described the traditional distinction between spirits that are entirely antagonistic and those which are potentially supportive. This sort of distinction is now explicit in the Christian usage adopted by the vast majority of Hulis, but it is expressed as a conflict between God and all *dama*, which are now seen to be Satan and his demons, and so are necessarily evil.

A number of issues, including the particularly energetic and efficient proselytising activities of the various missionary groups in this area, have led to a preoccupation with Christianity and opposition to traditional practices. The pidgin word *kanaka*, elsewhere used as a derogatory term for rural bumpkins unsophisticated in modern ways, has been adopted by Hulis to refer to pagans. (The Latin *pagani* also meant 'countrymen' before it came to mean 'heathen'.) Those few who have resisted the pressure to join the church may refer to themselves as *kanaka* with some pride. But for the majority, who are no longer *kanaka*, traditional practices are seen as dangerous from two aspects: they will incur God's anger, and could unleash *dama* that may be difficult to control. Even talking of past religious practices may be seen as dangerous. One informant made this prayer before he felt able to talk about the *kebanda* ceremony: 'Father God, you are truly the leader, you are there. Now we are not making bad talk, we are not thinking bad thoughts, this is not *kanaka* work. I am recounting stories, Father God, I am telling the lore, I am telling of our origins. Help me' (*aba ngode i ore homogo o aba ngode i kego o ayu iya bi ko ndo mini ko ndo o aba ngode ganage biabe ndo te laro aba ngode te mana laro honowini nguai laro bia mogo bibe*). Another prominent ritual leader who had joined the church became ill a few months after he had spent some time with me talking of his former practice. The members of his church ascribed his illness to his having talked of traditional religion, and insisted that he should not take the risk again.

God as a new spirit

In former times, one of the most straightforward and common responses to major illness was to assume that it was caused by a *dama*, and to sacrifice a pig to the *dama* assumed or divined to be responsible. A diagnosis of *dama* attack is still common, but now the usual response is to ask for God's help. For example:

Case thirty-nine. A woman aged about fifty became very weak and unwell (she was suffering from malaria). Both she and her husband had recently joined the Roman

Spirits and God

Catholic Church, and they ascribed her illness to his *dama*. They felt that the *dama* to which he had previously sacrificed was angered at being deserted, and was attacking her in revenge. In addition to hospital treatment, they prayed frequently for God's protection.

The conception of God is in some respects similar to the traditional view of *dama*. Like a *dama*, God is vengeful if neglected, as in this case:

Case forty. A man aged about forty had been a convert for about ten years. Since adolescence he had suffered recurrent exacerbations of polyarthritis. He ascribed his present recurrence to his having drifted from the church, neglecting to attend services and failing to observe restrictions upon smoking, eating pork, drinking tea and so on. When his condition improved he ascribed this to his return to the church rather than to the hospital treatment he had received.

Sacrifices were also performed to enlist a *dama*'s support in hastening recovery from an illness which it was not suspected of causing. Sacrifice of this sort has been almost entirely supplanted by Christian prayer or other largely Christian ceremonies, now that the outcome in illness is seen by most people to be influenced mainly by God's will. Private prayers asking for God's help in illness are therefore commonplace. More formal prayer meetings are less common, though the morbidity study in the Hambuali area showed that on 10.5% of days when people suffered potentially serious symptoms they held such services.

In most cases there is a clear continuity between traditional and Christian ideas of spirit attack, with prayers for divine assistance or exorcism replacing sacrifice as the appropriate treatment. However, on occasions there can be tension between the Christian and the traditional view. The abandonment of traditional practices may be deemed necessary to gain God's protection, but the neglect of such practices may represent an equivalent threat. Where illnesses are held to be relatively unresponsive to modern cures and so the danger of forgoing traditional treatment is great, such treatments are still performed. We saw this in the treatment of *agali*. This is seen as a particularly Huli illness, and so Huli cures are still applied even in the case of Christians if their illness is severe. In other circumstances the fear of the consequences of either acting or neglecting to act in a traditional, that is non-Christian, way, can lead people to respond in an ambiguous manner in the face of illness. This sort of quandary is illustrated in the following case:

Case forty-one. A woman of about thirty-five became acutely ill with chest pain (*dama yandare*), weakness, shortness of breath and cough. Her first husband had died about a year before, and she had recently remarried. As a Christian she had not mourned her dead husband in the traditional manner, for which she should have painted her body with white clay, decked herself in Job's tears, worn a long skirt, and stayed near his mourning-hut tending a smokey fire, among other observances. As she did not mourn him properly she felt that his shade (*dinini*) had attacked her. She had made herself particularly vulnerable by marrying again. Traditionally, widows protected themselves from the anger of their dead husbands before remarrying through the *ira*

165

giambe ritual. As a Christian this too was forbidden her. Her condition deteriorated, she became delirious, and was taken to Tari Health Centre where she recovered (she was suffering from lobar pneumonia).

A pig kill (*nogo homane*) was traditionally held some four days after a funeral, and this was said to help the dead person's shade on its journey to the place of the dead (*humbirini andaga*). As Christians, this man's relations had not performed *nogo homane*. While the woman was in hospital, they now held a pig kill where they asked God to drive the troublesome shade away. Apart from the prayers, the occasion was very similar to a *nogo homane*, though it was being held a year after the man's death.

In cases which are loosely ascribed to *dama*, the patient and those in attendance may feel that prayers are insufficient, and in accordance with traditional practice they sacrifice pigs. Such ceremonies are known as *tuguli nogo* (church pig: *tuguli* means 'church' from the pidgin *skul*, school). Roman Catholics are more willing to allow such eclectic ceremonies than Protestants, but *tuguli nogo* is performed by members of these churches as well. I will describe one instance:

Case forty-two. A man of about fifty years had been ill for four days with pain in his chest, spitting blood and fainting. He was known to suffer from *hagara* (chronic bronchitis), but he had gone into a rapid decline. He lived near the aid post, but did not want to be taken there for treatment. Instead, he asked a woman of his clan whose prayers were said to be effective to conduct a *tuguli nogo* service for him. He and his group were Roman Catholics. They stood a cross by the earth oven, and prepared three pigs for killing. She prayed 'Father, master, rich man. We are wretched. He has *bu* (bronchitis) within him. The badness that is in him, wash it out.' (*Aba, anduane, homogo. Ina ko biaga kamagoni. Bu kabenaha ko weruagani domo wahai habe.*) She touched his chest and belly with her hand, and then they killed the pigs. Then she added 'Do (with him) whatever you wish.' (*Ininaga hameme hangu bibe.*)

There are obvious differences between this and traditional sacrifices, such as the presence of the cross. The style of the dedication of the pig also differs. In sacrifices to *dama*, the officiant is making an intimate covenant and not a public address. He also addresses a *dama* more as an equal, and would not adopt this tone of passive humility. But in general the form of the ceremony, the dedication of the pig and the later statements to accompany the oblation of cooked pig that is thrown into the fire are clearly in continuity with the form and intention of traditional sacrifices. Another response for Christians to the quandary that strongly indicated ceremonies are forbidden to them is to allow others who are still *kanaka* to perform the ceremony for them.

The moral implications of Christian diagnoses

Prayer in these circumstances implies that people place the illness in a Christian context, though in most cases there is no specific interpretation of the roles of God or *dama* in causing the illness. Where spiritual influence is given a specific interpretation, the Christian view departs significantly from past conceptions. In general *dama* were thought to attack people merely to satisfy their greed for flesh, and to be largely indifferent to the moral implications of people's thoughts or deeds. One exception was Datagaliwabe, but he was concerned only with the most serious misdemeanours, and even then was thought to intercede extremely rarely. The moral code was upheld through constant personal interaction and negotiation, the implications of each act depending as much upon the particular response it evoked from others as on any universal standard of proper conduct. Acceptance of Christianity is one of the influences which has led to the transformation of this particularistic morality and to its becoming more universalistic. This change is apparent in explanations and actions in illness. For example:

Case forty-three. A boy of four months became ill with fever, cough and shortness of breath. The mother thought that God had caused the illness to punish her. She had had 'bad thoughts' (*mini ko*), and had stolen small items from her husband's relatives when they annoyed her or did not treat her fairly.

That emotions can led to illness in oneself or in others is a traditional Huli concept. Desire, fright, sorrow, jealousy and anger can lead to a variety of ill effects, as I have explained (pp. 136–44). The Christian teaching to which the Huli have been subject has also been concerned with the effects of the emotions. One of the common preoccupations of sermons is the need for self-control, and the idea that excessive emotion, whether expressed or just experienced, is not Christian. This concern, and the chord that it finds in Huli thinking, is commonly seen in interpretations of illness.

Case forty-four. A woman felt that her husband neglected her and her children. He never gave her help or money, and was always away visiting. She aired her grievance, and they had a furious argument. When her baby of five months developed pneumonia, she assumed that God was punishing her for becoming angry.

Anger can lead to divine punishment even when it is not openly expressed:

Case forty-five. A woman of about sixty was given a pig to look after by her brother. Later, her brother's wife came to her, furious that her husband had farmed out the pig, saying that as he had a wife it was for her to look after his pigs. The wife struck her sister-in-law. The woman did not hit back, or say anything, but when she became ill with malaria she thought that God was punishing her for being angry 'inside' (*kabaneha*).

Such explanations have a clear effect in supporting the moral code, both in terms of underpinning aspects of Huli values that are still current, and in reinforcing the acceptance of introduced ideas of proper conduct, particularly those stressed by the missions. As I have pointed out, *dama* were traditionally seen as largely disinterested in the moral implications of men's dealings with each other. However, they were evoked in oath-taking (*tiari*), where two disputants would each declare the truth of their version of an event, and the particular *dama* invoked caused disease and misfortune to the man who has lied or to his relations. Such oath-taking continues, though God, rather than a *dama*, is invoked. For example:

Case forty-six. A man stole a pig from his wife's brother. He was suspected of being the thief, but he denied it. At the village court hearing he still denied it. He was told to put up his hand to heaven so that God would see, and to say that he had not stolen the pig. He did this. His wife thought all along that he had been lying, and when her baby son became ill with shortness of breath her suspicions were confirmed.

A number of the examples of illness interpreted as divine punishment that I have cited indicate the potential influence explanations of this sort can have as a means of social control. Divine displeasure is a serious threat, and it is now intimated in circumstances where spiritual influences would traditionally not have been suspected. Concern over the potential consequences of acts deemed to displease God may lead people to modify their behaviour in a number of ways. They may be more compliant than otherwise, be moderate in their habits, abstain from tobacco, alcohol or whatever their particular mission prohibits, repudiate theft, avoid emotional displays and so on. Where wives' misfortunes may be interpreted as being consequent upon their disobeying their husbands, women become more compliant. Where polygamy may lead to divine retribution, fewer people are willing to expose themselves to the risks. In addition to these influences upon people's demeanour, habits and relations with each other, the dangers of God's displeasure, and ability of Christians to enlist God's help in casting out *dama*, leads people to be submissive towards those in authority in the various churches. Besides the immediate threat of illness, miscreants also risk the later misery of a hell that is most graphically described to them. I will illustrate aspects of Christian interpretations of illness by the following case history:

Case forty-seven. A newly married woman developed malaria (*wabi warago*), then began to have fits. Her husband took her to the health centre. She was treated for cerebral malaria. Her condition became so poor that women began to gather at the health centre, grieving quietly, waiting for her finally to expire. At one time she was thought to be dead (*buhe ereba haya*, literally 'her breath has disappeared'), but then they saw some movement in her chest (*bu emene biri laya*). The nurse in charge gave her oxygen and sucked mucus from her throat. At that point, three pastors came in who had come to visit another patient. They asked her husband if they could pray for her, and he agreed, though they were from a different mission from his own. The prayer was as follows: 'Father God, today this woman has died, and her breath is gone. We are here in sorrow. You are the master of everything, you are on high. Now bring back her life so that all the people that are here will see your strength. Then they will know that you are there. Then they will change their hearts. Raise her up now.' (*Ina aba ngode ayu ibu homayidago buhe ereba hayidago dara ore kamago ini anduane mbirale bibahendenaga wahene li kego ayu ibu buhe mo dai bi la waliagali o karu inaga hongo ayu hondolo. Ngode henemane harua lo manda bilo ani bialu tinaga bu mo ariari bilo ayu ibu mo hea ha.*) Then one of the pastors told the nurse to give the woman some water to drink. The nurse was reluctant as she had been told to give nothing by mouth, but the pastor told her that God wanted the patient to drink, so the nurse complied. The pastor called her name, and she grunted. They prayed again several times. A pastor turned to all the watching relations and said that he had prayed, and she had got up (*heaya*). They must all have one thought in their minds, of God in heaven, and if they had any bad thoughts (*dindini ngagonaga*, literally 'of things that are of the earth'), then she would die again. Her brother took her hand, and the pastor asked him if he went to courting parties (*dawanda*), drank beer, fornicated or smoked. He did not answer, and the pastor told him that he did all those things, so he could not hold his sister's hand. Later she had a fit, and the pastor said to her 'What is your name?' She grunted something like 'Ea.' He asked her if she had another name, and the grunt sounded like 'Oa.' The pastor said that she was naming the two *dama* that were within her, a man and a woman. He then called to the *dama*, 'Go outside, go outside!' (*tagira pu, tagira pu*). Later that night she was much better, and was talking. A pastor of their own church came, but the three pastors asked him to leave. They stayed with the couple, praying and talking for much of the night. The woman left her own church for that of the pastors. The husband became a more devout member of their original denomination, and gave up smoking and drinking.

The dangerous immediate or longer-term consequences of divine displeasure represent a largely new sanction, and awareness of them influences behaviour in a number of ways, particularly amongst the more devout. Public testament and confession compel people to admit to improper acts where previously they would have been loth to do so. The spiritual implications of particular acts are interpreted mainly by those in authority in the various churches: the local pastors, deacons and senior members of the congregation. The influence they gain by this means makes the church an important agent in the current changes in Huli disputes and dispute settlement. The acceptance of their view is reinforced by the threat of illness, death and damnation.

Determinants in these diagnoses
Dama attack

I consider here only those cases where the explanation of *dama* attack was unequivocal, was an expression of traditional Huli religious concepts and where it was treated by sacrifice. I am therefore excluding from this discussion numerous cases where *dama* were alluded to in a vague way as possible agents, and those where *dama* attack is best seen in the Christian context. During my field work between 1977 and 1979 I saw only six cases conforming to these criteria. The current rarity of what in former times was a common response to serious illness is an index of the degree of acceptance of Christianity and modern treatments. Those who continue in their traditional observances are the subject of continual pressure to join the church and may be exposed to mockery and insults. These six cases of illness therefore tell us as much about the attitudes of these patients as about belief in *dama* attack in general.

All six patients were men, and their ages ranged from about fifty-five to eighty years. They shared a conviction that they owed their resilience to their traditional practices. Non-Christians commonly make negative comparisons between themselves and churchgoers, saying how poor is the skin of the others, deriding the way they live with their wives and making the claim that no one else of their generation has survived. They consort primarily with each other, though this is simply a preference, and not because they are ostracised by Christians. The importance of associates in maintaining a non-Christian stand is shown in case thirty-four above, where the man found himself isolated and would have succumbed to church pressure if the severity of his illness had not intervened and he had not been able to stay later with another non-Christian. The successful outcome of the *kebanda* ceremony confirmed him in his conviction that he should stay outside the church. Similarly, others of this group attribute recovery from particular past illnesses, or success in their affairs, to sacrificing to their *dama*, and are thus determined to continue.

Their illnesses were all incapacitating. Five of them involved severe pain, which was attributed to the *dama* consuming the flesh. In three of the cases, no use was made of Western medicine. In such serious illnesses it in unusual not to seek any aid post or health centre treatment. There is no incompatability between traditional treatments and Western medicine, but it is an index of these men's commitment to their own cures that they did not seek Western treatment.

Christian explanations

Hulis seek God's assistance in illnesses of all sorts, though in most cases they propose no particular divine involvement in the causation of the illness. But this response implies a Christian context for the illness. Prayer-meetings are common. People may pray for relief from relatively minor complaints. For example, amongst the over-forties with aches and pains the morbidity study showed that formal prayers for relief were said on 13% of days that they suffered symptoms. In general, prayer-meetings became a more common response with advancing age. They are held on 3% of all days with symptoms in the under-fives, increasing to 9% in the over-forties. They are most common in severe illness in adults. For example, prayer-meetings were held on 17% of days that the over-forties suffered respiratory illness with shortness of breath (*bu*).

In addition to the large number of cases of illness which were viewed loosely in a Christian context, between 1977 and 1979 I saw twenty-four cases where divine intervention of the sorts I have described was specifically postulated. I will examine some of the features of these cases and suggest factors which predispose to a diagnosis of this sort. Age and sex distribution is shown in table 23.

This diagnosis is applied primarily in the illnesses of children and adult women. The children's diagnoses are based mainly upon the statements of their mothers, so that nearly all these diagnoses are effectively the opinions

Table 23 *Age and sex distribution of those suffering from illnesses attributed to divine intervention*

Age (years)	Cases	
	Male	Female
Under 5	5	3
5–19	1	1
20–29		4
30–39	1	1
40–49		2
50–59		3
60+	1	2

Table 24 *Relationship between the patient and the person attributing his illness to divine intervention*

			Cases
Man	blames himself	his own illness	1
Woman	blames herself	her own illness	9
Woman	blames herself	her child's illness	5
Pastor	blames man	man's illness	1
Pastor	blames woman	woman's illness	1
Pastor	blames woman	her child's illness	1
Husband	blames wife	his wife's illness	2
Wife	blames husband	his child's illness	4

of adult women. This conforms with the tendency for women to be more devout than men. But the diagnosis of divine displeasure is a moral statement and we must therefore examine the social contexts in which it is made. In particular we must look at the sorts of people who apply this diagnosis. The relationship between the patient and the person attributing the illness to divine displeasure is shown in table 24.

We find that women are willing to attribute illnesses in themselves or their children to God's displeasure at their own misdeeds, usually anger and 'bad thoughts' (14 cases). Apart from spouses, the only people who feel entitled to ascribe responsibility for illness of this sort are pastors and other church leaders. Wives may ascribe illness in their children to their husbands' refusal to join the church (2 cases), or to God's displeasure at their husband's misdeeds (one case of anger, one of theft). In turn, husbands may attribute their wives' illnesses to their disobeying the husband's wishes (2 cases). Incidents such as these are common, of course, so that the ascription of illness to God's punishment for them, and the acceptance to this diagnosis, must depend largely upon the attitudes to Christianity of those involved.

Table 25 *Diagnoses in illnesses attributed to divine intervention*

Diagnosis	Cases
Respiratory infections	10
Malaria, fevers (*warago*)	8
Diarrhoea, osteomyelitis, polyarthritis, hydatidiform mole, laceration, malignant melanoma	1 of each

The main feature of the medical conditions of those whose illnesses were ascribed to explanations of this sort is that they were mainly serious, and affected primarily internal organs. The diagnoses are shown in table 25.

Of these twenty-four cases, only one did not make any use of Western treatments (the woman with the cut hand, case forty-eight), showing that Christian and medical approaches to healing are quite compatible in Huli thought. But for them the scientific approach to illness possesses little explanatory power. They make frequent use of such treatments, but their commitment to them is limited in comparison with their commitment to Christian healing.

10

Patterns of response

My concerns in this study have been to examine Huli concepts of illness, and to analyse the expression of these concepts in their responses to the range of illnesses that affects them. This task has involved my presenting data of rather different sorts. I have included more information about the burden of illness and its medical nature than is usual in an anthropological account. Conversely, details of a society's social organisation and cosmology usually have little place in a medical study, which would be more epidemiologically based. With some notable exceptions, an extended portrayal of the society's historical experience would not appear in a work of either sort. In this final chapter I draw together these various strands more explicitly than I have attempted to do as yet. First, I examine the main influences upon the decisions concerning interpretation and action that individuals must make when faced by illness. Secondly, I look at the relationship between the Huli medical system and other aspects of their society. And thirdly, I examine the relevance of this research to the study of social change.

Decisions in illness

This study is based upon the examination of a large number of cases of illness, comprising the totality of illness in one geographical area and a large number of cases from other places. I adopted this approach for a number of reasons. It allowed representative conclusions concerning the differential stress that individuals place upon the wide range of alternative responses available to them when ill. It helped to minimise any bias arising from my own theoretical interests. It also produced findings sufficiently broadly based to be of practical use in planning improvements in health services, though this aspect of the work is not discussed here. However, the stress upon representativeness has the unavoidable disadvantage of taking attention away from individual patients and the influences that guide day-to-day decisions concerning management. I have attempted to counter this tendency by drawing extensively on case material, and have considered issues that may prompt particular responses. Here I reconstruct the Huli medical culture from the point of view of the individual patient.

173

Fig. 61 Home care: a sick man attended by his sons and a brother

Most illness is managed most of the time at home. The domestic organisation of care follows from a number of the features of Huli society that I have described. Illness may be shameful where health and social value are intertwined. Men in particular prefer not to be seen in the state of decrepitude that illness may bring: the contrast between a man's normal public aspect and his appearance when ill, wigless, dusty and hunched, can be very striking. Homes are separate and private, so that visitors may be unwelcome under normal circumstances. In illness large gatherings at the house of the patient are therefore rare. They occur where some particular event is being planned or executed, such as a prayer-meeting or pig kill, and also when the word has gone out that a person is dying. Whatever their private feelings about what could be seen as evidence of others' esteem for them, most patients who are not actually moribund are irritated by such gatherings.

The 'therapy managing group' is therefore much smaller than that described by Janzen (1978) for the Kongo. Most of the time patients take their own counsel if they are well enough, or old enough, to do so. Otherwise they may discuss the issue with others in the household. In severe illness, a sick adult may receive help from a variety of sources, and the range of relationships represented reflects the facility with which Hulis can mobilise a wide range of links, including friendship. One or two people will spend much of their time caring for the sick person's immediate needs (fig. 61). The patient may also spend much time alone. People say that while it would be bad to be neglected, too many visitors are a nuisance. From this base, the sick person, those caring for him or her, or the parents in the case of a child, make their decisions as to the diagnosis and proper treatment of the illness. Huli healers were willing to offer help to their close associates, but in general traditional treatment was organised on a contract basis. If the patient or those caring for him did not possess the necessary skills in diagnosis or treatment, they sought a consultation with a specialist who was expert in the area they themselves deemed relevant, and whose treatments had a reputation for efficacy. If they disagreed with his conclusions (or her conclusions, for many healers were female in former times), or were unimpressed with the effects of the treatment, they would take further action, either alone, or with the assistance of another specialist.

This is still the dominant picture today. Patients, with or without a small group of associates, make their own decisions about the nature and implications of an illness. If they are not able to take the action they feel is indicated themselves, they will either send for assistance or emerge to seek the desired treatment. Even where they make use of modern health services, people are constantly assessing the value of the treatment they receive. Only 4% of those prescribed a course of penicillin at aid posts completed the course of five treatments. Of those admitted to Tari Health Centre, 28% discharged themselves before the doctors intended them to leave. The domestic location of care is illustrated in fig. 62, which is derived from the findings of the Hambuali morbidity study. This gives a misleading impression of the proportion of cases where action is taken, as, in fact, action of the three main sorts may be taken in the same illness.

Much of the time people took no specific action at all. Measures of the sorts included under self-help and Christian healing were generally performed at the instigation of the patient or those in attendance, and conducted at home. Aid post treatments were sought quite commonly. Here again, the decision to seek treatment at the aid post generally comes from the patient or parent, who then makes the necessary sortie to receive the medicine. The aid post orderly's assessment is likely to coincide with that of the patient or parent, so that the drug or drugs prescribed are usually the desired ones. One-half of health centre treatments are given to out-patients, so that patients must sleep away from home on only 1% of the days that they are ill.

Next, I look at the factors that guide patients or their parents through the processes of diagnosis and treatment.

Diagnosis

In this study I have arranged patients' diagnosis in an inclusive hierarchy which began with descriptive observations on the symptom (what the illness is), moved on to their concepts of the bodily processes underlying the illness

175

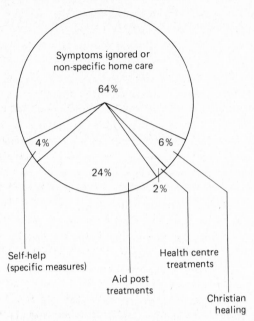

Fig. 62 Relative resort to the various treatment strategies as a percentage of symptom days

(how the illness came about) and finally their explanations of what caused the particular patient to become ill (why the illness occurred).

In most cases patients, or parents, become aware of bodily disorder and refer to it in descriptive terms only. If asked why the illness has occurred, they will answer '*bamu*', 'for no reason'. The lack of more elaborate explanation does not necessarily reflect a lack of concern. Many of these complaints are trivial, but others, such as *bu* (shortness of breath) and *ti* (diarrhoea), are not, and are regarded as serious by the Huli. In other cases, in addition to offering a descriptive diagnosis, they may express an opinion about how such illnesses come about. These are general statements, and do not specify what caused the illness in the particular instance under discussion. When asked why the illness occurred, the answers in such cases would include 'old age', 'because it is the time for head colds', 'worms', 'blood', or any of the other explanations that I elaborated in chapter 6. When asked why the illness affected them and not someone else, the answer would again be '*bamu*', 'for no reason', or '*manda nabido*', 'I don't know'. It is perhaps misleading to gloss *bamu* as 'for no reason'. The distinction between those illnesses which occur *bamu* and those which do not is more between illnesses which are given no socially or spiritually significant explanation, and those that are given such explanations. Where explanations such as assault, spirit attack or pollution

176

are given, the illness did not occur *bamu*. In the vast majority of cases, where such explanations are not invoked, the Huli are satisfied with their naturalistic explanations.

Their willingness to be satisfied with naturalistic explanations of illness is apparently unusual in comparison with other studies of illness explanation in such societies. This raises the question of the extent to which this disparity reflects a genuine difference between the Huli and other societies, or is an artefact that follows from differences in methodology. Methodological differences are certainly important. Most anthropological studies of illness have been concerned with diagnoses of the 'why?' sort. As Gillies (1976) points out, this interest has given a probably spurious impression that the societies studied do not explain illness in naturalistic terms. Here I have defined my area of study largely upon external criteria, though I found that my view of what constituted illness largely corresponded with theirs. An alternative approach might have been to concentrate upon the relationships between illness and selected aspects of their cosmology: pollution fears or spirits, for example. If I had followed that course their acceptance of naturalistic explanations might have been less apparent, and in my view the study could have become unrepresentative of modern Huli society.

But besides these methodological considerations, the Huli may be genuinely unusual in the extent of their acceptance of natural causes for illness. Gilbert Lewis (1975) also defined illness upon external criteria, and found that 57% of Gnau illnesses were unexplained, in the sense that they were not explained in terms of spirits, sorcery or breaking a taboo. In this study, only 10% of illnesses were explained in terms which supplied an answer to the question 'why me?', and less than 2% were explained in terms of spirits, sorcery or pollution. These differences between the Huli and Gnau are explained in part by my inclusion of more minor illness, but they also appear to reflect major differences in the sorts of explanation favoured by these two societies. (I should repeat the point I made above on pp. 73 and 170 that the Huli diagnoses involving spirits, sorcery or pollution that I included in the quantitative study of frequencies of the various explanations were unequivocal diagnoses which led to specific actions. In addition, a much larger number of patients may see their illnesses in a Christian context and so pray for God's assistance, or vaguely suspect pollution but discount it when they recover with non-specific measures.) They show considerable interest in physical and pathological processes. Examples I have discussed include: their interest in the movement of blood and pus; their ambitious surgical practices; their interest in bodily changes at autopsy; and their detailed interest in the timing of menstruation, conception and pregnancy. Similar features may be found in other New Guinea societies, but the level of the Huli's interest in empirical knowledge about illness appears unusual.

The likelihood of their being satisfied with naturalistic explanations relates to a number of features of the illness, and of the patient suffering from it. First, these are likely to be relatively minor complaints, including coughs, colds, aches and pains, skin lesions and so on. Secondly, where the illnesses are more severe, they are often relatively common occurrences in the age group of the person affected. Examples here include dyspnoea or diarrhoea in young children, and *amali* (generally chronic obstructive airways disease) in older people. Thirdly, apart from the illnesses of old age, they are generally of relatively short duration. Where a child is continually sickly, or an adult's illness does not resolve, they are more likely to seek an answer to the question of why that person became ill when they did.

The patient or parent, with or without the advice of one or a few associates, may come to consider that a descriptive diagnosis is insufficient. In addition to the opposites of the above three features of the illness (that is: its severity; its relative rarity in people of the patient's age group; or its chronicity) we can isolate three other issues which may prompt the selection of a diagnosis of greater explanatory power. The first is the relationship of the illness to specific Huli theories of illness; the second is the social situation of the illness; and the third is the religious significance attached to it. These issues may be closely interrelated, but I will deal with them in turn.

Relationship of the illness to theoretical knowledge

The Huli recognise a number of discrete illness categories which are supported by detailed theoretical views as to their causation, typical symptomatology and likely natural history. Diagnoses of this sort that I have discussed in some detail include those attributed to female pollution (*agali*), fright (*mogo laya*) and covetousness (*lingi*). Here I will review the issues that come to bear in the selection of these diagnoses in actual instances of illness. The problem is to differentiate between whether their ideas about the cause of the illness carry more weight than the manifest symptoms of the illness in the selection of the diagnosis. I begin by considering the main features that lead men to diagnose *agali* (illnesses in men attributed to female pollution).

Huli concepts are precise as to the causation, underlying bodily changes and symptomatology of *agali*. In the event of actual illness they may weight the various elements in this ideal conception differently, and may forgo some of these expected features entirely. The unity of this syndrome rests primarily on the ideas concerning its causation. It can therefore include a variety of disease types. But this is not a diagnosis by aetiology alone. The precision of the Huli notion of the 'typical' presentation of *agali* leads them to consider the nature of the symptoms of an illness in the process of diagnosis. In the event, the nature of the symptoms proves to be of limited importance in assigning the diagnosis, and may be little more than supportive evidence.

Lingi (illness brought about by covetous glances) is also said to have a specific cause and typical symptomatology. But in this case the aetiology may be assumed on the basis of the symptoms (usually diarrhoea in a child).

Patterns of response

I have illustrated the interaction between aetiology and symptomatology in *agali* (fig. 53) and *mogo laya* (fright illness, fig. 56). What I am concerned with here is the relative stress that the Huli place on either of these variables in different illnesses. *Agali* is primarily, though not entirely, diagnosed on the basis of the patient's exposure to the illness. In *lingi* it is more common for the parent to assume exposure on the basis of the symptoms. Fright illness is intermediate between these two diagnoses in this respect. While the child is usually known to have been startled, when the symptoms are 'typical' the child is often only assumed to have been startled, by a dream for example. The relative stress that is placed upon the aetiology or the manifestations of these illnesses varies with the verifiability of the impingement of the causative agent. Huli views of female pollution are so specific that a man can usually be quite certain whether or not he has exposed himself to it. The diagnosis of *agali* is thus based to a large extent upon exposure. Victims of *lingi* are usually young children, and so cannot report on the occurrence of covetous glances. Such glances are in any case fleeting. Mothers may therefore deduce exposure from the symptoms. Mothers usually notice if their children are startled, but when a child has just the symptoms a mother would expect in fright illness she may assume because of this that her child must have been startled without her noticing.

The social situation of illness

I have examined the strategic use of illness and the place of illness in the patterns of retribution and exchange that are central to Huli society in chapter 8. I will not repeat those points here. I will consider only the broad influences that such considerations may have upon the decisions of the patient, parent or their associates.

The presence of any illness raises doubts as to the threat that it may represent, and questions as to the proper course of action. We have seen that in most cases, Hulis are willing to consider illnesses as random discontinuities in normal functioning. They may theorise about the process underlying the illness, but they do not in general come to definite conclusions concerning the reasons why particular patients became sick when they did. One set of circumstances where people do put forward diagnoses of such specificity is when the illness is seen to extend into the patient's or parent's social relations. The simplest example of this is where a victim demands compensation for trauma unequivocally caused by an assault. But as we have seen, an intercurrent illness that might otherwise have been disregarded may take on great significance where the patient has an outstanding grievance. And the duration of an illness may coincide with the duration of litigation concerning the assault to which the illness is attributed. Such grievances are common, and Huli ideas about the bodily effects of trauma are such that a wide range of illnesses may be explained in these terms. The processes of establishing diagnoses of this sort and resolving the social implications of the illness involve extending the range of people directly involved in the management of the illness beyond the close range of immediate associates. I return to this point when I consider decisions about treatment below.

The religious significance attached to the illness

Any illness can be given a religious dimension. In traditional terms this might imply attack by a malicious *dama*, or the withdrawal of support by a normally benevolent *dama*; in Christian terms, attack by Satan, or punishment by God. Such influences may be suspected in a vague way in many cases of illness. A number of factors may transform suspicions into diagnoses. Severe and extended illnesses are more likely to be viewed in these terms, though the specific form of the illness is not usually relevant. But the key issue here is the particular attitude of the patient, his parents or close associates towards traditional religion or Christianity. In general, we find that people's interpretations of illness are consistent with their preceding committment to particular religious views. Normally devout Christians are more likely to interpret illness in themselves or their children in terms of their faith. The few practising traditionalists interpret their illnesses more readily than others in terms of Huli religious ideas. Instances of illness, especially serious illness, can also cause people to revise their usual religious allegiances. The opinions of others outside the patient's immediate circle are often important here. Pastors, other committed Christians or practitioners of Huli healing may offer their interpretations of the illness. As we have seen, such interventions may lead to patients and those close to them revising their religious allegiances.

Selection between treatments

We have seen that the Huli are very willing to use Western treatments in conditions of all sorts. This acceptance of Western medicine corresponds with the abandonment of most traditional cures, but in most cases this shift does not imply any direct conflict between traditional and Western therapies. Their pragmatic approach to most illnesses has led them to take advantage of those treatments offered by the Department of Public Health which they judge to be more efficacious than their own methods. Patients, or their mothers in the case of small children, decide for themselves that some medicine might be beneficial, and present themselves for treatment. But, while they are very willing to use Western treatments, their utilisation of health services often appears ambivalent and uncommitted. One issue here is that they are uncertain of their rights in gaining access to government services. But we must also consider the area of their medical culture occupied by Western medicine. They have only limited knowledge of the premises underlying the prescription of these treatments. The germ theory of disease has been explained in formal and informal health education, but only those aspects which accord loosely

180

with their own view have been widely accepted. For them, Western treatments are largely on a par with their own treatments for conditions explained in terms of proximate causes. They are seen mainly as techniques which act directly upon the illness. Where a more complex explanation of the illness is suspected, Western treatments may be helpful, but they cannot be expected to eradicate the cause of the illness. We therefore find that illnesses that are diagnosed in social, moral or religious terms are usually treated with specific measures as well as, though not to the exclusion of, Western medicine.

With illnesses explained in terms of the acts of others, particularly assault, dispute settlement can constitute treatment of the illness, though aspirin and other medicines may be used. Such illnesses cannot be resolved privately. To succeed, patients must mobilise as wide a range of support as possible. They will make the illness public knowledge by frequent complaining, regular visits to the aid post and graphic portrayals of their affliction, such as fainting or stooping. They commonly seek medical evidence to support their case, either in the form of an X-ray or a doctor's letter from Tari Health Centre, or the verbal support of an aid post orderly. They will approach local government councillors and village court magistrates in the pursuit of their claims. Sufferers of complaints that arise in social relations must seek their resolution there, and so forgo the quiet and privacy of their homes, the environment they normally prefer when ill.

While traditional treatments have been largely eclipsed by Western medicine with little friction between these alternative approaches, Christian healing is in explicit conflict with traditional measures. Most of the moral and spiritual aspects of the traditional medical system are now seen in a Christian context, as I have explained in chapter 9. Such interpretations are often private and the response, prayer, is also private, or restricted to a small circle. But on occasions such treatments may become more public. The patient or other church members may feel that a larger service is indicated, or they may decide to kill pigs. This is one circumstance where the usual autonomy of the patient and those in attendance may not be respected. The Christians' conviction of the correctness of their view makes them willing to intrude upon the affairs of others in a way which is not usual in Huli society.

Traditional cures are now practised in the main by and for the few older men who for their own reasons have repudiated Christianity. When they are ill these men usually keep to themselves, or consort with others of like mind. They are committed to their Huli beliefs, and so perform traditional cures where the diagnosis indicates a particular treatment. The question in these cases, therefore, is why these particular individuals choose to withstand the current trend of abandoning traditional observances? I have discussed this on pp. 169–70. But it is also interesting to consider which traditional cures are still sought by those who in health would decry such practices. These include treatment for female pollution in men (*agali gamu*), removal of the parasitic mass, *kuyanda* (*kuyanda duguaga*), removal of *nambis poisin* (*nambis poisin duguaga*) and the removal of Ibatiri's arrow (*tawa timu duguaga*). Western medicine is known to be effective in many conditions, but it is not thought capable of countermanding the influence of particularly Huli phenomena, such as spirits and pollution. Christianity is said to be 'like *gamu*' (the term for spell or rite) in being capable of counteracting all harmful influences. There are clear continuities between Christianity and Huli religious views, and the Huli interpretation of Christianity has absorbed many traditional concerns. But there are no satisfactory modern responses to some fundamentally Huli problems. The frequency with which some traditional ceremonies are performed, despite the general atmosphere of disapproval, therefore indicates certain lacunae in the ability of medical or Christian means to remedy Huli afflictions.

Kuyanda and *agali* both relate to their complex of ideas surrounding female pollution, and I have discussed the modern practice of healing of these conditions in chapter 7. The continued practice of the removal of Ibatiri's arrow (*tawa timu duguaga*) by people who are otherwise Christians is explicable on rather different grounds. This traditional ceremony has now been adapted for the treatment of the new condition, 'coastal' sorcery (*nambis poisin*). These two conditions have become conceptually linked. There is some confusion as to whether the removal of coastal sorcery (*nambis poisin duguaga*) is really a pagan (*kanaka*) practice. The confusion here stems from the linkage in people's minds between 'traditional' and 'non-Christian'. This treatment was not known in former times, so some maintain that it is not unchristian (*kanaka*). In addition, 'coastal' sorcery is a novel illness, and people assume that it should be treated by specific means of the sort used by 'coastal' people. Some of the methods used are new, but the coincidental similarity between these and their own ceremony for the removal of Ibatiri's arrow (*tawa timu duguaga*) has led them to use this traditional cure for the new illness.

Illness and society: reciprocal influences

The particular mix of diseases, concepts, techniques and organisation that constitutes each society's medical culture relates in various ways to other aspects of the society. An obvious example of the concordance between social and medical systems in the West is the caricature of family roles presented by the relationship between the hospital doctor (father), in benevolent though somewhat distant authority, the nurse (mother), deferential to the doctor and entrusted with the continual minor tasks of caring for the patient (child), who is the passive recipient of these attentions. In small-scale societies such interrelationships may be more clearly drawn. Here I will consider the ways in which the Huli medical system is embedded in the social order, and reflects the values particular to this society.

At the most immediate level we saw that the frequencies of some complaints are understandable in terms of the division of labour and other features of Huli society which lead to differing experiences and activities for males and females. Examples included differences in the common sorts of pain complained of by men as opposed to women, and different sorts of skin lesion. But in these simple examples social influences are operating primarily in effecting the differential exposure of individuals to traumata and other environmental insults. The socially patterned meaning of the lesion to the sufferer is of little importance.

More complex interactions between the social and medical spheres are revealed in the attribution of illness to assault and the consequent judicial mode of treatment. Men and women attribute illnesses to different sorts of injury. Men are more concerned by arrow wounds, and women by blows with sticks, and these differences reflect the different sorts of violence to which either sex is subject: men suffer the effects of injuries received in battle, while women are concerned with the effects of domestic violence. But illnesses of this sort do not simply reflect the level of violence. They are also claims. Balance is a central concern in Huli society. Relations between individuals are marked by reciprocity. This takes the material form of the exchange of food and wealth, but people are also concerned with balance in their relationships and are highly sensitive to slights or other evidence of disrespect. The imbalance that follows a verbal insult can be repaired by the payment of compensation. Illness may be seen to constitute evidence of the legitimacy of the injured person's claim, though the physical insult may be less important to the sufferer than the affront that an assault represents. Whatever the course of the disease process, these illnesses therefore may represent negotiations for respect on the part of the aggrieved person. The identification of the illness with the social process of redress is explicit in Huli behaviour and idiom, as when the arrow stops 'growing' when compensation has been paid.

The pattern of such illness shows that it may be seen as a form of coercion by those whose access to other means of redress may be limited. Most of these cases concerned married women. In comparison with many highland societies, Huli women are more able to assert their wishes and prevail. They are able to initiate and secure divorce. But in saying this one must not exaggerate their autonomy. A forceful woman may be capable of asserting her wishes whatever the opinions of her affines and her natal group. But most women are not sufficiently determined to stand against both their brothers and their husband. A husband's ill-treatment may lead to little support. But if he should harm her or cause her to become sick through his ill-treatment, her plight becomes publicly recognised and she is more likely to achieve the reparation she desires, or a divorce should she wish it.

Other sorts of illness explanations can be seen as extensions of the relations between men and women. When mothers attribute the illnesses of their children to fright and the fright was caused by their husbands' violence to them, we could say that the women are gaining redress from their husbands for ill-treatment. Similarly, the attribution of illness to divine displeasure reveals strategies of social control. Men may say that their wives' illnesses follow from divine displeasure at their not being subservient. Women may attribute their children's illnesses to their husband's unchristian behaviour. Church leaders may influence the behaviour of their flock by attributing illness to behaviour of which they disapprove.

Male–female relations are surrounded by elaborate codes of belief and practice. The ordering of sexual relations is strict. In former times men and women were expected to lead very separate lives. Men grew and cooked their own food, lived apart from women, were concerned with the bachelor cult until marriage and then strove through a variety of means to limit the harmful influences of women upon them. Many of these restrictions are no longer observed by most men, but the attitudes they express have proved to be amongst the most resistant to change. Ideally, sexuality is concerned only with the proper production of children. The rules that guide this focus are subsumed by the dangers for men of weakness, failure in public roles and death through specific illnesses. These illnesses, as penalties for flouting the rules surrounding sexuality, constitute evidence for the need for such rules. The danger of illness also supports other values in Huli society to do with male–female relations. The dangers of illegitimate sex may protect marriage. By 'stepping over' his wife and satisfying himself adulterously a man places the health of his children at risk, besides exposing himself to the danger of *agali*.

A number of other explanations of illness may buttress moral values. 'To be struck down by heat' (*tawaneme baya*) is an extreme penalty for impropriety. The victim, incidentally ill, dies solely from being in the presence of someone whom he has wronged. The spirit Datagaliwabe may intervene and cause death as a punishment for moral transgressions (see also Glasse 1965:37, 48–9). *Tawaneme baya* and Datagaliwabe are invoked most uncommonly. But their existence as concepts makes complete the complex of ideas concerning the implications to oneself and to others of private thoughts and feelings. In traditional society there were no institutions that allowed individuals to exert influence over others in any predictable way. Modern institutions, such as the village court, have not altered the means most people must use to induce others to give them support when they require it, which consist largely of an effective presentation of self. Eloquence is essential, but some qualities are thought to act directly upon an audience. These arise within, and find expression primarily in the state of the skin. The direct effect of this inner state of health upon others is expressed in the idiom of the 'open nose'.

When they are thwarted or feel themselves abused, ill-effects can follow. Hulis talk of strong emotions as if they act autonomously. They are sensitive to the possible implications of powerful emotions in others, and are wary of eliciting them. When someone commits suicide through anger, whoever caused their anger is held responsible for the death. If you refuse someone what they wish, they may harm you through spite (*madane*). If you do not share food with someone, their desire (*hame*) for what you have may itself cause you to become ill through *lingi*, though they intended you no harm, and are not held culpable for the illness. These direct effects of feelings upon others contrast with the lack of formal means of gaining redress. Those who have performed highly improper acts may be able to avoid any consequences by leaving the parish of those they have wronged, and settling elsewhere. The possibility of automatic punishment for wrong-doing seen in *tawaneme baya*, or the power of Datagaliwabe, offer a means of enforcing the moral code where their social institutions are not adequate to do so. This aspect of the Huli view of morality is occasionally supported by the ancestor spirits, Kebali, or by other spirits in oath-taking (*tiari*). But in general the effects of improper behaviour I have described are said to follow directly from the act without the intervention of the spirits. The religious significance of these implications of immoral acts has been adapted and reinforced by the present preoccupation with Christianity.

Another aspect of illness beliefs which may relate to the wide range of cross-cutting ties in Huli society is sorcery. We saw that traditionally the feared sorcerers and techniques were those of the surrounding cultures. Whatever the frequency of illness attribution to sorcery in former times, it is now rare. The commonest modern form of sorcery is a novel technique which is said to come from peoples unknown in former times. The boundaries of malignity have been pushed yet further as knowledge of other places has increased. The lack of stress upon sorcery within Huli society may follow in part from the interconnectedness of each group and the mobility of individuals, who travel widely throughout the Huli area. These aspects of their social organisation make the definition of in-groups and out-groups less tenable.

The quality of Huli illness descriptions accords with the quality of their public life. The ethos of individualism and their vigorous style combine to make this a volatile society. Meetings can quickly become fractious. People talk as if any quarrel might erupt into war. There is in fact comparatively little violence in modern Huli society, but frequent rumours of dire events lead to a charged atmosphere. Their view of illness is similarly volatile. The body is fragile. The spirit is skittish, and death may follow suddenly from some minor insult. They suspect the worst very quickly, so that when a person faints they may be dying. People are at risk whatever their state of health. Similarly, they see society as under constant threat from the disorder that may follow the conflicting wishes of its members.

Medical pluralism: continuity and change

The study of belief in times of rapid social change can be problematical, especially where there is considerable disagreement between individuals about the extent that old and new ideas are pertinent, where the range of available ideas is considerable and where the relationship between assertion and behaviour may be unclear. The study of the response to illness offers a valuable introduction to these areas. Illness that is perceived as serious demands reference to available knowledge, both to explain it and to guide treatment. Social change may challenge previously accepted ideas, posing both the problem of choosing between alternative explanations, and the problem of reconciling what was already understood before with newly presented possibilities, and making them intelligible. Ideas introduced by social changes both modify and are modified by pre-existing schemes of knowledge. The study of responses to illness allows us to examine the use of novel concepts in explanation, and their effects upon action, with precision.

The majority of treatments now used by the Huli were unknown to them thirty years ago. The data concerning illness behaviour that I have presented provides an index of change in this area of Huli life. We can expect people to accept or reject according to the fit of the new, though they may also abandon some practices and adopt others under duress. For example, the Huli abandoned warfare largely as a result of the administration's superior strength. But in the health field, while the administration insisted upon a number of changes such as the interment of corpses, specific coercion has played little part in the transformation of the Huli medical culture. One element here that I have already commented upon at length is their empirical approach to much illness. Their willingness to experiment with Western medicine was noted by Yelland, who led the first medical patrol in the Tari Basin in 1954. He wrote (1955: 32) 'Each morning there would be more people volunteering to have treatment, and it was not unusual to see the Medical Orderly surrounded by people, all pointing to sores and asking for attention'. Aspects of traditional therapeutics have simply atrophied in the face of what the Huli regard as more effective treatments. This is particularly the case in treatments which have little cosmological significance.

In addition to this simple process of replacement by modern medicine, traditional healing has also been actively discouraged by the missions. The abandonment of traditional religious practices has certainly been the aim of the majority of missionaries, and they and the Huli evangelists they trained have approached this end through a well-organised programme of proselytisation. In other respects there are many similarities between the aims of the missions and those of the administration, but the Huli have not in general felt that compliance with the missions was obligatory. One set of reasons for their interest in Christianity concerns their dependent status. During the 1940s a number of disturbances, some fortuitous and some secondary to European exploration, caused the Huli to experiment with the *mara gamu* cult taught to them by the Enga. The 1950s and 1960s brought administrative control and the permanent presence of European administrators and missionaries. The political and technical superiority of the Europeans raised many questions and people sought some answers by reinterpreting their own mythology. The only coherent presentation of European knowledge was supplied by the missions, so that Christianity has come to be known as *tuguli* (school). The missions and administration also run primary and secondary schools for children, but the only generalised system of adult education is that offered by church services and individual counselling. The teaching offered to adults is thus concerned almost entirely with the Bible. Implicit in this teaching, and the Huli's understanding of it, is the sense that European authority and competence is somehow underpinned by biblical knowledge. Their eagerness to acquire such knowledge can therefore be seen as a wish to obtain the lore (*mana*) relevant to modern circumstances now that their own lore has proved inadequate in some areas of modern life.

Against this ostensible current of abandoning former practices, in illness we find perseverence with a number of traditional responses. The first of these is the ascription of illness to assault, and the consequent demand for compensation. This is in conflict with Christian teaching, as Christians are not supposed to demand compensation for injury. To do so is not disapproved as strongly as, say, a sacrifice, but Christians demanding compensation can find themselves under strong pressure to desist. Nevertheless, this response to illness is still common. We could perhaps predict this from what we know of the Huli. This finding confirms the centrality of exchange and retribution which could be termed a 'core concept' (Prins 1979) in this society. Secondly, the divisions in sexual relations were highly marked in traditional society, and these concerns with sexuality, its control, and with fertility, continue today. The study of illness behaviour confirms that these concerns also express basic Huli values. Such ideas have been modified in various ways, but their specificity and the lack of any detailed parallels in European thought have caused the Huli to retain significant areas of these beliefs and the practices that follow from them.

We can also see the retention of core concepts in the wider religious sphere. The fervour of their adoption of Christianity stems in part from a number of propitious similarities between the concerns of their own religion and the aspects of Christianity that have been stressed to them. One set of continuities between traditional and Christian preoccupations is in the concern with the social and personal implications of thought and feeling which I have considered in chapter 8. Another is in the similarity between Huli *dama* and Christian devils that I have considered in chapter 9. The millennial aspect of Christianity which has been stressed to them also accords strongly with their traditional religious concerns. Christian teaching has caused them to change the emphasis they place on some aspects of traditional lore. But there are clear parallels between, on the one hand the past crucifixion and the imminent Judgement Day, and on the other the past death of Bayebaye and the return of *mbingi*. Christianity therefore offers an enduring vehicle for their former concerns. Despite the obvious differences between the past style of traditional observances and the present form of Christian worship, the Huli themselves stress the clear continuities between former and current religious preoccupations.

The spread of Western medicine, as well as the complexities of most traditional medical systems, usually require that responses to illness must be investigated as aspects of 'medical pluralism', which Janzen (1978:xviii) defines as 'the existence in a single society of differently designed and conceived medical systems'. Janzen's study is valuable in demonstrating the multiplicity of choices available to the group he studied, and the process whereby patients may shuttle back and forth between different types of treatment. He points out that while the various sorts of treatment available may be organisationally and conceptually distinct, they are not in direct conflict with each other. Each type of therapy may have its place in the broad set of diagnostic ideas of the people he studied, and 'the widespread pattern of lay therapy management prevents separate therapy systems from becoming irreconcilably disparate' (ibid:222). He refers to this peaceful coexistence of differing approaches to treatment as 'complementary medical pluralism'.

The term 'medical pluralism' has slipped into common usage without the definitional wrangle that attended the introduction of the term pluralism into the anthropological analysis of political institutions. The study of political pluralism belongs to two quite distinct traditions. The earlier interest was in the coexistence of a variety of relatively autonomous political, religious, professional and economic groupings in modern Western societies. Writers such as Tawney (1920) regarded these groupings as counters to what they saw as the dehumanising effects of *laissez-faire* capitalism. The second approach to pluralism has grown largely from the work of Furnivall, whose analysis of the economics of colonial societies led him to identify 'plural societies' which in their purest form are characterised by 'different sections of the community living side by side, but separately, within the same political unit' (1948:304). The two applications of the idea of pluralism have quite contradictory implications. In the first view the product of pluralism is harmony. In the second, pluralism is the product of sectional domination (Kuper 1969). It is this second view of pluralism that has been adopted by anthropologists.

What does the definitional debate concerning other pluralisms tell us about the way that the term 'medical pluralism' is used? In my view very little. This literature, for example the work of M. G. Smith (1969), by concerning itself primarily with institutional forms, has taken insufficient note of the ways in which individuals can meander through a variety of groupings or institutions as their needs or whims dictate. The focus upon individuals is particularly important in the medical sphere, as it is unusual for people to maintain their contact with a healing institution in times of health. Such allegiance does occur, in the cults of affliction for example, but the resorts utilised in times of illness do not in general have the enduring influence that, say, political and economic institutions have.

Instead, medical pluralism usually denotes a plurality of medicines rather than a distinct category of pluralism as this term is used in either school of political theory. Nevertheless, the use of the term 'medical pluralism' is justified in terms of a third tradition: in the philosophical sense, pluralism is a system of thought where more than one ultimate principle is recognised. The medical culture of societies such as the Huli is clearly pluralistic in this sense. However, in applying the term we must guard against assumptions that may follow from more restricted uses of the term, particularly the assumption that for these societies medical pluralism is necessarily a modern phenomenon.

The interest in pluralism in the wider anthropological literature was prompted largely by the effects of colonial and post-colonial changes. These made the former portrayal of societies as discrete, homogeneous, cultural units increasingly untenable. These same changes, including the introduction of Western medicine and the development of spiritualist churches, increased the range of medical responses. But this should not be taken to mean that previous medical systems were invariably monistic. The change in style in anthropological studies of illness is as much a reflection of changes in anthropologists' conceptions as it is of the changes experienced by the peoples they study. Janzen (1981) points out that Evans-Pritchard's *Witchcraft, Oracles and Magic among the Azande*, a work which has come to be taken as the model representation of a closed system, is also a portrayal of medical pluralism. The critical measure of the success of an anthropological analysis of another medical culture is no longer assumed to be the congruity of the intellectual, symbolic and sociological coherence that it reveals. The extent to which other medical cultures are systematised must be a matter of empirical observation rather than a reflection of the dictates of the discipline. Last (1981) prompts us to accept the extreme case of a 'non-system', where the value of some remedies 'lies in their very strangeness, in their *not* being part of a known system of medicine' (ibid:389).

When they are ill, individual Hulis may choose between the broad categories of Western medicine, Christian healing, litigation and traditional healing, and will make more decisions within each of these categories of treatment. Each of these types of treatment is likely to involve different specialists: an aid post orderly or doctor, a pastor, a magistrate and a

189

practising healer respectively. The picture that emerges is one of diversity. But diversity was a feature of the traditional medical culture. Each of the components of the modern medical scene had its equivalent strategy in former times. One could even say that there was greater diversity in traditional Huli medicine, for a wide range of healing rituals and methods of divination as well as mechanical techniques have now been abandoned. The route by which the term 'pluralism' has entered the anthropological lexicon must not be taken to imply that in societies like the Huli medical pluralism is the outcome of the introduction of colonial medicine and other recent innovations. Individual Hulis have always had available to them a wide array of resorts in illness.

My main aim here has been to identify the variety of different influences on people's current responses to illness. I have not categorised these influences by their source or their institutional base, such as naturalistic, *kanaka*, Western medical, Christian, judicial and so on, but have considered them together as alternative components of a single medical culture. The various types of treatment available to the Huli are organisationally quite distinct. But a key quality of the Huli medical culture, despite its diversity, is its coherence to the individual Hulis who make use of it.

References

Ackerknecht, E. H. (1946) 'Natural diseases and rational treatment in primitive medicine', *Bulletin of the History of Medicine*, **19**:467–97.
Ackerknecht, E. H. (1947) 'Primitive surgery', *American Anthropology*, **25**:45–9.
Barnes, J. A. (1962) 'African models in the New Guinea Highlands', *Man*, **62**:5–9.
Barth, F. (1975) *Ritual and Knowledge among the Baktaman of New Guinea*. Yale University Press, New Haven.
Biocca, E. (1945) 'Estudos etno-biológicos sobre os índios da região do Alto Rio Negro – Amazonas. Nota II – Transmissão ritual e transmissão criminosa da espiroquetose discromica (Purú-Purú, Pinta, etc.) entre os índios do Rio Icana', *Arquivos de Biologia (São Paulo)*, **29**:7–12. (Translated for me by Dr Christine Hugh-Jones.)
Blong, R. J. (1985) *The Time of Darkness: Local Legends and Volcanic Reality in Papua New Guinea*. University of Washington Press, Washington, D.C.
Brown, P. and G. Buchbinder (eds.) (1976) *Man and Woman in the New Guinea Highlands*. American Anthropological Association Special Publication 8.
Cohn, B. S. (1980) 'History and anthropology: the state of play', *Comparative Studies in Society and History*, **22**:198–221.
de Lepervanche, M. (1967–8) 'Descent, residence and leadership in the New Guinea Highlands', *Oceania*, **38**:134–58, 163–89.
Devereux, G. (1956) 'Normal and abnormal: the key problem of psychiatric anthropology'. In *Some Uses of Anthropology: Theoretical and Applied*, eds. J. B. Casagrande and T. Gladwin. Anthropological Society of Washington, Washington, D.C.
Evans-Pritchard, E. E. (1937) *Witchcraft, Oracles and Magic among the Azande*. Clarendon Press, Oxford.
Fabrega, H. (1972) *Disease and Social Behaviour*. The M.I.T. Press, Cambridge, Mass.
Feachem, R. G. A. (1977) 'Environmental health engineering as human ecology'. In *Subsistence and Survival*, ed. T. P. Bayliss-Smith and R. G. A. Feachem, 23–61. Academic Press, San Diego, Ca.
Fortune, R. F. (1932) *Sorcerers of Dobu*. Routledge and Kegan Paul, London.
Frake, C. O. (1961) 'The diagnosis of disease among the Subanun of Mindanao', *American Anthropology*, **63**:113–32.
Frankel, S. J. (1976) 'Mass hysteria in the New Guinea Highlands', *Oceania*, **47**, no. 2:106–33.
Frankel, S. J. (1979a) *Kebanda* (a film record: copies of this and the following films are held on video cassette in the archives of the Department of Social Anthropology, Cambridge, and the Institute of Papua New Guinea Studies, Port Moresby.)
Frankel, S. J. (1979b) *Ogoanda* (a film record).

191

References

Frankel, S. J. (1979c) *Nogo golo* (a film record).

Frankel, S. J. (1979d) *Ega kamia hangaga* (a film record).

Frankel, S. J. (1979e) *Tawa timu duguaga* (a film record).

Frankel, S. J. (1984) 'Peripheral health workers are central to primary health care: lessons from Papua New Guinea's aid posts', *Social Science and Medicine*, **19**(3):279–290.

Frankel, S. J. (1985) 'Social and cultural aspects of family planning programmes', *Papua New Guinea Medical Journal*, **6**(3):155–62.

Frankel, S. J. and D. Smith (1982) 'Conjugal bereavement amongst the Huli', *British Journal of Psychiatry*, **141**:302–5.

Frankel, S. J. and D. Lehmann (1984) 'Oral rehydration therapy: combining anthropological and epidemiological approaches in the evaluation of a Papua New Guinea programme', *Journal of Tropical Medicine and Hygiene*, **87**:137–142.

Frankel, S. J. and D. Lehmann (1985) 'Oral rehydration: what mothers think', *World Health Forum*, **6**:271–3.

Frankel, S. J. and G. A Lewis (eds.) (forthcoming) *Medical Pluralism in Papua New Guinea*. D. Reidel, Dordrecht.

Freidson, E. (1970) *Profession of Medicine*. Harper and Row, New York.

Furnivall, J. S. (1948) *Colonial Policy and Practice*. Cambridge University Press.

Gillies, E. (1976) 'Causal criteria in African classifications of disease'. In *Social Anthropology and Medicine*, ed. J. B. Loudon, pp. 358–95. Academic Press, San Diego, Ca.

Gillison, G. (1980) 'Images of nature in Gimi thought'. In *Nature, Culture and Gender*, eds. C. MacCormack and M. Strathern, pp. 143–73. Cambridge University Press.

Glasse, R. M. (1963) 'Bingi at Tari', *Journal of the Polynesian Society*, **72**:270.

Glasse, R. M. (1965) 'The Huli of the Southern Highlands'. In *Gods, Ghosts and Men in Melanesia*, eds. P. Lawrence and M. J. Meggitt, pp. 27–49. Oxford University Press.

Glasse, R. M. (1968) *Huli of Papua: a Cognatic Descent System*. Mouton, Paris.

Glick, L. B. (1968) 'Foundations of a primitive medical system'. Unpublished Ph.D. thesis, University of Pennsylvania.

Glick, L. B. (1967) 'Medicine as an ethnographic category', *Ethnology*, **6**:31–56.

Golson, Jack (1982) 'Agriculture in New Guinea: the long view'; 'Agricultural technology in New Guinea'; and 'New Guinea agricultural history: a case study'. In *A Time to Plant and a Time to Uproot. A History of Agriculture in Papua New Guinea*, eds. D. Denoon, and C. Snowden, pp. 33–64. Institute of Papua New Guinea Studies.

Good, B. (1977) 'The heart of what's the matter', *Culture, Medicine and Psychiatry*, **1**:25–58.

Harley, G. W. (1941) *Native African Medicine*. Harvard University Press, Cambridge, Mass.

Hides, J. (1936) *Papuan Wonderland*. Blackie, Glasgow.

Janzen, J. M. (1978) *The Quest for Therapy in Lower Zaire*. University of California Press.

Janzen, J. M. (1981) 'The need for a taxonomy of health in the study of African therapeutics', *Social Science and Medicine*, **15B**:185–94.

Junod, H. A. (1912) *The Life of a South African Tribe*. I. *The Social Life*. Attinger Fréres, Neuchâtel.

Kleinman, A. (1980) *Patients and Healers in the Context of Culture*. University of California Press.

Kuper, Leo (1969) 'Plural societies: perspectives and problems'. In *Pluralism in Africa*, eds. Leo Kuper and M. G. Smith, University of California Press.

References

Langness, L. L. (1964) 'Some problems in the conceptualization of Highlands social structures', *American Anthropology*, Special Publication on New Guinea, **66**:162–82.

Langness, L. L. (1968) 'Bena Bena political organization', *Anthropological Forum*, **2**:180–98.

Last, M. (1981) 'The importance of knowing about not knowing', *Social Science and Medicine*, **15B**:387–92.

Leach, E. R. (1961) *Rethinking Anthropology*. Athlone Press, London.

Lewis, A. J. (1953) 'Health as a social concept', *British Journal of Sociology*, **4**:109–24.

Lewis, G. A. (1975) *Knowledge of Illness in a Sepik Society*. Athlone Press, London.

Lewis, I. M. (1976) *Social Anthropology in Perspective*. Penguin Books, Harmondsworth.

Maddocks, I. (1978) 'Pari village'. In *Basic Health Care in Developing Countries*, ed. B. S. Hetzel, pp. 11–37. Oxford University Press.

Malinowski, B. (1922) *Argonauts of the Western Pacific*. Routledge and Kegan Paul, London.

Meggitt, M. J. (1964) 'Male–female relationships in the Highlands of Australian New Guinea', *American Anthropology*, Special Publication on New Guinea, **66**:204–24.

Meggitt, M. J. (1965) *The Lineage System of the Mae-Enga*. Oliver and Boyd, Edinburgh.

Meggitt, M. J. (1973) 'The sun and the shakers', *Oceania*, **44**, no.1:1–37; no.2:109–26.

Newman, P. L. (1964) 'Religious belief and ritual in a New Guinea society', *American Anthropology*, Special Publication on New Guinea, **66**:257–72.

Oldfield, F., P. G. Appleby and R. Thompson (1980) 'Palaeoecological studies of three lakes in the Highlands of Papua New Guinea, *Journal of Ecology*, **68**:457–78.

Parish List (1980). Southern Highlands Project, Mendi, P.N.G.

Pethybridge, M. (n.d.) *From Fear to Freedom*. Lakeland.

Prins, Gwyn (1979) 'Disease at the cross-roads: towards a history of therapeutics in Bulozi since 1876', *Social Science and Medicine*, **13B**:285–315.

Prins, Gwyn (1981) '"What is to be done? Burning questions of our movement"', *Social Science and Medicine*, **15B**:175–83.

Raich, H. (1967) 'Ein weiteres Fruchtbarkeitsidol aus dem westlichen Hochland von Neuguinea', *Anthropos*, **62**:938–9.

Riley, I. D. (1979) 'Pneumonia in Papua New Guinea'. Unpublished M.D. thesis, University of Sydney.

Rodrigue, R. B. (1963) 'A report on a widespread psychological disorder called *lulu* seen among the Huli linguistic group in Papua', *Oceania*, **33**:274–9.

Rubel, A. J. (1964) 'The epidemiology of a folk illness: *susto* in Hispanic America', *Ethnology*, **3**:268–83.

Schieffelin, E. R. (1982) 'The *bau aa* ceremonial hunting lodge'. In *Rituals of Manhood*, ed. G. H. Herdt, pp. 155–200. University of California Press.

Shryock, R. H. (1948) *The Development of Modern Medicine*. Victor Gollancz, London.

Sillitoe, P. (1979) *Give and Take*. St Martin's Press, New York.

Simons, R. C. and C. C. Hughes (1985) *The Culture-Bound Syndromes*. D. Reidel, Dordrecht.

Sinnett, P. F. (1975) *The People of Murapin*. Institute of Medical Research, Papua New Guinea, Monograph Series no. 4.

Smith, M. G. (1969) 'Institutional and political conditions of pluralism'. In *Pluralism in Africa*, ed. Leo Kuper and M. G. Smith, University of California Press.

Strathern, A. J. (1968) 'Sickness and frustration', *Mankind*, **6**:545–51.

References

Strathern, A. J. (1972) *One Father, One Blood*. A.N.U. Press, Canberra.

Strathern, A. J. (1973) 'Kinship, descent and locality: some New Guinea examples'. In *The Character of Kinship*, ed. J. Goody, pp. 21–33. Cambridge University Press.

Strathern, A. J. (1977) 'Why is shame on the skin?' In *The Anthropology of the Body*, ed. J. Blacking, pp. 99–110. Academic Press, London.

Strathern, A. J. (1981) '"Noman": representations of identity in Mount Hagen'. In *The Structure of Folk Models*, ed. L. Holy and M. Stuchlik, pp. 281–303. Academic Press, London.

Strathern, M. (1968) '*Popokl*: the question of morality', *Mankind*, **6**:553–61.

Strathern, M. (1972) *Women In Between*. Seminar Press, London.

Strathern, M. (1980) 'No nature, no culture: the Hagen case'. In *Nature, Culture and Gender*, eds. C. MacCormack and M. Strathern, pp. 174–222. Cambridge University Press.

Tawney, R. H. (1920) *The Acquisitive Society*. Harcourt, New York.

Topley, M. (1970) 'Chinese traditional ideas and the treatment of disease', *Man*, **5**:421–37.

Turner, V. (1967) *The Forest of Symbols*. Cornell University Press, N.Y.

Twyman, E. (1961) *The Battle for the Bigwigs*. Unevangelised Fields Mission, Melbourne.

Vines, A. P. (1970) *An Epidemiological Sample Survey of the Highlands, Mainland and Island Regions of the Territory of Papua New Guinea*. Department of Public Health, Port Moresby, Papua New Guinea.

Wood, A. W. (1980) 'Food cropping in the Tari basin', paper presented at the Second Papua New Guinea Food Crops Conference, Goroka, July 1980.

Wurm, S. A. (1961) 'The languages of the Eastern, Western and Southern Highlands, Territory of Papua and New Guinea', In *Linguistic Survey of the Southwestern Pacific*, ed. A. Cappell. Noumea.

Yelland, L. C. (1955) 'Tari sub-district patrols numbers 1, 2 and 3 from January to June, 1954', *Papua New Guinea Medical Journal*, **1**, no.1:29–32.

Index

abdominal pain, 83, 85–6, 106, 116, 117, 140, 141, 149; Huli descriptions of, 87, 88; treatments for, 89, 94
abortion, 101
abscesses, 67, 82, 85, 130; treatment for, 89
aches and pains, 64–6, 178; treatments for, 89, 92; *see also* abdominal pain; backache; chest pain; headache; injuries; joint pain
administrative control, development of, 10–15, 28, 29
adultery, 102, 110, 184
aetiology, 1, 7, 8, 118, 127, 129; interaction between symptomatology and, 119, 123, 137, 141, 178–9; *see also* explanations of illness
agali (illness in men caused by female pollution), 106–8, 113–23, 137, 163, 165, 178–9, 182, 184; traditional healing of, *see agali gamu; nogo tini gamu*
agali gamu, 106–8, 114, 115, 120–2, 181
agnates, agnation, 39–51 *passim*
agriculture, 26–7
aid post treatments, 15, 75, 77–9, 131, 170, 175; accessibility as factor in use of, 92–5
Ain's cult, 28–9
amali (chronic chest disease), 27, 74, 86, 87, 130, 133, 162
Amazonian peoples, attitudes to skin disfigurement among, 3–4
Ambua, Mount, 22
anatomical knowledge, Huli, 81; *see also* bodily processes
ancestors, *see* founding ancestors
angawai (rite to recall and bind the soul within the body), 54, 136, 139
anger (*keba, popokl*), illnesses attributed to, 143–4, 167, 185
angua ('stepping over'), harm caused by, 102, 106, 156, 184
arrow wounds, 65, 88, 127, 128, 130, 131, 183; treatment for, 90–1

arthritis, 130; arthritic knees, 65, 92, 158; *see also* polyarthritis
Asia Pacific Christian Mission (Evangelical Church of Papua), 14, 15, 33
assault, illnesses attributed to, 52, 124–36, 176–7, 179, 181, 183, 187; *see also* injuries
ayumbu ('axe') ritual, 21–2

bachelor cult, *see ibagiya*
backache, 64–5, 82, 83, 106, 116, 130, 155, 163; treatments for, 90, 91, 92
Bainage parish, 41, 42
Baiyage Horo (mythical giant), 41
bamu (for no reason), illnesses which occur, 73, 176–7
Bareagua, 17
Barina (dead brother of Huli leader), 11
Bayebaye myth, 23, 25, 31, 32, 188
Bebenete sacred site, 19, 21–2, 23, 98
behavioural disorders, 4–5
bereavement, 142–3
'Besoso', *see* Dabure-Puya
Bibipaite sacred site, 22, 23
'big men', 45
birth rate, 62, 63
blood (*darama*), 47, 82–3, 126, 177; blood-letting, 90–1; 'burst blood', 82–3, 90; 'good' and 'bad' blood, 99, 100; *see also kuyanda;* menstrual blood
bodily processes, Huli concepts of, 9, 81–4, 125–6, 177
body fluids, changes in, 73, 74
bones, 47–8, 134; *see also* fractures
breath, *see bu;* dyspnoea; shortness of breath
'broken neck', 116, 117
bronchitis, chronic, 27, 74, 83, 86, 87, 130, 162, 166
bu (breath, life force), 81, 83–4, 87, 130, 136, 137, 141
burns, 67, 68

195

Index

Capuchin Catholics, 14
causes of illness, *see* aetiology
Champion, Ivan, 14
change, *see* social change
chest: operation to remove blood from (*kuabe*), 90, 91; pain, 64, 89, 165, 166; *see also amali* (chronic chest disease)
chicken pox, 27, 62
childbirth, 101, 156
children, illness in, 62, 67–72 *passim*, 85–6, 101, 111–13, 136–42 *passim*, 178–9; treatment of, 77–8, 92, 94, 139, 142; *see also* protective (strengthening) rituals
Chimbu healer, 148–9
Chinese fright illness, 138
Christian healing, 60, 75, 77, 80, 92, 139, 172, 189; in cases of *agali*, 114, 122, 123; in cases of spirit attack, 165–6; and traditional cures, 181–2; *see also* prayer meetings
Christian missions, 10, 14, 15, 25, 32–4, 186–7; and *Damene* Cultural Centre, 31–2
Christianity, Christians, 17, 30–7 *passim*, 74, 154; attitudes to *dama* (spirits), 154–6, 157, 164–7, 169–70; continuities between traditional lore and, 16, 23, 32, 35–7, 187–8; explanations of illness, 166–72, 177, 180; and traditional healing and ceremonies, 111–12, 114, 115, 120, 146, 161, 165–6, 182, 186; views on compensation payment for injury, 132–3, 187; *see also* Christian healing; Christian missions; *kanaka* (pagan, non-Christian)
'coastal sorcery', *see nambis poisin*
cognition, terms referring to, 84
cold, illness attributed to excessive, 86
colds (*homama*), 74, 86–7, 90, 130, 178
compensation for injury, 44, 125, 131–6, 137, 138–40, 187; 'compensation neurosis', 131; influence upon course of illness, 66, 124, 127, 131–2, 179, 183
conception, 47, 100, 109, 110, 134, 177
convulsions, 137, 138
cough, 62, 69, 165, 178; treatments for, 89, 90, 94
counting system, Huli, 23–4
courting parties (*dawanda*), 44, 110, 126, 169
covetousness, *see hame; lingi*
creation myths, Huli, 6, 17, 19, 25, 41, 45, 151, 152, 158
cultural influences in definition and patterning of illness, 3–6
cures, *see* treatment strategies
cutaneous lesions, *see* skin lesions
cystitis, 130

Daberanda, 19, 25

Dabu-Togoiya (ritual specialist), 19
Dabure-Puya ('Besoso'), 11–13
daburuli sorcery, 145
Dagima parish, 61
Dagiwali, *see* Hana
daloali (teacher in bachelor training house), 55, 103
dama, see spirit(s)
Damene Cultural Centre, 30–2, 36
Dandayi (spirit), 163
Datagaliwabe (spirit), 144, 154, 167, 184, 185
dawanda, see courting parties
dead, place of the, *see humbirini andaga*
death, 59, 84
deba paliaga rite, 160, 161
debility, 82, 130
decline, moral and physical, Huli preoccupation with, 18–19, 23–4, 26; *see also dindi gamu; mbingi* myth
Department of Public Health, 60, 75, 139, 180; *see also* aid post treatments; Tari Health Centre
descent groups, 43, 45, 47–51
desire, illnesses attributed to, 140–2; *see also hame; lingi*
developmental career, Huli, 100–4
diagnosis, 8, 9, 72, 73, 74, 81; factors guiding patients through process of, 175–80; moral implications of Christian, 166–9; *see also* explanations of illness
diarrhoea, 69–71, 85, 106, 137, 140, 141, 172, 176, 178; treatment of, 89, 92
diet, 39, 75, 85
dindi gamu ('earth spell', major earth fertility ritual sequence), 16, 17, 18–26 *passim*, 27, 30–2, 35, 99, 158
dindi malu (genealogy linking present parish members to founding ancestors), 45, 47, 48, 152
dindi pongone ('knots of the earth', major sacred sites), 19
dinini (spirit, soul, shade), 83, 84, 136–9, 150, 151, 165
dirt, harmful effects of, 73, 74, 85
disease, definition of, 5
dispute settlement, 169, 181; *see also* compensation for injury
divination, 17, 32, 152, 155, 190
divine displeasure, illness attributed to, 2, 154, 167–9, 170–2, 180, 184
division of labour, 39; and illness, 52, 65, 66, 124, 183
divorce, 51–2, 183
dressings, 89, 96
drugs, modern, 123, 175
Duguba peoples, 16–17, 19–21, 31, 38, 41, 145, 146, 147

196

Index

Duna people, 16, 17, 28, 31, 38, 41, 145, 151
dyschromic spirochaetosis, *see pinta*
dysentery, 27, 70, 126, 130
dyspnoea, 83, 86, 178

earache, 88, 160; treatment for, 89; *see also* otitis media
eclipses of the sun, 36
education, 187
ega kamia hangaga rite, 160, 161
Egari, Lake, 27
emotions, 83; and illness, 102, 136–44, 167, 184–5
Enga people, 14, 16, 17, 22, 28, 29, 51, 145, 158, 187
enteritis necroticans, 86, 130
environmental influences, 1, 6; illness produced by, 84–6
epidemics, 24, 27–8
Etoro people, 16, 21, 146
Europeans, arrival of, 7, 10–15, 24–37, 186–7
Evangelical Church of Papua, *see* Asia Pacific Christian Mission
exchange, 44, 45, 55; centrality of, in Huli society, 133, 157, 179, 183, 187
exorcism, 33, 34, 157, 165
explanations of illness, Huli, 72–4, 150; naturalistic, 176–8; relating to sexuality and growth, 97–123; *see also* assault; divine displeasure; emotions; environmental influences; female pollution; sorcery; spirit attack
eyes, 58, 160; treatment of infections, 89

Fasu people, 16
female pollution, 52, 55, 57, 74, 85, 99, 104–6, 109–10; *see also agali*; *guyu naya*; 'heat', women's; *kuyanda*
fertility, 97; ritual, 104–5, 155; *see also dindi gamu*
fever, 62, 71–2, 172; treatment of, 89; *see also* malaria
Foi people, 16
founding ancestors, 25, 32, 41, 45, 47, 98, 144, 150–2, 160; *see also* Kebali
fractures, 91, 96
fright, illnesses attributed to, 136–40, 178, 179, 183

gamu (spell), 92, 113
gastro-intestinal illness, 69–71, 142; *see also* diarrhoea; dysentery; vomiting
Gelote sacred site, 19, 21, 24, 151
Gendo parish, 41, 42, 51–2
genealogy, Huli, 23–4, 41–4, 45, 144; *see also* descent groups; *dindi malu*
geography, Huli sacred, 16–26

geria sorcery, 145
germ theory of disease, Huli acceptance of, 180–1
girls, training of, 104, 111
Gnau people, 177
God, Huli conception of, 164–6; *see also* divine displeasure
Goroka, 28
greed, *see lingi*
grief, *see* sorrow
growth of children, 101–2
guyu naya ('scorching' of children by women's 'heat'), 104, 113

hagara (chronic bronchitis), 87, 92, 166
hair, 81, 103; pulling out of, 90; *see also manda hare*
Hambu Hiliawi sacred site, 41
hambu sorcery, 17, 145, 146–7, 149
Hambuali Aid Post, attendance at, 75
Hambuali-Hira, 41
Hambuali-Kamianga, 41
Hambuali-Malubi, 41
Hambuali parish, 17, 41–51 *passim*, 61, 72, 74, 165, 175
Hambuali-Puli, 41
Hambuali-Taiabe, 41
Hambuali-Yuli, 41, 42
hame (desire, yearning), 110, 140, 141, 142, 143, 151, 185
hame gamu ritual, 104, 113
hameigini, *see* parishes
Hana (Hanawali, Dagiwali), 98–9, 110, 152, 156, 157, 158, 160, 163
Hari Hibira sacred site, 19–20
headache, 62, 64, 66, 106, 116; treatment of, 90, 92
health, Huli view of, 53–7, 58
health centre, *see* Tari Health Centre
health services, 5, 15, 34, 173, 175; *see also* Department of Public Health
heat: of *dama* (spirits), 159; effects of excessive, 86; *see also* 'heat', women's; *poboneme*
'heat', women's, 98, 109; dangers of, 104, 106, 113
Hela (founding ancestor), 16
Heolabe (spirit), 151, 152, 153, 156, 163
Hewa peoples, 16, 31
Hides, Jack, 10–14
himugu ere hiraga rite, 160
himugu hangaga rite, 160
historical perspectives, 6–7, 10–37
history, Huli view of, 6
Hiwari parish, 41
Holi gamu (possession state said to indicate presence of Holy Spirit), 36

197

Index

Holy Spirit (*dinini holi*), 36, 150
homama, see colds
home care of patients, 174–5
homes, settlement patterns, 38–9, 44, 60; *see also* residence and land-holding patterns
Hona-Hana, *see* Hana
Hona-Ni, *see* Ni
honde taribu (ritually unclean after childbirth), 156
hoop pines, sacred groves of, 19, 21, 25, 32, 41, 88
Hubi-Hondomogo (ritual specialist), 19, 24, 25, 28
Huli language, 38; terms used to describe illness, 8–9, 82–3, 85, 87–8, 125, 160; vocabulary relating to parts of the body, 81
Huli society, 38–52, 110, 185; *see also* social change
Hulia, River, 21
Hulia-Hewabe (ritual specialist), 25
humbirini andaga (the place of the dead), 11, 151, 166
Hunabe (Kebali), 157
hunguli wiagada (worthless person), 58
hysterical collapse, 130

iba gamu (water spell), 106, 107, 108, 114, 121
ibagiya (bachelor cult), 10, 51, 55, 58, 103–4, 109, 110, 154, 184; *ibagiya* myth, 99–100; *ibagiyanda* (bachelor training house), 29, 55, 99, 104, 110
Ibatiri (water spirit), arrows of: illness caused by, 147, 161; removal of, *see tawa timu duguaga*
ibatiri (scruffy, ineffectual individual), 51, 58, 97, 110
igiri yango (unrelated friends), 43, 49
illness, ill health, definitions of: cultural variations in, 3–6; Huli, 5, 57–9
impotence, 130
in-patient treatment, *see* Tari Health Centre
individualism, Huli ethos of, 44, 49–50, 144, 185
influenza, 27, 130, 146
inhalations, 90, 94
injuries, 1–2, 64, 66; *see also* assault; compensation for injury
intestines, 81–2, 106, 107–8, 114
Ipili people, 16, 28, 29
ira giambe hangaga ritual (for protection against shades of the dead), 151, 165–6
iriyale (children born with too little interval between them), 103
irritants, illness ascribed to, 86

Jesus Christ, Huli conception of, 23, 32
joint pain, 64, 65; treatment of, 89; *see also* arthritis
Judgement Day, Huli preoccupation with, 34, 35, 36, 188
judicial mode of treatment, *see* litigation

Kagua people, 147, 148
Kaluli people, 16, 21
Kaman people, 22
kanaka (pagan, non-Christian), 113, 164, 166, 169–70, 181, 182
Kebali (ancestor spirits), 41, 150–1, 152, 153, 155–7, 163, 185
kebanda, see sacred sites
Kebe (founding ancestor), 25, 32
kidneys, 81; *see also* nephrotic syndrome
Kikori River, 16
knee pain, 65, 92, 125, 158
Komo, 10, 15, 41
Kopiago District, 15
Koroba District, 15, 38
kuabe (release of blood from the chest), 90, 91
Kuarimago (spirit), 158–60
Kuk site, Western Highlands, 26
Kutubu, Lake, 14, 16, 34, 38
kuyanda (leech-like parasitic mass), 3, 101–2, 109, 110, 111–12, 139–40, 142, 143; treatment of, 54, 101, 112, 182
kwashiorkor, 86

language, *see* Huli language
leadership, 44–5, 49
leprosy, 88
Lidu (spirit), 160
life expectancy, 62, 63
life force, *see bu*
Linavin parish, 61
lingi (illness caused by others' covetousness), 102, 111, 140–2, 178–9, 185; *lingi duguaga*, 140, 142
litigation, judicial mode of treatment, 66, 124, 131, 179, 183; *see also* compensation for injury
liver, 81
Long Island, volcanic eruption on (*c.* 1700 A.D.), 17
lulu (acute dissociative state), 29–30
lungs, 81

ma hiraga (scorching taro) ceremony, 54, 102
ma ibira gamu rite (to strengthen child in preparation for birth of sibling), 54, 102–3
Mae Enga, lineage system of, 51
Malaita, 34

Cambridge Studies in
Social Anthropology

Editor: JACK GOODY

*ALSO AVAILABLE AS A PAPERBACK